The Federal Estate Tax

The Federal Estate Tax

History, Law, and Economics

David Joulfaian

The MIT Press
Cambridge, Massachusetts
London, England

This book was set in Palatino LT Std by Toppan Best-set Premedia Limited. Printed and bound in the United States of America.

Library of Congress Cataloging-in-Publication Data

Names: Joulfaian, David, author.
Title: The federal estate tax : history, law, and economics / David Joulfaian.
Description: Cambridge, MA : The MIT Press, [2019] | Includes bibliographical
  references and index.
Identifiers: LCCN 2018055026 | ISBN 9780262042666 (hardcover : alk. paper)
Subjects: LCSH: Inheritance and transfer tax--United States.
Classification: LCC HJ5805 .J68 2019 | DDC 336.2/760973--dc23 LC record available at
  https://lccn.loc.gov/2018055026

10 9 8 7 6 5 4 3 2 1

To Alex, Ani, Dave, and Steph

Contents

Preface   ix

1.   Introduction   1

2   A Brief History   7

3   Description of the Tax   25

4   Profile of Taxpayers   41

5   The Beneficiaries   65

6   Fiscal Contribution   85

7   Behavioral Effects Related to Saving and Labor
     Decisions   101

8   Other Behavioral Effects   135

9   A Critical Assessment   175

     Notes   179
     References   189
     Index   197

Preface

The estate tax is arguably one of the most neglected taxes. Aside from legal scholarship and practice, there is very little in the way of study of the tax by academics. And so, not surprisingly, much less of the structure of the tax and its consequences are familiar to the population at large as well as to many policymakers.

There is an obvious void in the study of the estate tax and the general understanding of its scope. In an attempt to fill this void, this book provides a description of the tax, its historic evolution, and a review of its economic consequences in a format that is accessible and yet comprehensive. There is no judgment on my part on the pros and cons of estate taxation, as this would require the difficult task of addressing an alternative source of revenues as well as the compromises that policymakers have to make in choosing from estate, corporate, and personal taxes and excises to fund their programs. Nevertheless, the book addresses many aspects of the estate tax to help guide readers in learning about the tax.

I have been fortunate to have served as an economist at the U.S. Department of the Treasury, Office of Tax Analysis, where the constant flow of tax proposals and discussions on tax-related matters have influenced the writing of this book. Five anonymous reviewers provided extensive and insightful comments that have shaped the manuscript. My colleagues at Treasury and coauthors on a number of estate tax–related papers have provided critical feedback on many aspects of the presentations in the book. I have greatly benefited from the wisdom and legal scholarship of Katherine Hughes. And at the MIT Press, Emily Taber, Laura Keeler, and Virginia Crossman have been helpful throughout the process of getting this manuscript published. Nathan Born, Parisa Manteghi, Roman Mookerjee, Siobhan O'Keefe, and Anna Rakhman have provided invaluable research assistance over the years. The views expressed in this manuscript are mine alone, and should not in any way be attributed to the U.S. Department of the Treasury.

1 Introduction

Taxes take a variety of forms, and include levies on individual and business income, personal expenditures, and wealth. Often governments design tax systems and levy taxes for reasons other than to just fund their programs and operations. Indeed, the form and reach of some of the taxes imposed are designed, among other purposes, to shape behavior as in the case of the income tax deduction for charitable giving or the case of tobacco taxes, and to reflect on the ability to pay as well as to correct for inequalities in the income distribution as in the case of progressive income taxes and wealth levies. The latter may take the form of annual wealth taxes and inheritance taxes typically applied to the wealthiest of estates. The ensuing tax system unavoidably reflects a set of compromises by governments and the difficult choices its legislators encounter, as they levy taxes on their constituencies when they are raising and educating their children, starting or expanding a business, during their retirement years, and after their death.

Inheritance taxes represent one of the oldest forms of taxation. Such taxes may be traced back to ancient Egypt, during the reign of Psametichusi in the seventh century BC. A tax on inheritances was also introduced by the Romans some two thousand years ago. Reflecting on the difficult choices that policymakers have to make, and faced with the prospect of having a land tax levied instead to provide for housing for veterans, in the year AD 6 the Roman Senate approved Emperor Augustus's proposed inheritance tax, the *vicesima hereditatium*, as an alternative source of funding.[1]

Inheritance taxes take several forms, and are often labelled as death duties or death taxes because they typically apply after the death of the wealth holder. Inheritance tax rates may vary by size of the monetary transfer and type of relationship between the deceased and the heir.

These taxes may be paid by each beneficiary after receiving an inheritance, or alternatively can be paid by the estate of decedents with the total tax liability determined by the size of the bequests to each beneficiary. Inheritance taxes may also take the form of an estate tax for which the tax liability is determined by the size of wealth held by the estate irrespective of the nature of the beneficiaries, with after-tax wealth distributed to the heirs. The modern variant of these taxes also applies to wealth transfers during life in the form of gift taxes aimed primarily at preempting tax avoidance.

Death taxes took the form of feudal charges or payments to the lord or sovereign during the Middle Ages. By 1694, and burdened by the cost of the French Wars, England enacted a stamp tax that applied to legal documents related to the probate of wills; this required the purchase of a stamp in the amount of five shillings in case of personal property worth over twenty pounds.[2] The stamp tax was converted in 1796 into a tax on the value of transfers of personal property applied at tax rates ranging 2 to 6 percent depending on the nature of the relationship of the heirs. The tax, often referred to as a legacy tax, was modified over the years and evolved into an estate duty that applied to all assets held at death by 1894.

In the formative years of the American Republic, a very limited array of revenue sources was available to the federal government. These primarily included custom duties, sale of public land, and select excises. To raise additional revenues, especially at times of crises, the federal government experimented with different forms of inheritance taxes. It enacted the Stamp Act of 1797, a tax in a way similar to the English taxes imposed on receipts from personal estates, before eventually also settling on the estate tax in 1916 that extends to all property held at death.[3]

The tax evolved over the years into the federal unified transfer tax, which is more commonly referred to as simply the estate tax. It currently consists of the estate tax that applies to wealth held at death, the gift tax that applies to lifetime transfers, and an additional generation-skipping transfer tax (GSTT) that applies to both bequests at death and gifts made during life to grandchildren and other beneficiaries that skip a generation. Following general practice, the federal unified transfer tax hereafter will often be referred to as the estate tax. It is the only form of wealth taxes levied by the federal government.[4]

In the 1930s, the tax accounted for up to 10 percent of federal receipts. This declined to about less than 1 percent in recent years, and is paid by well under one-tenth of 1 percent of the estates of the 2.7 million decedents annually; precisely 5,219 estates reported tax liability on returns filed in 2016, the latest year for which data are available.[5] Despite the seemingly limited exposure of the population to the tax, this form of taxation has become controversial and the subject of heated debates over the two past decades. The many recent and continuous calls for its repeal should not be surprising as inheritance taxes in the United States have repeatedly fallen victim to good times as well as swings in the prevailing political sentiment.

These debates are not unique to the estate tax. All taxes are controversial as they have implications for efficiency and equity. In the case of efficiency, the concern is whether the tax distorts economic behavior and induces individuals to take actions they would not take in the absence of the tax. Efficiency implications include whether the estate tax reduces saving, risk taking, and entrepreneurship. Equity concerns relate to whether all individuals pay their fair share of taxes in defraying the cost of services provided by the government and whether tax liabilities reflect the ability to pay principle. There has always existed tension between efficiency and equity considerations, between concerns over the tax system impeding economic growth and job creation, and having the tax burden fall disproportionately on the less well off.

Both Adam Smith and David Ricardo, in part, objected to wealth transfer taxation on the grounds that it is a tax on capital, and reflecting on the tax induced distortions of saving.[6] In many ways this forms the basis for arguments in opposition to the estate tax to date. Proponents of the tax find its "protective" nature of the tax base appealing; it can act as a backstop to the income tax and offset the erosion in its base due to tax evasion and avoidance, as well as bolster the progressivity of the tax system.[7] But the passionate debates leading to the enactment of the estate tax a century ago transcended the traditional efficiency and equity (and revenue needs) arguments. Supporters viewed large concentrations of wealth as dangerous to a democracy, and large inheritances were considered inconsistent with democratic ideals of equal opportunity.[8]

Some of the recent heated debates for and against the estate tax have gone well beyond the traditional positions that each of the proponents and opponents have staked. With the prospect of estate tax repeal in 2001, proponents all but abandoned their traditional support of the estate tax as contributing to the enhancement of equal opportunity and reducing inequality. Indeed, very little of the century-old passion that led to the enactment of the estate tax and the expansion of its scope was visible.

In an interesting twist, the cries for fairness and morality of taxing wealth transfers became the mantra of the opponents of the estate tax. They passionately, and successfully, made their case in 2001 that the tax is unfair as it penalizes success, and morally obnoxious as it obstructs parents from leaving legacies to their children. Even mainstream economists joined the estate tax "unfairness" chorus. As an example, Gregory Mankiw of Harvard University, at the time he served as the chairman of the Council of Economic Advisers of President George W. Bush, stated that the estate tax "unfairly punishes frugality" and claimed "There are no principles of good tax policy that support this tax."[9]

In their 2006 book, Yale University professors Michael Graetz and Ian Shapiro provide interesting insights into the debates and the political maneuvering on the planned repeal of the federal estate tax in 2001.[10] They describe the political mystery of how the anti-tax coalition was put together, with support from the majority of the U.S. population—virtually all of whom will not be touched by the estate tax. Indeed, a poll conducted by CBS News/ New York Times in 2001, around the time proposals to repeal the estate tax were being advanced, found that 71 percent of Americans opposed the tax.[11] And political affiliations had little effect on these poll results, as 74 percent of Republicans objected to the tax compared to 69 percent for Democrats.

Aside from the works of legal scholars, there are few empirical studies on the estate tax and its economic consequences to guide and shape public policy and inform academics, students, and the public at large. This book serves several purposes as it aims to fill some of the void in studies of the estate tax. It provides a comprehensive and accessible review of the estate tax and its economic effects. It also provides students and researchers of estate taxation with a valuable resource that documents historic changes in tax law and the population impacted by the tax.

Chapter 2 provides a brief history of the federal estate tax and its evolution into its current form. It traces developments in the estate tax, and the economic and political currents that may have shaped it, since its inception in 1916. Changes in tax law are documented, including those related to changes in tax rates, exemptions, and deductions.

These also include the temporary provisions introduced by Congress in 2001 and modified in 2010, as well as the changes introduced in 2013 and again in 2017. It also provides detailed time series of the various tax parameters, such as tax rates and exemptions in effect.

Chapter 3 provides a description of the structure of the tax and its inner workings. This includes the determination of the tax base and the various exemptions, deductions, tax credits, and tax rate schedule that apply in determining the tax liability. It also reviews provisions related to administering the tax. The latter include asset valuation conventions, filing requirements, and installment payment provisions in particular in the case of estates consisting of sizeable business holdings. Wherever appropriate, the chapter also provides a brief history of individual provisions.

Chapter 4 sketches the profile of taxpayers and their attributes, providing the size distribution of wealth and its composition, with a similar exercise carried out for gifts. Next, the number of taxpayers is traced over time for both estate and gift taxes. Chapter 5 extends the discussion to the beneficiaries, both heirs and charitable organizations.

Chapter 6 traces the fiscal contribution of the estate tax. It provides annual time series on the tax revenues collected for both the estate and gift taxes. This is followed by a discussion of the underlying factors that may have influenced observed trends, such as changes in tax rates, exemptions, and the underlying economic activity, including the recent turbulent trend in lifetime gifts and the seismic changes observed in 2012. Chapter 6 also reviews trends in enforcement and administration of the tax.

Chapters 7 and 8 discuss the economic effects of the tax and review the available empirical evidence in the literature. Chapter 7 addresses labor responses to estate taxation, as well as its effects on saving and wealth accumulation. The latter includes the choice between gifts and bequests and the timing of gifts, as they alter the size of wealth accumulated by donors. And chapter 8 addresses the effects of estate taxation on other economic activities. These include charitable giving (both in life and at death), forms of life insurance ownership, capital gains realizations, interstate mobility, and tax evasion.

Chapter 9 concludes with a critical assessment of the estate tax. It highlights key outstanding criticisms of the estate tax and addresses some of its shortcomings.

2   A Brief History

Much of the taxes levied in the earlier and formative years of the American Republic reflected spending decisions and the expanding role of the government.[1] During this period, revenues were collected primarily from import duties, the sale of public lands, and select excise taxes. The country experienced an explosion in the size of the population, which grew from five million to 76 million in the nineteenth century. It also experienced a number of financial crises and wars, internal and external. All of these had the effect of increasing the demand for government services. As the role of the public sector expanded, so did the need for additional sources of revenues.

The Civil War brought about a significant increase in government expenditures. In 1862, a number of new measures were introduced to fund the growing needs. These included the enactment of the first inheritance tax, what was known at the time as a "legacy tax," to apply at a maximum tax rate of 5 percent to personal property.[2] The tax was supplanted with a succession tax with a maximum tax rate of 6 percent to apply to real estate.[3] Awash with revenue surpluses in the aftermath of the Civil War, there was considerable pressure to roll back many of the taxes levied to finance the war, including the inheritance tax. The tax was repealed in 1870, and very shortly afterward the income tax was repealed as well.

Following the financial Panic of 1893 and business failures, the federal government reenacted the Civil War-era income tax in 1894 to meet its expenses.[4] The new income tax was slightly different from its predecessor in determining the tax base. Gifts and inheritances received, for instance, were included in income and taxed at a rate of 2 percent on the excess over $4,000. In effect, the new legislation integrated the income and wealth transfer taxes into what is commonly known as an accession tax. The income tax contained a number of flaws and was eventually repealed when the Supreme Court declared it unconstitutional.[5]

With the onset of war between the United States and Spain in 1898, additional sources of revenues were once again needed. Given the strong opposition to the enactment of an income tax, Congress instead passed the War Revenue Act of 1898 which included an inheritance tax with a maximum tax rate of 5 percent. The bill also provided for additional sources of revenues such as taxes on some corporate receipts (oil and sugar), excise taxes, and stamp duties. This time, the Supreme Court upheld the inheritance tax, although the Court did disapprove of some of the specifics.[6] In 1902, hostilities with Spain ended and federal expenditures decreased.[7] With expanding budget surpluses, the tax was repealed in 1902 and with it much of the remaining Spanish-American war taxes.[8]

Concerned over the regressive nature of the existing tax code, which relied heavily on consumption taxes, and the perceived rise in wealth concentration, President Theodore Roosevelt proposed a progressive inheritance tax in 1906. The tax was to be "framed so as to put it out of the power of the owner of one of these enormous fortunes to hand on more than a certain amount to any one individual."[9] The Panic of 1907, marked with sharp declines in stock prices, held Roosevelt back from implementing his social vision. There was another attempt to introduce an inheritance tax in 1909, and such a provision was included in the Payne-Aldrich Tariff Act of 1909. However, it was dropped from the final version under pressure from conservatives and states who viewed inheritance taxes as their domain.[10] Instead the corporation income tax was introduced, and an amendment to the Constitution for a federal personal income tax was submitted to the states.[11]

The Modern Estate Tax Is Born

Shortly after the ratification of the Sixteenth Amendment, the personal income tax was introduced in 1913. The tax applied to income in excess of $3,000 with a maximum rate of 7 percent. World War I, with its depressing effects on trade, had led to a sharp reduction in revenues from tariffs. In addition, the military buildup significantly increased government expenditures. To meet the nation's growing fiscal needs, Congress enacted the Emergency Revenue Act of 1916. This act increased individual income and corporate tax rates. In addition, it introduced the estate tax. The adoption of the estate tax form of taxing inheritances, instead of a pure inheritance tax, was primarily driven by its revenue yield and its relative ease of administration.[12] At the time of its enactment, it applied to the wealth of decedents with estates in excess of $50,000 with a tax rate schedule ranging from a low of a rate of 1 percent to a maximum rate of 10 percent for assets transferred over $5 million in value.

Following the outbreak of World War I, the projected deficit for fiscal year 1917 stood at $177 million, or about 20 percent of the revenues collected in 1916.[13] As a consequence, the federal government enacted a comprehensive tax package, the Revenue Act of 1916, which also included the introduction of the estate tax, to help finance the deficit and defray the cost of the war preparedness campaign. As with all taxes, the revenue yield was certainly the primary reason for the enactment of the estate tax in 1916. However, this could not have been the sole and immediate reason for its enactment, since Congress could have easily raised revenues and met the country's immediate needs from other sources. Indeed, the very same enabling legislation in 1916 also increased personal income and corporate taxes. There is little doubt that the choice of the source of revenues reflected objectives other than those merely related to the short-term need of financing budget deficits and government programs; it most certainly reflected a desire to redistribute the tax burden in particular as consumption taxes made up the bulk of the revenue source. This is especially the case given the relatively small contribution of the estate tax to governmental finances at the time. Indeed, and while government revenues increased from $0.8 to $3.7 billion between fiscal years 1917 and 1918 in the aftermath of the legislated tax increases, less than $48 million of this increase was contributed by the newly enacted estate tax; only $6 million was collected in fiscal year 1917.[14]

Due to pressing needs to fund the war effort, estate tax rates were raised twice in 1917. In the first, the Act of March 3, 1917, the tax rate schedule was increased by 50 percent with the maximum tax rate increased from 10 to 15 percent again for estates greater than $5 million in value; it was increased from 1 to 1.5 percent for the smallest taxable estates. Estate tax rates were again raised by the War Revenue Act of 1917, enacted on October 3, 1917, to a maximum of 25 percent on assets in excess of $10 million. It also raised the tax rate from 1.5 to 2 percent for the smallest estates. This War Revenue Act exempted the estates of servicemembers with death resulting from injuries inflicted during the war. On net, the act was estimated to raise about $2.5 billion in its full-year effect on revenues needed for the war effort, with only $5 million generated from the estate tax.[15]

Additional funds were again needed to fund the war. The Revenue Act of 1918, with delayed presidential signing on February 24, 1919, raised about $5.8 billion in additional revenues, or about one-half of the war budget of the previous year. Much of the revenue was raised by increased tax rates on personal income and excises. Reflecting on the opposition to federal estate taxation, and despite the urgent revenue needs, estate tax rates were slightly reduced for smaller estates in lower tax brackets. For those with taxable estates under $1.5 million, tax rates were reduced by 1 to 2 percentage points. More important, a deduction for charitable bequests was introduced for the first time. On the other hand, and moving in the other direction, the tax base was also expanded, by extending the estate tax to life insurance proceeds in excess of $40,000 received by the estate, its executors, or its beneficiaries. On net, and despite the tax rate reductions for the smaller estates, the estate tax was projected to raise $60 million from the total of $5.8 billion in new revenues in the first full year after enactment.[16]

With more funds needed, the Revenue Act of 1924 brought about sweeping changes. The estate tax was supplanted with a gift tax in 1924 in an attempt to minimize estate and income tax avoidance. In that same year, the maximum estate tax rate was raised from 25 to 40 percent. The estate tax base was also expanded to include jointly held property in the taxable estate, as well as property where the decedent had any control or power of attorney.

In addition, the estate tax was modified by a new tax credit introduced to offset state inheritance taxes and set equal to 25 percent of the federal estate tax liability. This had the effect of reducing the maximum estate tax rate from 40 to 30 percent depending on the inheritance tax burden estates face in different states.

In many ways, the federal estate tax generated strong opposition from the states that viewed such a tax as their main preserve. The introduction of the credit for state death taxes was aimed at minimizing the objection of the states to the estate tax. The tax credit reflected the federal government's intention to have states adopt inheritance taxes "equivalent to 25% of the federal tax."[17] The intent here was to impose uniform state inheritance taxes and minimize interstate competition for the wealthy.[18] At the time of the enactment of the credit, Florida adopted a constitutional amendment to prohibit the enactment of inheritance and income taxes in November 1924. This was an obvious attempt to compete for the wealthy and encourage their migration to the state; the state of Nevada followed with its own constitutional amendment in July 1925.

Following budget surpluses and growing opposition, however, the gift tax was repealed retroactively in 1926. The estate tax increases introduced in 1924 were also repealed retroactively. The exemption of $50,000 was expanded to $100,000, and the maximum estate tax rate was further reduced from 40 to 20 percent on transfers over $10 million.[19] Furthermore, the credit for state death taxes was set equal to 80 percent of the federal estate tax, a provision that virtually denied much of the revenue from this source to the federal government. At prevailing tax rates, this is equivalent to a maximum credit rate of 16 percent of taxable estates, or 80 percent of a tax rate of 20 percent effectively reducing the maximum federal tax rate to 4 percent only for states employing inheritance taxes.

Faced with an expansion in government expenditures and declining revenues during the Great Depression, the reach of the estate tax was expanded once again by the Revenue Act of 1932. The estate tax exemption was reduced from $100,000 to $50,000, and the maximum tax rate was raised from 20 to 45 percent for transfers in excess of $10 million.

The estate tax may be viewed as means to pre-empting the erosion of the income tax. But it too can be easily avoided through lifetime gifts. In dynastically motivated families, individuals may transfer funds directly to grandchildren in life or at death and thereby minimize wealth transfer taxes. To counteract these tendencies, a revamped gift tax was also introduced by the 1932 act in an attempt to reduce estate and income tax avoidance, and applied to cumulative lifetime gifts in excess of $5,000.[20] The stated purpose of the proposed introduction of the gift tax in the House Committee report was "To assist in the collection of the income and estate taxes, and prevent their avoidance through the splitting of estates during the lifetime of a taxpayer."

While the gift tax was put in place in 1932 to minimize the erosion of estate and income taxes, its structure at the time reflected another objective. In a seemingly deliberate attempt to accelerate the cash flow to the U.S. Treasury, the gift tax rate schedule was set at 75 percent of that of the estate tax to encourage gifts. Such a rate differential was believed to enhance the incentives for making gifts and deliberately set so as to result in an acceleration of tax revenues more in the form of gift taxes and less in estate taxes that would be paid much later.[21]

The estate tax was once again increased, this time by the Act of May 10, 1934. The maximum tax rate was increased to 60 percent, with the gift tax rate increasing to 45 percent (75 percent of the estate tax rate). The estate tax rate was again raised by the Act of August 30, 1935, to a maximum of 70 percent, and 52.5 percent for gifts, and the exemption was reduced from $50,000 to $40,000.

With revenue needs rising, to fund the military buildup prior to World War II in 1940, a 10 percent surtax was imposed by the Revenue Act of 1940. And per the Act of September 20, 1941, the maximum estate tax rate was raised to 77 percent (57.5 percent for gifts). In effect this change combined the surtax and regular tax to form a single tax rate schedule, with the top rate applying to transfers in excess of $50 million.

Estate and gift taxes were again changed per the Act of October 21, 1942. The estate tax exemption was increased from $40,000 to $60,000, and in exchange the $40,000 life insurance exemption was abolished. The exemption for cumulative lifetime transfers was reduced to $30,000 for gifts, with an annual exclusion of $3,000 down from $4,000 provided for gifts. In addition, the act required that only the portion a married decedent had contributed to the acquisition of jointly-owned assets or community properties be included in the taxable estate.

Post–World War II Reforms

The treatment of marital property was revisited by the Revenue Act of 1948. Sidestepping the complications of figuring out the acquisition cost of contributed property by each of husband and wife, the act introduced a marital deduction for spousal bequests limited to 50 percent of the value of the property transferred, in an attempt to bring parity between the community property and non-community property states. Bequests in excess of this limit continued to be fully taxable.

The tax laws governing transfers were codified by the Internal Revenue Act of 1954. While the purpose of the latter was to merely codify existing rules, it also introduced some changes in the process. Examples include the simplification of the computation of the credit for state death taxes introduced in 1926. Rather than having estates calculate the tax credit by applying 80 percent to the estate tax rate schedule dating back to 1926, an equivalent tax credit rate schedule was devised ranging from zero to 16 percent applied to the taxable estate to calculate the amount of tax credit. More details on these computations are provided in chapter 3, and table 3.2 in particular. The act also excluded life insurance proceeds from policies not owned by the insured and where the insured did not control or have any incident of ownership.

To help liquidity-constrained estates to meet their tax liabilities on time, the Small Business Tax Revision Act of 1958 allowed taxpayers to pay the tax in installments. Estates with certain closely held business were allowed to pay tax attributable to the business over ten equal annual installments—rather than as one payment made within fifteen months after the date of death—subject to a 4 percent interest rate. To qualify, the value of the closely held business, generally defined as 20 percent or more ownership, must at least exceed either 35 percent of the gross estate (roughly total assets) or 50 percent of the taxable estate.

It was not until 1976 that the tax rates and exemptions put in place in 1942 were modified, and the estate tax revisited with substantial reforms. The Tax Reform Act of 1976 (TRA76) lowered the maximum estate tax rate from 77 to 70 percent. It replaced the separate estate and gift tax exemptions with a unified tax credit of $30,000, which effectively doubled the size of exempted estates to $120,666 in 1977 and set the exemption to increase in steps to $175,625 by 1981. It introduced a special use valuation for businesses and farms in order to exempt up to $500,000 of the value of the qualifying real property. TRA76 also integrated the gift tax with the estate tax under the unified transfer tax, sharing a common tax rate schedule. This rate schedule applied to cumulative transfers in life and at death. Consequently, the maximum gift tax rate was increased from 57.75 percent, i.e. 75 percent of 77, to 70 percent for gifts made in 1977 and beyond.

In addition, TRA76 modified the transfer tax system so that both estate and gift taxes were complemented with a generation-skipping transfer tax (GSTT) intended to reduce tax avoidance through generation-skipping transfers. However, the GSTT only applied to indirect transfers from trusts and did not extend to direct transfers from donor to grandchildren and other beneficiaries skipping a generation or more. Prior to TRA76, individuals could have created a life estate in their assets for their children, which was then followed by life estate for the grandchildren, and so on down the generations. These trusts are typically directed to pay all income to the children, with the remainder passed on to the grandchildren at their death, and so on. In other words, each generation receives income from these trusts or life estates during their lifetime. But recipients' interest in the underlying property expires at death and escapes taxation as these assets do not form part of their estates. While the initial donor or grantor may have been subject to transfer taxes, given these assets would have formed part of the taxable transfers, all transfers to future generations escape taxation altogether even though each generation may have enjoyed the income from these trusts during their lifetime.

On top of the changes in the estate tax, TRA76 repealed step-up in basis for inherited assets and replaced it with basis carryover.[22] In other words, and in addition to the estate taxes, when these assets are sold by the heirs at some point in the future they may become liable for capital gains taxes on past gains accrued by the decedent. Adjustments to basis, or the acquisition cost of property purchased by donor, were made for estate taxes paid to avoid double taxation by both the estate and capital gains taxes. Only appreciation beyond 1976 accrued by the donor during her life would become taxable when the underlying assets were sold by the beneficiaries; gains accrued before 1977 were "grandfathered" because the basis of property acquired before December 31, 1976, was to be stepped up to this date. The Revenue Act of 1978 extended the effective date for taxing past gains from the end of 1976 by three years to permit a review of the implications of carryover. But the basis carryover provision eventually was repealed as provided for by the Crude Oil Windfall Profit Tax Act of 1980.

In a sea of political changes, the Economic Recovery Tax Act of 1981 (ERTA81) introduced a number of significant changes that dramatically curtailed the reach of the estate tax. The maximum tax rate was reduced in stages from 70 in 1981 to 50 percent by 1985;[23] the maximum exemption, by virtue of increases in the unified credit, was expanded in steps from $175,625 in 1981 to $600,000 by 1987; the marital deduction was made unlimited, as it was expanded from about one-half the estate, thus fully exempting spousal transfers from taxation; spousal transfers to qualified terminable interest property (QTIP) trusts were made deductible; the special use valuation exemption was raised to $700,000; and the annual gift tax per donee exclusion was increased from $3,000 to $10,000.

Concerns over the generosity of the tax cuts introduced by ERTA81, and the expanding budget deficit, led Congress to enact the Tax Equity and Fiscal Responsibility Act of 1982 (TEFRA) to scale back some of the benefits of the previously enacted changes. The act reduced the existing 100 percent exclusion of retirement assets to a maximum of

$100,000 for individuals dying in 1983 and beyond. For the first time, retirement assets became taxable. The exclusion was repealed altogether by the Deficit Reduction Act of 1984 (DEFRA), and all retirement assets henceforth are included in the gross estate. DEFRA also froze the maximum estate rate at 55 percent through 1987, from the pending 50 percent in 1985. The Omnibus Budget Reconciliation Act of 1987 (OBRA87) again froze the tax rate at 55 percent for a period of five years, which the Clinton administration made permanent by enacting OBRA93.

Motivated by a simpler tax code, with lower tax rates and a broader tax base, to provide improved growth incentives and better tax compliance, the Reagan administration ushered the Tax Reform Act of 1986 (TRA86). The act, which was designed to be revenue neutral, made for significant reductions in individual and corporate tax rates in exchange for limitations on deductions and exemptions. It did not touch the estate tax with one primary exception; it drastically expanded the GSTT to apply to all transfers, both direct from donor and indirect as in distributions from trusts to beneficiaries. TRA86 set the GSTT tax rate equal to the maximum estate tax rate to apply to cumulative intergenerational transfers in excess of $1 million per donor. A temporary exemption of $2 million per donee was introduced to expire in 1989.

The Tax Relief Act of 1997 expanded the size of exempted estate to $1 million in steps, to take effect in 2006, beginning in 1998 with the exemption expanded to $625,000. It also indexed for inflation the annual gift tax exemption ($10,000), as well as the GSTT ($1 million) and the special use valuation ($750,000) exemptions. In addition, it provided family-owned businesses an exclusion of up to $675,000 as well as 40 percent exclusion of the value of land for permanent conservation easements.

Under temporary legislation enacted in 2001, the Economic Growth and Tax Relief Reconciliation Act of 2001 (EGTRRA), the reach of estate and gift taxes was curtailed through 2009, with both the estate tax and the GSTT—but not the gift tax—set to be repealed in 2010;[24] the maximum estate tax rate was reduced in steps to 45 percent and the gift tax rate to 35 percent in 2009; the size of estate and GST exemption was exempted in steps to $3.5 million in 2009 with the gift tax exemption capped at $1 million. It also reduced the amount of tax credit for state death taxes by 25, 50, and 75 percent over the years 2002 to 2004, and then replaced the credit with a deduction effective in 2005. At the expiration of this temporary legislation, and in 2011, the estate tax and GSTT were to be reinstated to reflect the law in effect prior to the enactment of the changes in 2001. Similarly, the gift tax was reset to prior law as well.

Before the estate tax was reintroduced in 2011, and under legislation enacted on December 17, 2010, the Tax Relief, Unemployment Insurance Authorization, and Job Creation Act of 2010 (TRUIAJC) extended the EGTRRA temporary provisions for two more years, through 2012, modified to provide for an estate tax exemption of $5 million (indexed) with a maximum tax rate of 35 percent. Unused portions of this exemption can be claimed by the surviving spouse for a combined total of $10 million (indexed), and is hence "portable." In other words, if the first spouse had an estate that used an exemption of $2 million only, then the estate of her surviving spouse is enabled to claim the remaining $3 million unused exemption in addition to his own $5 million (indexed) exemption. TRUIAJC also provided estates of decedents in 2010 with the option to be taxed under the 2011 estate tax regime instead of the basis carryover regime of 2010.

By the stroke of midnight, December 31, 2012, the temporary tax provisions expired, and the law reverted to that in effect in 2001. Congress, meeting on New Year's Day, enacted the American Taxpayer Relief Act of 2012 (ATRA) to take effect on January 1, 2013. ATRA made the provisions in TRUIAJC permanent, retaining the indexation of the $5 million size of exempted estate but setting the maximum estate and gift tax rate at 40 percent.

The latest legislation to shape the estate tax, the Tax Cuts and Jobs Act (TCJA), was signed into law on December 22, 2017, by President Trump. TJCA doubled the size of the exempted estate from $5 to $10 million (indexed as of 2011) for decedents after December 31, 2017. This exemption will remain in effect until the end of 2025, after which it will revert to the law in effect in 2017.

Major developments in estate and gift taxation are captured in tables 2.1, 2.2, and 2.3. These include the historic trend in estate and gift tax rates, and key exemptions, deductions, and tax credits, dating back to the enactment of the estate tax in 1916. Table 2.4 summarizes the temporary changes in effect between 2002 and 2012. And last, table 2.5 provides further details on the legislative changes introduced since 1916.

Table 2.1
Historical Features of the Estate Tax

Year	Tax Rate Range	Exemption or Equivalent Amount	Unified Credit	Maximum Marital Deduction	Special Use Exclusion for Closely Held Business
1916	1–10%	$50,000	N.A.	N.A.	N.A.
1917	1.5–15	50,000	N.A.	N.A.	N.A.
1917	2–25	50,000	N.A.	N.A.	N.A.
1919	1–25	50,000	N.A.	N.A.	N.A.
1924	1–40	50,000	N.A.	N.A.	N.A.
1926	1–20	100,000	N.A.	N.A.	N.A.
1932	1–45	50,000	N.A.	N.A.	N.A.
1934	1–60	50,000	N.A.	N.A.	N.A.
1935	2–70	40,000	N.A.	N.A.	N.A.
1941	3–77	40,000	N.A.	N.A.	N.A.
1942	3–77	60,000	N.A.	N.A.	N.A.
1949	3–77	60,000	N.A.	50% of Adj. Gross Estate	N.A.
1955	3–77	60,000	N.A.	50% of Adj. Gross Estate	N.A.
1977	18–70	120,667	$30,000	50% or $250,000	$500,000
1978	18–70	134,000	34,000	50% or $250,000	500,000
1979	18–70	147,333	38,000	50% or $250,000	500,000
1980	18–70	161,563	42,000	50% or $250,000	500,000
1981	18–70	175,625	47,000	50% or $250,000	600,000
1982	18–65	225,000	62,800	100%	700,000
1983	18–60	275,000	79,300	100%	750,000
1984	18–55	325,000	96,300	100%	750,000
1985	18–55	400,000	121,800	100%	750,000
1986	18–55	500,000	155,800	100%	750,000
1987	18–55	600,000	192,800	100%	750,000
1996	18–55	600,000	192,800	100%	750,000
1998	18–55	625,000	202,050	100%	750,000
1999	18–55	650,000	211,300	100%	760,000
2000	18–55	675,000	220,550	100%	770,000
2001	18–55	675,000	220,550	100%	800,000
2013	18–40	5,250,000	2,045,800	100%	1,070,000
2014	18–40	5,340,000	2,081,800	100%	1,090,000
2015	18–40	5,430,000	2,117,800	100%	1,100,000
2016	18–40	5,450,000	2,125,800	100%	1,110,000
2017	18–40	5,490,000	2,141,800	100%	1,120,000
2018	18–40	11,180,000	4,417,800	100%	1,140,000

Note: Year reflects period when feature took effect. See table 2.4 for temporary provisions in effect for 2002–2012. The estate tax exemption was scheduled to increase from $600,000 in 1997 to $1 million in 2006 (TRA97).

Table 2.2
Historical Features of the Gift Tax

Year	Tax Rate Range	Annual Exclusion per Donee	Exemption or Equivalent Amount	Unified Credit	Maximum Marital Deduction
1924	1–40%	$500	$50,000	N.A.	N.A.
1926	N.A.	N.A.	N.A.	N.A.	N.A.
1932	0.75–33.5	5,000	50,000	N.A.	N.A.
1934	0.75–45	5,000	50,000	N.A.	N.A.
1936	1.5–52.5	5,000	40,000	N.A.	N.A.
1942	2.25–57.75	4,000	40,000	N.A.	N.A.
1943	2.25–57.75	3,000	30,000	N.A.	N.A.
1949	2.25–57.75	3,000	30,000	N.A.	50% of Gift
1955	2.25–57.75	3,000	30,000	N.A.	50% of Gift
1977	18–70	3,000	120,667	$30,000	50% of Gift
1978	18–70	3,000	134,000	34,000	50% of Gift
1979	18–70	3,000	147,333	38,000	50% of Gift
1980	18–70	3,000	161,563	42,000	50% of Gift
1981	18–70	3,000	175,625	47,000	50% of Gift
1982	18–65	10,000	225,000	62,800	100%
1983	18–60	10,000	275,000	79,300	100%
1984	18–55	10,000	325,000	96,300	100%
1985	18–55	10,000	400,000	121,800	100%
1986	18–55	10,000	500,000	155,800	100%
1987	18–55	10,000	600,000	192,800	100%
1996	18–55	10,000	600,000	192,800	100%
1998	18–55	10,000	625,000	202,050	100%
1999	18–55	10,000	650,000	211,300	100%
2000	18–55	10,000	675,000	220,550	100%
2001	18–55	10,000	675,000	220,550	100%
2013	18–40	14,000	5,250,000	2,045,800	100%
2014	18–40	14,000	5,340,000	2,081,800	100%
2015	18–40	14,000	5,430,000	2,117,800	100%
2016	18–40	14,000	5,450,000	2,125,800	100%
2017	18–40	14,000	5,490,000	2,141,800	100%
2018	18–40	15,000	11,180,000	4,417,800	100%

Note: Year reflects period when feature took effect. See table 2.4 for temporary provisions in effect for 2002–2012. The annual exclusion is indexed to $11,000 in 2002 through 2005, to $12,000 in 2006 through 2008, and to $13,000 in 2009 through 2012. Note that the $50,000 exemption in 1924 is per calendar year. The gift tax exemption was scheduled to increase from $600,000 in 1997 to $1 million in 2006 (TRA97).

Table 2.3
Historical Features of the Generation-Skipping Transfer Tax (GSTT)

Year	Maximum Tax Rate (%)	Exemption per Donor	Exemption per Donee
1916	N.A.	N.A.	N.A.
1977	70	$250,000	N.A.
1982	65	1,000,000	N.A.
1983	60	1,000,000	N.A.
1984	55	1,000,000	N.A.
1985	55	1,000,000	N.A.
1986	55	1,000,000	N.A.
1987	55	1,000,000	$2,000,000
1990	55	1,000,000	N.A.
1999	55	1,010,000	N.A.
2000	55	1,030,000	N.A.
2001	55	1,060,000	N.A.
2013	40	5,250,000	N.A.
2014	40	5,340,000	N.A.
2015	40	5,430,000	N.A.
2016	40	5,450,000	N.A.
2017	40	5,490,000	N.A.
2018	40	11,180,000	N.A.

Note: Year reflects period when feature took effect. See table 2.4 for temporary provisions during 2002–2012. GSTT rate and exemption are set equal to the maximum values of that of the estate tax.

Table 2.4
Temporary Features of the Estate and Gift Tax: 2002–2012

Year	Estate Tax Rate Range	Exemption or Equivalent Amount	Unified Credit	GSTT* Exemption	Gift Tax Rate Range	Exemption or Equivalent Amount
2002	18–50	1,000,000	345,800	1,100,000	18–50	1,000,000
2003	18–49	1,000,000	345,800	1,120,000	18–49	1,000,000
2004	18–48	1,500,000	555,800	1,500,000	18–48	1,000,000
2005	18–47	1,500,000	555,800	1,500,000	18–47	1,000,000
2006	18–46	2,000,000	780,800	2,000,000	18–46	1,000,000
2007	18–45	2,000,000	780,800	2,000,000	18–45	1,000,000
2008	18–45	2,000,000	780,800	2,000,000	18–45	1,000,000
2009	18–45	3,500,000	1,455,800	3,500,000	18–45	1,000,000
2010	Repealed**	Repealed	Repealed	Repealed	18–35	1,000,000
2011	18–35	5,000,000	1,730,800	5,000,000	18–35	5,000,000
2012	18–35	5,120,000	1,772,800	5,120,000	18–35	5,120,000

* GSTT tax rate is equal to maximum estate tax rate.
** Assets are subject to basis-carryover regime. As an alternative to basis carryover, estates may opt into the 2011 tax law that exempts from tax estates up to $5,000,000 in taxable value.

Table 2.5
Changes in Estate and Gift Tax Rates

Estate Tax Changes		Gift Tax Changes	
Dates in Effect	Description	Dates in Effect	Description
September 9, 1916	Estate tax introduced with maximum rate of 10 percent and exemption of $50,000.		
March 3, 1917 October 4, 1917	Minimum and maximum tax rates raised to 1.5 and 15 percent, respectively; raised once again to 2 and 25 percent.		
February 24, 1919	Minimum tax rate lowered to 1 percent; Revenue Act of 1918.		
June 2, 1924	Maximum rate increased to 40 percent; a tax credit for state taxes was introduced equal to 25 percent of federal tax. Effective after 6:55 pm.	January 1, 1924	Gift tax introduced.
February 26, 1926	Maximum tax rate lowered to 20 percent and state death tax credit rate raised to 80 percent; 1924 changes repealed retroactively. Effective after 10:25 am.	February 26, 1926	Gift tax repealed retroactively.
June 6, 1932	Maximum estate tax rate raised from 20 to 45 percent, effective after 5 pm.	June 6, 1932	Gift tax enacted with a maximum rate of 33.75 percent.
May 11, 1934	Rate increased to 60 percent. Act of May 10, 1934.	January 1, 1935	Rate increased to 45 percent.
August 31, 1935	Rates increased to 70 percent. Act of August 30, 1935.	January 1, 1936	Rate increased to 52.50 percent.
June 26, 1940	Temporary10 percent surtax effective through 1945. Enacted on June 25, 1940.	June 26, 1940	Same as estate tax.
September 21, 1941	Maximum rate set to 77 percent. Act of September 20, 1941.	January 1, 1942	Rate increased to 57.75 percent.

Table 2.5 (continued)

Estate Tax Changes		Gift Tax Changes	
Dates in Effect	Description	Dates in Effect	Description
October 22, 1942	Estate tax exemption increased. Enacted on October 21, 1942.	January 1, 1943	Gift tax exemption reduced.
January 1, 1949	Introduced marital deduction equal to 50 percent of estate. Enacted on April 2, 1948.	January 1, 1949	Same as estate tax.
January 1, 1959	Small Business Revision Act of 1958 introduced installment payments.	N.A.	N.A.
January 1, 1977	Rate reduced to 70 percent. Enacted on October 4, 1976 (TRA76).	January 1, 1977	Estate and gift tax unified, and maximum gift tax rate increased to 70 percent.
January 1, 1982	Maximum rate reduced from 70 to 50 percent over four years (1982–1985). Unlimited deduction for spousal transfers. Enacted on August 31, 1981 (ERTA81).	January 1, 1982	Same as estate tax.
January 1, 1983	Limit exclusion of retirement assets to $100,000.	N.A.	N.A.
January 1, 1985	Maximum rate frozen at 55 percent by legislation enacted on July 18, 1984 (DEFRA). Repeal exclusion for retirement assets.	January 1, 1985	N.A. Same as estate tax.
October 23, 1986	Generation-skipping transfer tax introduced with a temporary $2 million exemption per donee through 1989. Enacted on October 22, 1986 (TRA86).	September 26, 1985	Same as estate tax but retroactive to 1985.
January 1, 1988	Maximum rate again frozen at 55 percent. Enacted on December 22, 1987.	January 1, 1988	Same as estate tax.

Table 2.5 (continued)

Estate Tax Changes		Gift Tax Changes	
Dates in Effect	Description	Dates in Effect	Description
January 1, 1993	Maximum rate set at 55 percent permanently. Enacted on August 10, 1993 (OBRA93).	January 1, 1993	Same as estate tax.
January 1, 2002	Tax phased out in steps by 2010, to be reintroduced in 2011.* Enacted on June 7, 2001 (EGTRRA)	January 1, 2002	Maximum rate reduced in steps to 35 percent, and reset to 55 percent in 2011.*
January 1, 2011	Temporary two year reduction in maximum tax rate to 35 percent with an exemption of $5 million. Enacted on December 17, 2010.*	January 1, 2011	Same as estate tax.*
January 1, 2013	Changes enacted in 2010 made permanent but with 40 percent top rate. Enacted on January 1, 2013.	January 1, 2013	Same as estate tax.
January 1, 2018	Doubled size of exempted estate to $10 million (indexed to 2011). Enacted on December 22, 2017, and expires after December 31, 2025.	January 1, 2017	Same as estate tax.

* See table 2.4 for temporary rates in effect in 2002 through 2012.

Summary

About a century ago, the estate tax was enacted at a time of great financial need as the government prepared for the military buildup in advance of World War I. These applied to estates in excess of $50,000 (about $1 million in 2018) with a maximum tax rate of 10 percent. With growing expenditures and expanding deficits, the early years were a turbulent period that witnessed rapid changes in the estate tax that led to the increase in the top tax rate from 10 percent in 1916 to 40 percent by 1924.

With growing surpluses, the federal estate tax was dramatically reduced in 1926 as the maximum tax rate was reduced to 20 percent, with 80 percent of the tax remitted to the states. But with the onset of the Great Depression, the estate tax was revamped by a number of successive laws over a decade that saw the maximum estate tax rate rise to 77 percent, with little change in the size of the exempted estate.

History seems to repeat itself with turbulence revisiting the estate tax nearly a century after its first enactment. But this time it does so in reverse direction with the reach of the estate tax curtailed. While the estate tax applied in 1916 with a maximum tax rate of 10 percent to taxable estates over $50,000 (about $1 million in 2018 dollars), about a century later the maximum tax rate is 40 percent applied to wealth in excess of $10 million (indexed to inflation as of 2011), with an unlimited deduction for spousal and charitable bequests. A much higher tax rate applies to a much narrower tax base.

3   Description of the Tax

The estate tax underwent numerous changes since its inception as it evolved into the current unified transfer tax system encompassing the estate, gift, and generation-skipping transfer taxes. Many of these changes affect the definition of wealth and its composition, allowable deductions, exemptions, tax rate schedules, and credits. A description follows of the law in effect in 2017 and a summary of the changes introduced over time that shaped each individual provision of the tax, including the temporary changes in effect over the period of 2018 to 2025.

The Tax Base

The current estate tax base encompasses the value of real estate, cash, bank deposits, stocks, bonds, mutual funds, businesses, pensions, and proceeds from life insurance policies owned by the decedent. Together, these assets form the gross estate.

The gift tax applies to lifetime transfers of assets just as transfers at death are taxed under the estate tax. One major distinction between the estate tax and the gift tax is that the latter applies on a tax-exclusive basis, as long as the donor pays the tax. In other words, the gift tax is based on the amount received by the donee and not the total amount, including tax, relinquished by the donor as in the case of bequests.[1] For an illustration, assume a parent wishing to make a cash transfer of $10 million faces a hypothetical gift or estate tax rate of 50 percent. Under the estate tax, the estate pays a tax of $5 million, and the heirs receive $5 million. Under the gift tax, the beneficiaries receive $6.66 million with a tax liability of $3.33 million, for a savings of $1.66 million.

When transfers, either testamentary (at death) or inter vivos (between living persons), skip a generation, as in the case of a grandchild, the underlying assets become subject to the generation-skipping transfer tax. This tax, using the maximum estate tax rate, applies in addition to the estate and gift tax. Beginning with the Tax Reform Act of 1986 (TRA86), the GSTT has applied regardless of whether the transfer is made directly to a grandchild, or through a trust as provided for in the Tax Reform Act of 1976 (TRA76).

Valuations
In determining the value of the gross estate, assets are generally valued at their market value (or appraised value in the absence of a publicly tradable market). Because assets may depreciate or decline in value between the date of death and the date the estate tax is due, the tax code provides an alternative valuation date.[2] Under current law, estates may value their assets (net and gross) at either their market value at the date of death or at six months from such date. The alternative valuation date was set at one year from the date of death when first introduced in 1935.

The tax code also provides an alternative valuation method for real property used on farms or in businesses.[3] Under this special-use valuation method, the value of an asset is based on its value as an ongoing business when that amount is less than its market value.[4] The excess of the market value over the special use value is excluded from the gross estate. This exclusion was first introduced in 1976, and limited to a maximum of $500,000. The maximum exclusion was increased to $750,000 in 1983, and is now indexed for inflation as of 1997 as documented in table 2.1 of chapter 2. The heirs to such property are required to actively manage it, and failure to materially participate in its operations or disposal of the property within ten years of its inheritance will subject the heirs to recapture taxes.[5]

While assets are expected to be valued at their fair market value, a reduced value may be reported under certain circumstances. For example, if a decedent, or donor, owned a large block of publicly traded stocks, the market value reported for tax purposes would likely be discounted. The discounted value may reflect the reduction in the expected lower trading price of such stock if a large block were to be sold. This blockage rule is one of many valuation methods employed by estate planners.

Minority discounts provide another valuation method more commonly used to value inter vivos gifts, especially of closely held businesses. This valuation discount is also extended to estates when a minority position is maintained in an asset. The value of interest transferred may fall short of the pro-rata share of the value of the corporation or entity transferred due to the lack of control or marketability.[6]

Life Insurance

Life insurance proceeds are included in the gross estate depending on the form of ownership of the policy.[7] They form part of the taxable estate if the decedent had owned or in any way controlled the underlying policies. They are excluded if the beneficiaries, or trusts formed on their behalf, owned these policies and fully control them. More specifically, they are excluded when the beneficiaries retain the exclusive right to change the listed beneficiaries, to borrow against the policy or pledge it as collateral for a loan, to cancel the policy, or to surrender it for any cash value. Excluded proceeds are reported on Form 712 and typically attached to the estate tax return.

Life insurance proceeds first became taxable under the Revenue Act of 1918, enacted with delay in February 1919, introduced some two years after the enactment of the estate tax. Under the Act, proceeds in excess of $40,000 from life insurance policies owned or controlled by the decedent, as well as other proceeds from policies on the life of the deceased owned by others, were made part of the gross estate. This treatment was revamped by the Act of 1942, which made taxable all proceeds from insurance policies where the decedent paid the premiums or had an incidence of ownership.

The scope of the estate tax treatment of life insurance proceeds was further modified by the introduction of the Internal Revenue Code of 1954. The act was an attempt to consolidate all previously enacted laws through 1953, including those related to the estate tax. While it clarified the provisions of the several tax codes enacted to date, it also made some relatively minor changes. More to the point, and as enacted, it dropped the ownership "premium paid" test in defining what portion of life insurance proceeds are included in the taxable estates. Since then, only proceeds from policies owned or controlled by the insured form part of the estate and are potentially taxable.

Pension Assets

Retirement assets in all of its forms are included in the taxable estate. These pension assets were generally exempt from estate taxation and excluded from the gross estate prior to 1982. The Tax Equity and Fiscal Responsibility Act of 1982 (TEFRA) limited this exclusion to $100,000, as part of a legislative package aimed at scaling back the scope of the tax cuts introduced in ERTA81 and the shortfall in tax revenues it may have contributed to. Beginning with the Deficit Reduction Act of 1984 (DEFRA), assets held in qualified pension plans, individual retirement accounts (IRAs), and similar plans became fully included in the gross estate.[8] To avoid double taxation, however, an income tax deduction for estate tax paid on such assets is provided for distributions from qualified plans to the heirs. The estate tax allocated to retirement distributions is reported on the beneficiary's individual income tax return as "Federal estate tax on income in respect of a decedent" under "Other Miscellaneous Deductions" on Form 1040, Schedule A.

The Tax Reform Act of 1986 levied a tax rate of 15 percent tax on "excessive" accumulations in retirement plans, as an addition to the estate tax.[9] An accumulation is deemed excessive if it exceeds the present value of a hypothetical annual annuity (generally the greater of $150,000 and $112,580 indexed for inflation as of 1989) using the life expectancy of a person as old as the decedent. The tax was repealed by the Taxpayer Relief Act of 1997 (TRA97), a congressional motion that may have been greatly influenced by the writings of John Shoven and David Wise.[10] In their working paper, which was eventually published in 1998, these authors argued that savers may face tax rates of 92 to 99 percent when the excise tax is combined with estate and income taxes.

Family-Owned Business

As amended by the Internal Revenue Service Restructuring and Reform Act of 1998, TRA97 introduced a new provision benefiting family-owned businesses. Beginning in 1998, estates may deduct up to $675,000 of the interest in a family business in computing the taxable estate.[11] For those who claim the maximum deduction, however, the maximum exemption available by virtue of the unified credit is limited to $625,000 for a combined value of $1.3 million; the deduction would have been $300,000 in 2006 with the size of the exempted estate at $1 million had the 2001 law changes and those that have followed not been enacted.

To qualify for this treatment, the value of the business must exceed 50 percent of the adjusted gross estate. Furthermore, the heirs are required to materially participate in running the business. As the exemption level was expanded over time, and exceeded $1.3 million, this deduction is no longer applicable.

Conservation Easements

Beginning in 1998, permanent conservation easements may benefit from a 40 percent exclusion of the value of land up to a maximum of $100,000, depending on the location of the property (TRA97).[12] The exclusion rose to $200,000 in 1999, $300,000 in 2000, $400,000 in 2001, and $500,000 in 2002 and thereafter.

Exemptions and Exclusions

When first enacted, the estate tax provided for an exemption of $50,000, or about $1,100,959 in 2016 dollars, in computing the taxable estate. Over the years, as table 2.1 illustrates, the exemption fluctuated within a narrow band through 1976 when it was $60,000. TRA76 repealed this exemption and replaced it with a unified credit of $30,000 in 1977, which is equivalent to an exemption of $120,667.

The gift tax provides for an annual exclusion of $10,000, or $20,000 in split gifts by husband and wife, per donee or beneficiary, which is indexed for inflation as of 1998 as called for by TRA97.[13] Prior to ERTA81, the exclusion was limited to $3,000 (see table 2.2). When first enacted, the gift tax provided a specific, or lifetime, exemption of $40,000, above and beyond the annual exclusion. The exemption fluctuated very little over the years through 1976 when it was $30,000, as shown in table 2.2. TRA76 also repealed this exemption and replaced it with the unified credit as it integrated the estate and gift taxes.

The GSTT exemption is set equal to the size of exempted estate. It allows an exemption of $5 million (indexed for inflation as of 2011), increased to $10 million for the years 2018 through 2025, for cumulative generation-skipping transfers per donor. This is up from the $1 million exemption provided for by TRA86, and as shown in table 2.3.[14] Effective for transfers in 1999, the GSTT exemption, as provided for in TRA97, is indexed for inflation. The exemption was $250,000 when the GSTT was first enacted in TRA76 and applied only to indirect transfers such as those generally from trusts. TRA86 also provided for a temporary $2 million exemption per grandchild for transfers during the period October 23, 1986, through 1989.

Deductions

A number of transfers and expenses are deductible in computing the taxable estate. These include spousal bequests (marital deduction), bequests to charity, debts of the decedent, and expenses incurred by the estate. State and local estate and inheritance taxes are also deductible in deriving the taxable estate. But prior to 2005, the deduction took the form of a tax credit, the State Death Tax Credit, which was converted to a deduction by EGTRRA. This deduction, along with its earlier form, will discussed in the tax credits section that follows.

Marital Deduction

All transfers of property to a U.S. citizen spouse are deductible in computing the taxable estate and gifts.[15] Prior to ERTA81, the deduction for spousal bequests was limited to the greater of $250,000 or one-half the Adjusted Gross Estate. The latter is defined as the gross estate less funeral expenses, estate administrative expenses, and debts. Prior to TRA76, estates could deduct only 50 percent of the gross estate (see table 2.1), and prior to the Act of 1948 no deduction was allowed; only the surviving spouse's interest in community property was excluded from the estate. Limiting the deduction to one-half of the estate was motivated by a desire to equalize the tax treatment of transfers to spouses in common law states with those in community property law states.[16] The motivation for the unlimited marital deduction in ERTA81 was that husband and wife ought to be treated as one unit, and that estate taxes would be paid eventually at the death of the surviving spouse. However, the act left untouched the step-up in basis on assets transferred to the spouse at death and the tax code continues to treat the two as distinct economic units for capital-gains tax purposes.

As under the estate tax, all inter vivos transfers of property to a U.S. citizen spouse are also deductible from the gift tax base. Prior to 1982, the deduction for spousal gifts was limited to 50 percent of the lifetime gifts in excess of $200,000. However, the first $100,000 of spousal gifts was fully deductible and the next $100,000 was fully taxable. Prior to 1977, the deduction was limited to only 50 percent of the gift.

Charitable Bequests

Amounts donated to qualifying charitable organizations and federal, state, and local governments are deductible in computing the taxable estate and lifetime gifts.[17] The deduction was first introduced by the Revenue Act of 1918, two years after the enactment of the estate tax. Lifetime charitable contributions are also deductible in computing the taxable gifts and income of the donor. The Tax Reform Act of 1969 tightened the rules governing bequests to foundations, especially those engaged in dealings with the heirs. TRA86 expanded the deduction to encompass conservation easements.

Other Deductions

The gross estate is reduced by the amount of outstanding debts held at death and by estate expenses.[18] These debts include mortgages and outstanding medical expenses. Funeral expenses and costs for settling the decedent's estate, such as attorney and executor commissions, are also deductible under the estate tax.[19] Alternatively, rather than being deducted against the taxable estate, some of these expenses may be deducted against the estate's (fiduciary) income tax. Attorney fees, for instance, may offset the taxable income derived from assets in the period between the date of death and the settlement of the estate.[20] With the rising size of the exempted estate, more of these estate expenses are likely to be deducted under the income tax.

Prior to ERTA81, bequests to orphan children could also be deducted. This deduction was limited to $5,000 for each year the orphan child was under age 21. Another deduction, introduced by TRA86, was for the sale of employer securities to employee stock ownership plans (ESOPs). This deduction was repealed for decedents dying after July 12, 1989 (Omnibus Budget Reconciliation Act of 1989).

Tax Rate Structure

As of 2013, the tax rate schedule ranges from 18 percent on the first $10,000 of taxable estate and gifts up to 40 percent for the excess over $1 million. The computed tentative tax is then reduced by the unified tax credit that exempts $5.25 million in taxable estate in 2013, or $11.2 million in 2018 as provided for by TCJA, signed into law on December 22, 2017. This compares to the 55 percent rate for the excess over $3 million of taxable estate and gifts had the law not changed permanently in 2013 and reverted back to 2001 law.

Table 3.1
Estate Tax Rate Schedules

Taxable Estate		Tax Rates by Year in Effect				
over	but not over	2001	2002	2011	2013	2018
0	10,000	18%	18%	18%	18%	18%
10,000	20,000	20%	20%	20%	20%	20%
20,000	40,000	22%	22%	22%	22%	22%
40,000	60,000	24%	24%	24%	24%	24%
60,000	80,000	26%	26%	26%	26%	26%
80,000	100,000	28%	28%	28%	28%	28%
100,000	150,000	30%	30%	30%	30%	30%
150,000	250,000	32%	32%	32%	32%	32%
250,000	500,000	34%	34%	34%	34%	34%
500,000	750,000	37%	37%	35%	37%	37%
750,000	1,000,000	39%	39%	35%	39%	39%
1,000,000	1,250,000	41%	41%	35%	40%	40%
1,250,000	1,500,000	43%	43%	35%	40%	40%
1,500,000	2,000,000	45%	45%	35%	40%	40%
2,000,000	2,500,000	49%	49%	35%	40%	40%
2,500,000	3,000,000	53%	50%	35%	40%	40%
3,000,000		55%	50%	35%	40%	40%
Addendum						
Unified credit		220,550	345,800	1,730,800	2,045,800	4,417,800
Equivalent exemption		675,000	1,000,000	5,000,000	5,250,000	11,180,000

Note: See table 2.4 for temporary tax rates, unified credits, and equivalent exemptions in effect between 2002 and 2012, and table 2.1 for parameters in effect after 2013.

The current tax rate schedule is shown in the last column of table 3.1, along with the rate schedules in effect in 2001 as well as the temporary rate schedules in 2002 and 2011; recall that the temporary maximum rates in effect over the years 2002 through 2012 are reported in table 2.4 of chapter 2. This rate schedule applies to the gross estate less allowable deductions plus lifetime taxable gifts. When the estate tax was first enacted, the tax rates ranged from 1 percent to 10 percent. As shown in table 2.1, these rates have changed considerably over the intervening years.

From 1987 through 1997, the benefit of the graduated tax rate schedule, along with the unified credit, to be described below, was phased out for taxable estates between $10,000,000 and $21,040,000, creating a surtax of 5 percent or a marginal tax rate of 60 percent (OBRA87). Beginning in 1998 through 2001, as provided for in TRA97, the graduated rates were phased out completely at taxable estates of $17,184,000 as shown in table 3.3. EGTRRA in 2001, temporarily, and ATRA in 2013 permanently repealed the phaseout of the benefit of graduate tax rates.

Cognizant of the interplay between the gifts and bequests, and beginning in 1977, Congress modified the gift tax so that it shared a common tax rate schedule with the estate tax, including unified tax credit amounts. Like the estate tax rates, gift tax rates have fluctuated considerably over the years (see table 2.2). Prior to 1977, the gift tax rates were set at 75 percent of the estate tax rates. Unlike the estate tax, the gift tax did not expire in 2010, with the maximum tax rate set at 35 percent The GSTT rate is set equal to the maximum statutory estate tax rate, or at 40 percent in 2013, and shares the estate tax exemption (see table 2.3).

Tax Credits

Several tax credits are available under the estate and gift tax. These credits include the unified credit, the state death tax credit (replaced with a deduction in 2005), the estate tax credit for gift taxes paid, and the credit for previously paid death taxes.

The Unified Credit

The largest of the available credits is the unified credit, which has been relabeled as the applicable credit amount.[21] The credit amount is $4,417,800 in 2018, which exempts $11.18 million in taxable estate, as set forth by the Tax Cuts and Jobs Act signed into law on December 22, 2017. The credit was set at was $1,945,800 in 2011, which effectively exempts $5 million in cumulative taxable estates and gifts, and is indexed for future inflation. Unused amounts, when taxable transfers are below the exemption, can be carried over and used by the estate of the surviving spouse (i.e., they are portable).

The credit was first introduced by the Tax Reform Act of 1976 that provided for a tax credit of $30,000 in 1977, equivalent to an exemption of $120,667. As table 2.1 illustrates, the value of this credit increased over time, especially with the enactment of ERTA81. From 1987 through 1997, the value of the unified credit was fixed at $192,800, equivalent to an exemption of $600,000, for combined estate and gift taxes. Thus, the first $600,000 of a taxable estate was taxed at a zero rate. Consequently, the marginal tax rate for estates in excess of $600,000 began at 37 percent. Taxable estates over $21,040,000 faced a flat tax rate of 55 percent. The unified credit, along with the progressive rate structure, was phased out between $10,000,000 and $21,040,000. The unified credit was set at $202,050 in 1998 and increased in steps to $345,800 so as to exempt taxable estates under $1 million in 2006, as provided for in TRA97 and before the temporary changes introduced in 2001and the permanent changes made in 2013 and beyond.

The State Death Tax Credit

Through 2004, the second-largest credit was that for state death taxes. In 2001 and prior years, and as provided for in the 1954 Act, the maximum credit was determined by a rate schedule for a given "adjusted taxable estate," defined as the federal taxable estate less $60,000.[22] The credit rate schedule ranges from zero to a maximum of 16 percent, as shown in table 3.2. The credit acts to reduce the maximum federal statutory tax rate to 39 percent, down from 55 percent, for the wealthiest estates (see table 3.2). EGTRRA phased out the credit, and reduced the allowed amount by 25, 50, and 75 percent between 2002 and 2004. In 2005, it replaced the tax credit with a deduction in 2005, and the American Taxpayer Relief Act of 2012 made this change to a deduction permanent.

This credit was first enacted by the Revenue Act of 1924 in response to the criticism that the federal government had encroached upon the state domain of death taxes. It was limited to 25 percent of the federal estate tax liability. In 1926, the maximum credit rate was further raised while the estate tax rate was lowered. The credit rate was set at 80 percent of the 20 percent maximum federal marginal tax rate applicable in 1926, or effectively 16 percent, which remained part of the estate tax code through 2004. Prior to the Internal Revenue Code of 1954, it was necessary for estates to calculate the federal tax liability under the 1926 law to compute the maximum credit available for state death taxes.

A similar credit was not allowed for state gift taxes, and a deduction is not available now either. But because state taxes are not considered as part of the gift tax base, reflecting on its tax-exclusive nature, they are effectively treated as exclusions in computing federal gift and estate taxes and do not need a federal tax credit or deduction to avoid double taxation by both jurisdictions.

Estate Tax Credit for Lifetime Gift Taxes

Because estate and gift taxes apply to cumulative transfers, cumulative lifetime gifts are added back to the taxable estate in computing the

Table 3.2
State Death Tax Credit Rate Schedule

State Death Tax Credit Rate Schedule		
Adjusted Taxable Estate*		
over	but not over	maximum tax credit
$0	$40,000	$0
40,000	90,000	0 + 0.8% of 40,000
90,000	140,000	400 + 1.6% of 90,000
140,000	240,000	1,200 + 2.4% of 140,000
240,000	440,000	3,600 + 3.2% of 240,000
440,000	640,000	10,000 + 4.0% of 440,000
640,000	840,000	18,000 + 4.8% of 640,000
840,000	1,040,000	27,600 + 5.6% of 840,000
1,040,000	1,540,000	38,800 + 6.4% of 1,040,000
1,540,000	2,040,000	70,800 + 7.2% of 1,540,000
2,040,000	2,540,000	106,800 + 8.0% of 2,040,000
2,540,000	3,040,000	146,800 + 8.8% of 2,540,000
3,040,000	3,540,000	190,800 + 9.6% of 3,040,000
3,540,000	4,040,000	238,800 + 10.4% of 3,540,000
4,040,000	5,040,000	290,800 + 11.2% of 4,040,000
5,040,000	6,040,000	402,800 + 12.0% of 5,040,000
6,040,000	7,040,000	522,800 + 12.8% of 6,040,000
7,040,000	8,040,000	650,800 + 13.6% of 7,040,000
8,040,000	9,040,000	786,800 + 14.4% of 8,040,000
9,040,000	10,040,000	930,800 + 15.2% of 9,040,000
10,040,000	and over	1,082,800 + 16.0% of 10,040,000

* The adjusted taxable estate is equal to the taxable estate less $60,000. While the credit was repealed in steps by EGTRRA beginning in 2002, the replacement of the credit with a deduction was made permanent by 2013.

estate tax. Since lifetime gifts have already been taxed, the estate tax provides a tax credit for previously paid gift taxes to avoid double taxation.[23] In general, this treatment is relevant when progressive effective tax rates apply.

Estate Tax Credit for Prior Federal Tax Paid
To minimize excessive taxation of recently inherited wealth, the estate tax also provides a credit for previously paid estate taxes.[24] In computing the estate tax, a credit is set equal to the estate tax previously paid on inherited wealth. This credit is phased out over ten years, in two-year intervals, from the date of death. This credit, introduced in 1954, has its roots in the Revenue Act of 1918 that allowed a deduction for

Table 3.3
Federal Marginal Tax Rates after Unified and State Death Tax Credit (2001 Law Fully
Phased-In*)

Taxable Estate** ($1,000s)		Tax Rate after Unified Credit (%)	State Death Tax Credit Rate (%)	Net Federal Tax Rate (%)
over	but not over			
0	600	0.0	0.0	0.0
600	700	0.0	0.0	0.0
700	750	0.0	0.0	0.0
750	900	0.0	0.0	0.0
900	1,000	0.0	0.0	0.0
1,000	1,100	41.0	5.6	35.4
1,100	1,250	41.0	6.4	34.6
1,250	1,500	43.0	6.4	36.6
1,500	1,600	45.0	6.4	38.6
1,600	2,000	45.0	7.2	37.8
2,000	2,100	49.0	7.2	41.8
2,100	2,500	49.0	8.0	41.0
2,500	2,600	53.0	8.0	45.0
2,600	3,000	53.0	8.8	44.2
3,000	3,100	55.0	8.8	46.2
3,100	3,600	55.0	9.6	45.4
3,600	4,100	55.0	10.4	44.6
4,100	5,100	55.0	11.2	43.8
5,100	6,100	55.0	12.0	43.0
6,100	7,100	55.0	12.8	42.2
7,100	8,100	55.0	13.6	41.4
8,100	9,100	55.0	14.4	40.6
9,100	10,000	55.0	15.2	39.8
10,000	10,100	60.0	15.2	44.8
10,100	17,184	60.0	16.0	44.0
17,184	and over	55.0	16.0	39.0

* Fully phased-in by 2006 as called for by the Tax Relief Act of 1997.
** The taxable brackets are expanded to accommodate both the tax and state credit rate
schedules. The credit was temporarily repealed by EGTRRA and permanently by ATRA
in 2013. Under 2013 law, taxable estates face a marginal federal tax rate of 40 percent for
estates in excess of $5,250,000 (indexed).

taxes paid on property inherited within five years from the transferor's
date of death.

Due Dates

The estate tax, reported on Form 706, is due within nine months from
the date of death. When first enacted, the estate tax was due one year
after the date of death; estates with early payments within the year
were granted a discount of 5 percent. The gift tax on transfers in a given

calendar year, reported on Form 709, is due on April 15 of the following calendar year sharing the treatment of individual income tax filers. The deadline for filing returns can be extended for another six months on top of the initial nine-month-filing requirement.

At the discretion of the IRS, the time to pay the estate tax can be extended for up to one year.[25] This is requested on Form 4768, part III, with an explanation of the reasons for delay. Nevertheless, it is possible to re-extend up to a total of ten years for a "reasonable cause," with interest charges. As an example, if the estate is in some litigation with someone over asset ownership, then this would be considered a valid reason to delay payments as the estate attempts to recover its assets. In another example, the estate may not have the cash to pay the tax bill if some of its value is based on, for example, royalties from patents due in the future.

In general, however, and absent extension request approvals, delays in paying the tax liability in full would subject the estate to interest and penalties. Filing an estate tax return late will also subject the estate to penalties in the absence of valid reasons.[26] The penalty would be 5 percent of the tax liability for every month of delay, up to 25 percent of the tax bill.

Prior to 1981, the gift tax was also due on April 15 of the following year, except for gifts made in the first three quarters of the calendar year on which the tax was due on the fifteenth of the second month of the fourth quarter of the year. The GSTT is due on the dates the applicable estate or gift tax returns are due.

Tax Deferral

Estates with closely held businesses and farms may defer a fraction of the estate tax attributable to the business and pay the tax under the installment method.[27] This provision was first introduced by the Small Business Tax Revision Act of 1958 that provided for equal installment payments over a period of ten years, with a 4 percent interest rate, from the due date of the tax. The tax is now deferred for up to fourteen years from the otherwise due date (nine months from the date of death), with no principal payable during the first five years. Through 1997, interest payments were deductible against the estate tax. Calculating these interest payments was a cumbersome task that required the recalculation of the estate tax liability and the refiling of tax returns in each year of the deferral period. No similar provision is available for the gift tax.

The fraction of taxes deferred is equal to the ratio of the value of the qualifying interest in a closely held business to the adjusted gross estate, provided that this ratio is in excess of 35 percent (65 percent before 1982). Qualifying interest includes the value of proprietorships, and corporate stock or partnership interest if at least 20 percent of the voting stock or partnership assets is included in the estate, or if the corporation has no more than fifteen shareholders. A less generous deferral is also available to certain estates, such as those with severe liquidity constraints, at the discretion of the Commissioner of the Internal Revenue Service.[28]

Through 1997, and for qualifying estates, the tax was payable in installments at an interest rate equal to the short-term applicable federal rate (AFR) plus 3 percentage points. The tax on the first $1 million of the taxable estate, however, was deferred at a preferential interest rate of 4 percent. Due to the deductibility of interest expenses, the effective interest rate charged, for those in the 55 percent tax bracket, was 1.8 percent on the tax liability on the first million of taxable estate, $4 \times (1 - 0.55)$, and 4.05 percent for the tax liability on the taxable estate in excess of $1 million, assuming a 9 percent interest rate (or a 6 percent AFR).

Beginning in 1998, the interest rate charged on the tax on the first $1 million of taxable estate is set at 2 percent per TRA97. The $1 million threshold is in excess of the size of the exempted estate by virtue of the unified credit, and is adjusted for inflation after 1998. The interest rate charged on the tax liability on the taxable estate in excess of $1 million is set at 45 percent, or $1 - 0.55$, of the AFR. Interest charges are no longer deductible, which offsets the benefits of the lower interest rates. These changes significantly improve the administration of the tax because future recalculation of the tax liability and the filing of tax returns are done away with.

Summary

The current estate tax base can be characterized as a tax on the value of assets held at death with some adjustments. The latter include adjustments for changes in market conditions that may have depressed the assets' value before the filing of tax returns (alternative valuation date), as well as reduced valuations due to special tax preferences for businesses and farms, or resulting from private appraisals (minority discounts). The value of assets reported for tax purposes is then reduced by indebtedness and estate-related expenses.

The tax code allows full deductibility of transfers to charitable organizations, as well as spousal bequests. Assets transferred to spouses in trusts such as QTIPs, even though they are not necessarily under the full control of the surviving spouse, qualify for the marital deduction as the remainder of QTIP assets form part of her estate at death.

Reflecting on its cumulative nature, the resulting taxable estate is augmented with the sum of lifetime taxable gifts, and the tax rate schedule is applied to the combined transfers. The computed tentative tax is reduced by a number of tax credits, the largest of which is the unified credit that effectively exempts $11.18 million ($10 million indexed as of 2011) of taxable estates in 2018. Other tax credits include the credit for previously paid gift taxes, and credit for previously paid estate tax on inherited wealth. Generation-skipping transfer taxes are further added in deriving the total tax liability. Estates with sizeable business and farm assets are able to pay the tax in installments at low interest rates.

4   Profile of Taxpayers

The size and profile of taxpayers have varied over the years with the evolution of the estate and gift taxes. Rising filing thresholds and statutory exemptions on the one hand have led to a reduction in the number of individuals touched by the estate tax. Economic growth, on the other hand, often led to an expansion in the size of the population subject to the estate tax. The discussion that follows traces the population that is affected by the tax and sketches out its profile.

The Estate Tax

The number of tax returns filed during federal fiscal years 1933 through 2016 is shown in table 4.1. The number of estates has fluctuated over the years, and rose almost uninterrupted through the third quarter of the twentieth century as the reach of the estate tax was expanded. By the time the estate tax was codified in 1954, about 40,000 tax returns were filed. And the number of returns filed peaked in fiscal year 1977 at 248,000 returns. This growth was shaped exclusively by expansions in the economy and population growth, absent any tax law changes. But then it abruptly declined to 160,000 immediately after the doubling of the size of the exempted estate of $60,000 to 120,667 introduced by the Tax Reform Act of 1976.

As the size of the exempted estate expanded, the number of returns filed dramatically declined despite the performance of the economy and the expanding size of the population. TRA76, in addition to doubling the exemption in 1977, also expanded it in steps over the following years. ERTA81 further expanded the exemption from 175625 in 1981, in steps to 600,000 in 1987.

Table 4.1
Number of Estate Tax Returns Filed

Year	Returns	Year	Returns	Year	Returns
1933	8,504	1962	72,617	1991	63,988
1934	11,210	1963	79,426	1992	66,755
1935	13,133	1964	87,339	1993	73,389
1936	13,252	1965	94,051	1994	78,267
1937	15,244	1966	103,413	1995	82,860
1938	17,794	1967	113,081	1996	86,414
1939	18,265	1968	119,272	1997	97,267
1940	18,908	1969	123,495	1998	108,710
1941	19,044	1970	131,870	1999	117,226
1942	19,633	1971	149,432	2000	121,171
1943	18,430	1972	192,833	2001	121,715
1944	17,205	1973	201,975	2002	120,576
1945	17,927	1974	211,540	2003	91,679
1946	19,704	1975	215,918	2004	73,340
1947	23,209	1976	236,482	2005	65,703
1948	25,493	1977	248,316	2006	58,000
1949	28,472	1978	160,152	2007	49,924
1950	29,530	1979	159,404	2008	46,251
1951	31,896	1980	148,228	2009	47,320
1952	34,151	1981	145,617	2010	28,780
1953	37,000	1982	134,965	2011	11,128
1954	39,000	1983	111,415	2012	26,859
1955	40,000	1984	89,798	2013	32,288
1956	44,000	1985	76,729	2014	34,132
1957	49,000	1986	71,518	2015	36,343
1958	54,237	1987	60,755	2016	35,592
1959	61,250	1988	52,364	2017	34,340
1960	62,304	1989	54,700		
1961	69,405	1990	58,629		

Source: *IRS Data Book*, Internal Revenue Service, Washington, DC, various years.
Note: The number of returns reported in this table include amended and duplicate returns, as well as returns below the filing thresholds. They are generally larger than the number of estate tax decedents in a given year.

After fiscal year 1988, the number of returns filed resumed its upward trend, peaking around 121,000 in 2001. The enactment of EGTRRA dramatically expanded the exemption, and led to a significant reduction in the filing population in fiscal year 2003 and beyond. By fiscal year 2016, about 36,000 returns were filed. And these are likely to further trickle to a fraction following the expansion in the exemption to $11.18 million in 2018.

It should be noted that this time series of the number of tax returns filed includes amended and otherwise duplicate returns, as well as returns filed several years past the date of death. These may arise from audits, or from previously filed estate tax returns amended for mistakes, or from estates making use of the installment method requiring interest payments on deferred tax that also necessitate the recalculation of tax liability and filing of amended returns over some fourteen-year period. They may also include returns with gross estates below the required filing thresholds. As an example of the latter, estate tax returns with assets below the thresholds may be filed to make sure the statute of limitations apply, and avoid penalties in case of future audits outside the typical three-year statute of limitations. Thus, the figures overstate the actual number of final tax returns filed for decedents in a particular year.

Also, and critically because the fiscal year ends on September 30, these figures are bound to be different from those filed in a given calendar year, and certainly different from the number of those dying in a given year with estates required to be filed. Table 4.2 provides figures for estate tax returns filed in calendar year 2016, clean of any duplicate and amended returns. Given the delays in filing requirements, these returns for the most part represent decedents in 2015.

General Profile

By design, the reach of the estate tax is restricted to the wealthiest of estates, leaving untouched the overwhelming estates of decedents. As an example, about 2.7 million individuals died in 2015.[1] Of these, only about 12,411 left behind estates large enough to file estate tax returns in 2016. And of these, less than one-half were subject to tax.

As shown in table 4.2, only about 5,219, around one twentieth of 1 percent of all decedents, left behind estates with reported federal tax liability in 2016. This is possible because of the unified credit of $2,117,800 that exempts from tax estates with assets under $5.43 million, and along with the unlimited marital deduction that exempts all bequests to spouses, the charitable bequests, and a number of other deductions for estate expenses, which combined remove many from the tax rolls.

There are 7,052 estates with gross estates between $5 million and $10 million. Of these, only 4,842 are subject to tax. As with all filers, the $5 million exemption along with some of the other deductions explain much of the reduced number of taxable returns. With regard to the wealthiest estates—those with gross estates in excess of $50 million—434 estate tax returns were filed and only 300 are taxable. The

Table 4.2
Profile of Estate Tax Filers in 2016 (Amounts in $Millions)

Gross Estate ($Millions)	Gross Estate		Lifetime Gifts		Spousal Bequests		Charitable Bequests	
	Number	Amount	Number	Amount	Number	Amount	Number	Amount
< 5	1,218	4,073	1,145	4,352	432	779	232	110
5 < 10	7,052	49,293	2,790	4,765	3,615	13,110	1,276	1,926
10 < 20	2,635	35,824	1,431	3,617	1,418	12,235	624	2,091
20 < 50	1,073	31,587	739	3,234	553	11,472	369	3,079
50 and over	434	71,443	378	3,484	239	36,201	214	11,288
All	12,411	192,219	6,482	19,452	6,257	73,797	2,714	18,494
Taxable Returns Only								
< 5	611	1,964	585	2,566	35	35	131	39
5 < 10	2,402	17,254	1,292	3,037	190	268	492	226
10 < 20	1,293	17,974	812	2,504	227	1,052	362	555
20 < 50	611	18,285	477	2,473	151	1,944	239	1,316
50 and over	300	52,315	273	2,957	116	19,905	173	9,340
All	5,219	107,791	3,440	13,537	718	23,203	1,396	11,476

Table 4.2 (continued)

Gross Estate ($Millions)	Debts		State Tax Deduction		Tax		Tax % of Net Worth*	Tax % of Net Worth**
	Number	Amount	Number	Amount	Number	Amount		
< 5	820	124	327	54	611	347	10.2%	13.1%
5 < 10	4,842	1,767	1,418	580	2,402	1,975	5.4%	7.9%
10 < 20	2,000	1,286	612	583	1,293	3,838	12.8%	21.9%
20 < 50	848	1,555	270	517	611	4,577	17.0%	32.9%
50 and over	369	2,473	157	959	300	7,559	12.4%	39.7%
All	8,878	7,205	2,783	2,694	5,219	18,296	11.3%	22.6%
Taxable Returns Only								
< 5	493	48	186	34	611	347	19.9%	20.7%
5 < 10	2,037	392	773	384	2,402	1,975	14.0%	14.4%
10 < 20	1,163	549	458	548	1,293	3,838	25.2%	27.7%
20 < 50	559	780	212	504	611	4,577	29.0%	35.7%
50 and over	273	1,929	134	954	300	7,559	16.9%	40.3%
All	4,526	3,699	1,762	2,424	5,219	18,296	19.9%	29.9%

Source: IRS Statistics, https://www.irs.gov/statistics/soi-tax-stats-estate-tax-statistics-filing-year-table-1, and author's computations.

* Net worth is gross estate less debts and estate expenses.

** Net worth less spousal and charitable bequests, a proxy for bequests to heirs.

nontax status of the wealthiest estates is primarily due to the unlimited marital deduction and charitable bequests.

It is noteworthy that a sizeable number of estates below the filing threshold of $5 million have also filed tax returns. Indeed, 1,218 such returns were filed, or about 10 percent of the total number of filers. This should not come as a surprise, and it is not an anomaly. Technically, and reflecting on the cumulative nature of the estate and gift taxes, the filing threshold is the sum of the gross estate and cumulative lifetime gifts and not just the assets held at death. Otherwise, an individual may make a gift during life of say $10 million and leave behind an estate of $3 million and face no taxes on the latter. Indeed, the figures on lifetime gifts reported in table 4.2 confirm the important role gifts play in explaining the filing of the smallest of estates. Of the 1,218 estates under $5 million, 1,145 reported making taxable lifetime gifts totaling $4.4 billion.

Close to one-half of estate tax decedents provided for spousal transfers. In contrast, such estates make up about 7 percent of taxable estates. With the combination of the $5 million exemption and spousal bequests, most married decedents should leave behind estates free of estate taxes. The largest estates, perhaps not surprisingly, include a greater share of those providing spousal bequests. A total of $73.8 billion in spousal transfers are reported, which account for about one-third of the reported gross estate, a share that peaks at one-half the value for the group of largest estates; $36.2 vs. $71.4 billion for estates in excess of $50 million.

Charitable bequests represent another offset in computing the estate tax on the wealth reported at death. Over 20 percent of the estates provide for bequests to qualified charitable organizations. The fraction of estates giving to charities peaks at about 50 percent for the largest estates, whose owners gave away more than 15 percent of their wealth. A total of $18.5 billion in bequests are reported, with some 62 percent reported by estates in excess of $50 million.

The gross estate is further reduced by outstanding debts. These can be mortgages on residences and other real estate as well as personal loans. They may also include small amounts of unpaid medical bills and overdue taxes. About $7.2 billion in debts were reported, with about one-third reported by the wealthiest of estates, which interestingly appear more likely to be leveraged than the less well off.

Close to 25 percent of the estates deduct taxes paid to state and local governments on their taxable assets allocated to these jurisdictions.

They pay a total of $2.7 billion, which adds to the tax burden faced by these estates. A greater fraction of the wealthiest group claims this deduction and pays a greater share of these local taxes.

After subtracting all the deductions from the gross estate, applying the tax rate schedule and available tax credit, these estates report a total federal estate tax liability of $18.3 billion.[2] Defining the total tax liability as the sum of federal tax liability and the deduction for state death taxes, estates paid in taxes about 11.3 percent of their net worth less estate expenses, with "net worth" defined as gross estate less debts outstanding. This ranges from 5.4 percent for the estates between $5 million and $10 million, to a high of 12.4 percent for those with estates over $50 million. The tax liability as percent of net worth, less estate expenses and charitable and spousal bequests (essentially the effective tax rate on bequests to non-spouse heirs) is about 22.6 percent and ranges from a low of 7.9 percent to 39.7 percent for the wealthiest estates.

Asset Composition

Corporate equity makes up the largest category of assets held by estate tax decedents, as shown in table 4.3. A total of $72 billion in corporate equity is reported, $47 billion of which is in the form of publicly traded stocks, and $25 billion in the form of closely held stocks. The latter includes S corporations and C corporations where the decedent had at least a 20-percent share of ownership or control.

Of all the estate tax returns filed in 2016, 10,251, representing some 84 percent of all estates, reported holding publicly traded corporate stock, totaling $47 billion, which is about one-quarter of all assets held by the estates. There is little variation across estates both in terms of the fraction holding such stock or its share in the value of the gross estate.

About one-third of the estates, or 3,442 returns, reported holding closely held stock totaling $25 billion in value, or just under 13 percent of the gross estate. The very wealthy hold a disproportionately large share of these assets, which also form a larger share of their estates when compared to the other less well-off estates.

Virtually all estates hold cash, but it accounts for only 7 percent of the gross estate or $14.8 billion. The very wealthy hold a much smaller share of their assets in this form. As an example, for those estates with assets in excess of $50 million, cash makes up about 5 percent of all assets held, whereas it makes up close to 10 percent for estates under $10 million.

Table 4.3
Portfolio Composition of Estate Tax Filers in 2016 (Amounts in $Millions)

Gross Estate ($Millions)	Personal Residence		Other Real Estate		Real Estate Partnerships	
	Number	Amount	Number	Amount	Number	Amount
< 5	592	354	667	340	167	135
5 < 10	4,898	3,907	5,125	5,476	1,185	1,838
10 < 20	1,952	2,302	2,043	3,599	629	1,502
20 < 50	809	1,637	874	2,760	341	1,532
50 and over	325	1,214	374	3,159	176	5,352
All	8,576	9,415	9,083	15,334	2,498	10,359

Gross Estate ($Millions)	Closely Held Stock		Publicly Traded Stock		State and Local Bonds	
	Number	Amount	Number	Amount	Number	Amount
< 5	207	117	938	984	639	423
5 < 10	1,673	2,271	5,720	11,261	3,963	3,892
10 < 20	860	2,626	2,260	9,245	1,597	3,351
20 < 50	459	2,807	939	8,640	683	2,888
50 and over	243	17,025	393	16,526	296	3,778
All	3,442	24,845	10,251	46,656	7,178	14,332

Gross Estate ($Millions)	Cash		Retirement Assets		Other Limited Partnerships	
	Number	Amount	Number	Amount	Number	Amount
< 5	1,196	481	643	392	230	91
5 < 10	6,946	4,730	4,969	5,713	1,722	921
10 < 20	2,604	3,377	1,735	2,715	941	922
20 < 50	1,066	2,769	692	1,370	458	1,442
50 and over	433	3,473	249	834	257	3,568
All	12,243	14,830	8,288	11,023	3,608	6,943

Source: IRS, Statistics, https://www.irs.gov/statistics/soi-tax-stats-estate-tax-statistics -filing-year-table-1, and author's computations.

These estates also report holding about $14 billion in tax exempt bonds. These are also more likely to form a smaller share of the portfolios of the very wealthy. About 5 percent of the estates of those with assets over $50 million consist of tax exempt bonds compared to about 10 percent of those in the lower wealth groups. In contrast, much less is held in corporate bonds as well as federal bonds. About 40 percent of the estates reported holding $2.7 billion in corporate bonds. Similarly, a quarter of the estates held federal bonds totaling $1.9 billion.

Table 4.3 (continued)

Gross Estate ($Millions)	Farm Assets		Other Noncorp. Assets		Private Equity/ Hedge Fund	
	Number	Amount	Number	Amount	Number	Amount
< 5	130	151	149	47	51	15
5 < 10	1,011	2,852	1,427	796	484	159
10 < 20	378	1,415	806	795	348	249
20 < 50	140	613	405	901	237	507
50 and over	72	1,065	247	3,193	156	3,301
All	1,731	6,096	3,034	5,731	1,275	4,230

Gross Estate ($Millions)	Mortgages and Notes		Corp./Foreign Bonds		Net Life Insurance	
	Number	Amount	Number	Amount	Number	Amount
< 5	319	160	362	65	385	53
5 < 10	1,854	1,061	2,598	729	3,139	1,287
10 < 20	879	955	1,113	545	1,105	575
20 < 50	521	1,315	506	493	430	269
50 and over	280	3,329	217	862	175	261
All	3,853	6,820	4,795	2,694	5,234	2,445

Gross Estate ($Millions)	Art		Federal Bonds		Excluded Life Insurance	
	Number	Amount	Number	Amount	Number	Amount
< 5	121	15	218	37	277	619
5 < 10	847	138	1,659	382	1,071	4,322
10 < 20	540	185	633	270	547	1,645
20 < 50	326	330	291	253	240	1,189
50 and over	215	1,558	148	954	122	2,076
All	2,049	2,226	2,949	1,895	2,256	9,850

Source: IRS, Statistics of Income, https://www.irs.gov/statistics/soi-tax-stats-estate-tax
-statistics-filing-year-table-1, and author's computations.

Moving away from financial assets, about $45 billion in real estate-related assets were reported by these estates. Of these $9.4 billion were in the form of personal residences, $15.3 billion in other real estate, and $10.3 billion in the form of real estate partnerships. The latter partnerships are most highly concentrated and held by the top wealth group. About one-half of these partnerships, or $5.3 billion, is reported by the estates with assets over $50 million. Ownership of the "other real estate" category, which mostly includes rental property and vacation homes, is less concentrated with the wealthiest group accounting for about 20 percent of the real estate held. Ownership of personal residences is more dispersed with one noteworthy observation. About one-quarter of the estates do not report personal residences; only 8,576 out of 12,411 do.

In addition to the closely held businesses in the form of corporate equity and real estate already summarized, these estates also report holding other related forms of business assets. These include farm assets, noncorporate business assets and other limited partnerships, and private equity and hedge funds. About $6.1 billion is held in farm assets, with close to one-half concentrated in $5 million- to $10 million-sized estates. Close to $7 billion is held in the form of other limited partnerships, with over one-half held by the wealthiest group. An additional $5.7 billion is reported held in the other noncorporate business assets category, with one-half once again held by the top wealth group. Another $4.2 billion is held in private equity and hedge bunds, with three quarters held by those with estates over $50 million.

Retirement assets, which were once tax exempt prior to 1982, are sizeable too. These assets, whether in the form of Individual Retirement Accounts (IRAs), 401(k), or other type of pension vehicle, are reported by two thirds of the estates for a total $11 billion. The average pension value is about $1.3 million, and these assets are relatively well dispersed across all estates.

Life insurance policy proceeds, reduced by policy loans, are reported with a value of $2.4 billion, as shown in table 4.3. When compared to the total number of estates, these proceeds are reported by about 45 percent of the estates regardless of the estate size. They represent about 2 percent of the gross estate for all decedents, and peak at 0.4 percent for the wealthiest estates. But interestingly, another $9.4 billion in life insurance proceeds are missing and not reported. These proceeds are excluded from the estate and escape taxation because beneficiaries have direct ownership and control over the policies. When compared to included life insurance proceeds, the wealthiest estates report disproportionately more excluded proceeds. The excluded share of total insurance proceeds rises with the size of estate, and reaches about 90 percent for the estates with assets in excess of $50 million.

Asset Valuation
Estates have the option of valuing assets as of the date of death or six months from such date, and to report the value of the assets in the gross

estate using the minimum of the values obtained. Their chosen valuations form the gross estate for tax purposes. The total amount of assets
valued on the date of death is $193.3 billion, whereas the value reported
for tax purposes is $192.2 billion, a reduction in reported value of
$1.1 billion.

Another valuation method extended to estates, typically those with
extensive business and farm ownership as described in chapter 3,
allows estates to value business and farm assets on their capitalized
income as a going concern, which can be much lower than the market
value. As an example, a farm located near an urban center may elicit a
much higher value from a real estate developer than its value as an
operating farm. The difference between the market value and the capitalized value that can be excluded from the estate is capped at $1.14
million in 2018. The excluded amount due to this special valuation was
about $50 million in 2016 claimed by some fifty estates.

The third and largest valuation method relates to discounts that
estates claim in reporting the value of assets due to minority ownership
among other situations. These self-reported discounts are not sanctioned by Congress, and often reflect aggressive tax positions that have
been sanctioned by the courts.

The wealth reported on estate tax returns is reduced by $9.1 billion
in valuation discounts to arrive at the gross estate. These can be attrib-
uted to minority discounts and lack of marketability among other
attributes of assets held at death. Corporate equity accounts for slightly
more than 40 percent of these discounts, real estate in all of its forms
of ownership for 25 percent, and other limited partnerships for 13
percent, other noncorporate business assets for close to 9 percent, farms
for about 5 percent, and private equity and hedge funds for another 5
percent, as shown in table 4.4. Other remaining assets account for less
than 2 percent.

Decedent Spouse's Unused Exemption (DSUE)

In late 2010, the Tax Relief, Unemployment Insurance Authorization,
and Job Creation Act of 2010 (TRUIAJC) introduced the portability of
a decedent spouse's unused exemption (DSUE). Whereas estates under
the size of the exemption are not required to file tax returns, the introduction of the portability of DSUE created incentives for these small
estates of the first-to-die spouse to file tax returns to provide for an
expanded exemption for the estates of the second-to-die spouse. As an
example, an individual who passed away in 2011 with an estate of $3

Table 4.4
Valuation Discounts Reported on Estate Tax Returns Filed in 2016 (Amounts Are in
$Millions)

| | Valuation Discounts | |
Asset Type	Amount	Percent of Total
Total	9,056	100.0
Stock	3,730	41.2
Real estate	2,286	25.2
Other limited partnerships	1,190	13.1
Noncorporate business assets	779	8.6
Farms	475	5.2
Private equity and hedge funds	459	5.1
Other assets	137	1.5

Source: Author's calculations from sample of estate tax returns filed in 2016.

million, well below the $5 million allowed exemption and filing threshold, will be able to pass $2 million in unused exemptions to the surviving spouse for use by her estate; the unified credit was $1,730,800 in 2011, which exempted from tax estates under $5 million. This $2 million DSUE is in addition to the exemption that the surviving spouse is able to claim ($5 million in 2011).

Figures obtained from returns filed in 2016 show that 719 estates reported $2.3 billion in in used DSUE by the estates of surviving spouses. And, perhaps not surprisingly, most of these are used by the relatively smaller estates, although some of the larger estates benefit from them as well. As an example, in 2016 fifteen estates with assets in excess of $50 million claimed $34 million in additional exemptions.

Comparisons with Estates for the Year 2001

It would be informative to compare the most recent estate tax filings to those from a period before the expansion in the size of exempted estates. In 2001, for instance, the exemption threshold was $675,000, which is much smaller than the $5.43 million exemption threshold for those filing in 2016 (and that of $11.18 million in 2018). At the time, the number of deaths was smaller and the value of assets was lower as well. But on net, there were more estate tax filers as the filing threshold was lower.

For decedents in 2001, about 110,000 estates were filed with 50,000 reporting federal tax liabilities—about ten times the number of estates, including those taxable, filed in 2016. These estates reported $229 billion in gross assets. Unadjusted for growth and inflation, these estates are about 10 to 20 percent larger than those reported in 2016. Similarly, the federal tax liability is greater by about 30 percent, $23.9 vs. $18.3 billion. The former is weighed down by the availability of the credit for state death taxes, which is replaced by a deduction for the latest filers. And because some states abolished their inheritance taxes, a disproportionately smaller number of estates claim the deduction. The combined federal and state taxes, with the deduction or credit as proxy for latter, represent a higher share of wealth in 2001. In particular, this effective tax rate is much higher for the larger estates, although much of this difference between the two years disappears for the wealthiest group once we focus on the net federal tax liability only.

Estates by State

In addition to the size of the estate, another key variable of interest is the geographic distribution of tax filers and tax liability by state. Table 4.6 provides a geographical breakdown of estate tax returns filed in 2016. Perhaps not surprisingly, residents of the states of California, Florida, New York, and Texas account for about one-half of the universe of federal estate tax filers facing a tax liability. The taxes paid by these four states represent close to 40 percent of those paid by all filers nationwide.

The Gift Tax

As with transfers taking effect at death, transfers during life potentially require filing a gift tax return. But unlike estate tax returns, gift tax returns are required to be filed when the amount transferred, other than that for tuition and medical expenses, exceeds the annual exclusion of $10,000 adjusted for inflation as of 1998. Thus, an individual making a gift of $10,000 or less to his son, or a couple making gifts less than $20,000 (both indexed for inflation) in split gifts to each of their three daughters, may not file tax returns. Consequently, the majority of Americans are not subjected to the gift tax or its filing requirements. But because the filing threshold for the gift tax is much lower than that of the estate tax, we should expect disproportionately more filings of gift tax returns. As an example, the filing threshold was $14,000 for the transfers to individual recipients under the gift tax in 2016 compared to $5.45 million for gross estates in the case of the estate tax.

Table 4.5
Profile of Estate Tax Decedents in 2001 (Amounts in $Millions)

Gross Estate ($Millions)	Gross Estate Number	Amount	Lifetime Gifts Number	Amount	Spousal Bequests Number	Amount	Charitable Bequests Number	Amount
0.675 < 1	45,000	36,884	2,608	597	15,996	5,322	6,125	907
1 < 2.5	48,686	72,119	5,004	1,386	22,270	19,871	8,510	3,378
2.5 < 5	10,223	34,833	2,513	1,251	5,295	12,991	2,400	2,052
5 < 10	3,656	24,962	1,541	1,066	1,825	9,542	1,052	1,954
10 < 20	1,302	17,729	728	923	688	7,206	473	1,774
20 and over	695	42,493	504	1,383	388	17,178	337	9,590
All	109,562	229,019	12,898	6,606	46,462	72,110	18,897	19,653

Taxable Returns Only

Gross Estate ($Millions)	Number	Amount	Number	Amount	Number	Amount	Number	Amount
0.675 < 1	16,161	13,957	1,762	506	444	52	1,830	43
1 < 2.5	25,295	37,261	3,280	1,029	1,969	847	5,382	694
2.5 < 5	5,440	18,689	1,710	1,049	946	1,365	1,610	749
5 < 10	2,221	15,237	1,120	897	514	1,821	808	1,164
10 <20	833	11,368	544	769	264	2,105	377	1,106
20 and over	508	33,125	401	1,254	217	9,109	287	8,897
All	50,456	129,638	8,817	5,505	4,354	15,299	10,294	12,654

Gross Estate ($Millions)	Debts Number	Amount	State Tax Credit Number	Amount	Tax Number	Amount	Tax % of Net Worth*	Tax % of Net Worth**
0.675 < 1	31,035	874	22,185	433	16,161	659	3.1%	3.8%
1 < 2.5	35,118	2,272	25,976	1,360	25,295	5,612	10.2%	15.5%
2.5 < 5	8,092	1,261	5,678	930	5,440	4,774	17.4%	32.0%
5 < 10	3,016	879	2,259	951	2,221	4,280	22.2%	43.3%
10 < 20	1,123	658	834	848	833	3,085	23.5%	50.7%
20 and over	629	1,651	511	1,917	508	5,442	18.3%	54.6%
All	79,013	7,595	57,443	6,438	50,458	23,852	14.0%	24.2%

Taxable Returns Only

Gross Estate ($Millions)	Number	Amount	Number	Amount	Number	Amount	Tax % of Net Worth*	Tax % of Net Worth**
0.675 < 1	13,434	210	15,630	364	16,161	659	7.7%	7.8%
1 < 2.5	21,992	962	24,970	1,340	25,295	5,612	19.9%	20.8%
2.5 < 5	5,068	676	5,349	924	5,440	4,774	32.7%	37.2%
5 < 10	2,042	522	2,180	939	2,221	4,280	36.6%	46.3%
10 < 20	784	310	815	847	833	3,085	36.5%	52.1%
20 and over	478	1,185	497	1,914	508	5,442	23.4%	54.9%
All	43,798	3,866	49,441	6,328	50,458	23,852	24.7%	32.1%

Source: IRS, Statistics of Income, https://www.irs.gov/statistics/soi-tax-stats-estate-tax-statisti -filing-year-table-1, and author's computations.
* Net worth is gross estate less debts and estate expenses.
** Net worth less spousal and charitable bequests, a proxy for bequests to heirs.

Table 4.6
Estate Tax Returns Filed in Fiscal Year 2016, by State (Amounts in $1,000s)

State	Number	Amount	State	Number	Amount
U.S. Total	5,219	18,296	Montana	28	24
Alabama	49	190	Nebraska	28	52
Alaska	d*	d	Nevada	53	253
Arizona	71	209	New Hampshire	27	68
Arkansas	23	31	New Jersey	132	279
California	1,071	3,942	New Mexico	d	d
Colorado	66	206	New York	458	1,980
Connecticut	91	354	North Carolina	91	233
Delaware	d	d	North Dakota	d	d
District of Columbia	23	70	Ohio	105	310
Florida	704	3,029	Oklahoma	52	134
Georgia	92	309	Oregon	57	231
Hawaii	31	109	Pennsylvania	140	622
Idaho	d	d	Rhode Island	18	134
Illinois	220	611	South Carolina	38	118
Indiana	64	123	South Dakota	15	22
Iowa	44	84	Tennessee	58	136
Kansas	51	146	Texas	301	1,140
Kentucky	48	68	Utah	d	d
Louisiana	41	150	Vermont	19	34
Maine	22	66	Virginia	113	348
Maryland	88	231	Washington	72	180
Massachusetts	139	347	West Virginia	d	d
Michigan	117	747	Wisconsin	69	190
Minnesota	59	143	Wyoming	19	47
Mississippi	40	77	Other jurisdictions**	32	101
Missouri	61	238			

Source: IRS, Statistics of Income, Estate Tax Returns Study, October 2017.
* d = Data were deleted by the IRS to prevent disclosure of individual taxpayer data.
** Includes U.S. territories, U.S. citizens domiciled abroad at their time of death, and a small number of returns for whom state of residence was unknown.

The number of returns filed fluctuated over the years reflecting changes in the size of the annual exclusion as well as the state of the economy. As with the estate tax, the number of returns filed peaked in fiscal years 1977 at 386,802 as shown in table 4.7. And once again, as with the estate tax, this occurred just before the size of the exemption doubled from $60,000 to about $120,667. Similarly, the increase in the annual exclusion from $3,000 to $10,000 ushered by ERTA81 explains the drop in the number of returns filed in the early 1980s.

General Profile

Of the entire U.S. population in 2016, only 242,585 individuals filed gift tax returns in 2016, and reported a total of $70.5 billion in gifts.

Table 4.7
Number of Gift Tax Returns Filed

Year	Returns	Year	Returns	Year	Returns
1933	1,710	1962	95,874	1991	154,966
1934	3,619	1963	100,020	1992	167,680
1935	11,410	1964	107,172	1993	211,363
1936	22,590	1965	121,517	1994	214,302
1937	17,046	1966	133,646	1995	215,010
1938	16,601	1967	136,729	1996	226,334
1939	13,614	1968	138,514	1997	250,842
1940	14,435	1969	150,785	1998	257,722
1941	17,369	1970	147,693	1999	285,641
1942	30,048	1971	165,481	2000	304,558
1943	23,872	1972	190,743	2001	304,079
1944	20,772	1973	243,895	2002	278,926
1945	22,939	1974	252,653	2003	287,456
1946	23,554	1975	260,094	2004	249,019
1947	27,046	1976	302,464	2005	276,570
1948	30,603	1977	386,802	2006	255,651
1949	27,330	1978	195,194	2007	252,522
1950	32,155	1979	201,785	2008	252,286
1951	39,585	1980	215,993	2009	245,262
1952	45,656	1981	198,620	2010	230,007
1953	49,000	1982	99,533	2011	207,858
1954	48,000	1983	90,098	2012	249,451
1955	58,000	1984	87,216	2013	313,331
1956	68,000	1985	94,610	2014	334,641
1957	77,000	1986	102,965	2015	237,706
1958	79,520	1987	104,627	2016	249,302
1959	85,080	1988	102,569	2017	244,900
1960	91,132	1989	121,294		
1961	93,581	1990	146,014		

Source: *IRS Data Book*, Internal Revenue Service, Washington, DC, various years.

These do not include transfers in the form of payments by donor for beneficiary tuition or medical expenses; nor do they include gifts to certain political organizations.[3] They do include spousal transfers and charitable contributions, with the latter typically also deductible against the donor's taxable income. Gifts to spouses totaled about $1.6 billion, and another $12.6 billion in gifts to charities are made as shown in table 4.8.

Most of the charitable contributions, and to a lesser extent transfers to spouses, are made by individuals reporting small amounts of taxable gifts to other beneficiaries. As an example, those with zero taxable gifts reported gross gifts of $6.8 billion, of which $3.3 billion were transfers

Table 4.8
Gifts Reported on Gift Tax Returns Filed in 2016 (Amount in $Millions)

Taxable Gifts ($1,000s)	Current Gifts		Spousal Transfers		Charitable Gifts		Net Gifts	
	Returns	Amount	Returns	Amount	Returns	Amount	Returns	Amount
0	61,014	6,758	216	763	4,411	3,256	61,014	2,738
0.001 < 10	25,490	2,370	324	103	1,206	1,143	25,490	1,124
10 < 20	20,206	2,223	4	36	401	1,111	20,206	1,076
20 < 200	92,631	15,163	75	155	2,512	3,772	92,631	11,237
200 < 1,000	33,913	17,441	204	147	899	1,397	33,913	15,897
1,000 < 2,500	6,267	10,805	105	127	277	931	6,267	9,747
2,500 < 5,000	2,545	9,345	17	82	57	165	2,545	9,099
5,000 < 10,000	395	2,796	7	22	41	357	395	2,418
10,000 < 20,000	85	1,397	3	163	14	74	85	1,160
20,000 and over	39	2,206	0	0	7	358	39	1,848
All	242,585	70,503	956	1,598	9,826	12,563	242,585	56,342

Taxable Gifts ($1,000s)	Annual Exclusion		Taxable Gifts		Tax Liability		Prior Gifts	
	Returns	Amount	Returns	Amount	Returns	Amount	Returns	Amount
0	60,202	2,738	0	0	0	0	34,586	59,035
0.001 < 10	23,917	1,017	25,490	107	134	0	16,911	22,558
10 < 20	19,261	786	20,206	289	56	0	13,263	17,107
20 < 200	86,935	3,558	92,631	7,679	621	10	47,198	68,179
200 < 1,000	30,314	1,347	33,913	14,550	925	100	15,775	40,542
1,000 < 2,500	5,333	313	6,267	9,435	431	195	3,106	9,200
2,500 < 5,000	2,042	142	2,545	8,957	241	249	1,255	4,262
5,000 < 10,000	324	35	395	2,388	189	335	187	2,082
10,000 < 20,000	82	14	85	1,149	84	431	81	2,038
20,000 and over	36	7	39	1,890	39	746	36	2,724
All	228,444	9,958	181,571	46,444	2,719	2,066	132,398	227,728

Source: Author's calculations based on a sample of gift tax returns filed in 2016, and primarily reflect gifts made in 2015.

to charities. While the latter account for about one-half of the transfers for this group, they only account for less than 8 percent of the 61,014 returns filed.

These transfers netted a total of $56.3 billion transferred to children and other beneficiaries. These were also reduced by annual exclusions of close to $10 billion. This resulted in a total of taxable gifts of $46.4 billion reported on 181,571 gift tax returns. And of these donors, 132,398 individuals also made gifts in prior years with a cumulated value of $227.7 billion. After applying the tax rate schedule to the sum of current and past gifts, the unified credit, which exempts $5.43 million in transfers in 2015, and credit for previously paid gift taxes, the resulting gift tax liability is $2.1 billion. This was paid by only 2,719 individuals or slightly over 1 percent of all filers in 2016.

Taxable gifts between $10,000 and $200,000 represent the largest number of returns. About 113,000 such tax returns are filed, or some 47 percent of the total 242,585 gift tax returns filed. But these returns account for a tiny fraction of the reported gift tax liability, or $10 million out of $2.1 billion. Technically this should have been sheltered by the $5 million exemption (indexed). But cumulative gifts made in prior years by a small number of donors (677) may have pushed them up into the taxable status as they may have already used up the unified credit.

There are many gift tax returns filed that fall below the annual exclusion of $10,000 (indexed), the statutory requirement for filing a return, or do not claim the exclusion altogether. These are very likely gifts of future interest that do not qualify for the annual exclusion. Some of these may represent transfers to beneficiaries through a grantor-retained annuity trust (GRAT). A GRAT is a trust to which the grantor, that is, the donor, makes irrevocable transfers of assets and retains an annuity that has a value equal up to the value of the assets transferred; the trust may be required to make fixed payments for a term of fixed years (not longer than the donor's life expectancy). If the annuity is of equal value to the assets received by the trust, this is typically referred to as a zeroed-out GRAT. Once the annuity payment term is completed, the trust's remaining assets pass to its beneficiaries.[4] If the value of the annuity falls short of the value of the assets transferred, then the difference is treated as a gift of future interest (outside the fixed payment period), and it will not qualify for the annual exclusion. Unfortunately, reliable estimates on the aggregate volume of transfers to GRATS are not available. But the volume of gifts each valued under $1,000 reported in table 4.9 provides hints at the potential magnitude of such transactions.

Gifts by Type of Asset

In addition to information on the size of gifts made, equally interesting is the question of what types of assets are transferred during life. How many of these are cash, or cash-like, and how many are in the form of appreciable assets that are potentially governed by the basis-carryover regime? Table 4.9 provides a breakdown of the types of assets reported on gift tax returns filed by donors in 2016.

Unlike the estate tax, the largest category of assets transferred is cash. A total of $31.3 billion was transferred, or 46 percent of all gifts. The second-largest category is gifts of corporate stocks. About $15.2 billion in stocks was transferred, of which $3.5 billion are closely held stocks and $11.7 billion are other stocks.

Real estate makes up the third-largest category of assets. When transfers of personal residences, other real estate holdings, real estate partnerships, land, and real estate investment trusts (REITs) are aggregated, a total of $10.5 billion in real estate-related assets were transferred. Of these, $1.15 in personal residences were transferred. This may explain the missing ownership of residences in estates reported in table 4.3. Another $5 billion is reported for other real estate holdings, $1.7 billion in land, and $2.5 billion in real estate partnerships, among others real estate assets.

Noncorporate assets, as a group, make up the fourth-largest category, with a total value of $8.1 billion. Farm assets account for $2.4 billion of reported transfers. Limited partnerships account for 0.81 billion, family limited partnerships for $0.47 billion, hedge funds for 0.36 billion, and $4.2 billion for other noncorporate assets.

Other assets, primarily financial, include over $1 billion in state and local tax-exempt bonds, $0.6 billion in mortgages and notes, $0.36 billion in in hedge funds, $0.27 billion in life insurance policies, and $0.25 billion in corporate bonds and bond funds. There are $146 billion in annuities and retirement assets.

These figure are reproduced for returns filed in 2013, reflecting the unprecedented surge in the value of gifts made. Most of these returns represent gifts made in 2012, and it would be interesting to examine whether donors transferred a different portfolio of assets given they most likely expected the temporary exemption to decline from $5 to $1 million, and the tax rates to rise to a maximum of 55 percent. Total gifts

Table 4.9
Gifts by Type of Asset (Amounts in $Millions)

Assets	2016 Amount	Percent	2013 Amount	Percent
Cash, bonds, and notes	34,126	48.4	162,085	38.6
Cash	31,281	44.4	131,839	31.4
Bond funds	135	0.2	1,380	0.3
Corporate and foreign bonds	115	0.2	2,934	0.7
Mutual funds	85	0.1	1,091	0.3
Mortgages and notes	581	0.8	9,888	2.4
Other federal bonds	72	0.1	1,052	0.3
State and local bonds	1,857	2.6	13,901	3.3
Stocks	15,243	21.6	92,594	22.0
Closely held	3,529	5.0	38,569	9.2
Other	11,714	16.6	54,025	12.9
Real estate	10,515	14.9	72,857	17.3
Personal residence	1,150	1.6	7,399	1.8
Other real estate	4,956	7.0	32,579	7.8
Undeveloped land	1,671	2.4	10,383	2.5
Real estate mutual Funds and REITS	277	0.4	1,145	0.3
Real estate partnerships	2,461	3.5	21,350	5.1
Noncorporate assets	8,199	11.6	68,638	16.3
Farm assets	2,365	3.4	19,200	4.6
Family limited partnerships	469	0.7	2,734	0.7
Limited partnerships	813	1.2	19,039	4.5
Other noncorporate business assets	4,192	5.9	23,035	5.5
Hedge funds	360	0.5	4,630	1.1
Other	779	1.1	3,729	0.9
Insurance, face value	271	0.4	1,644	0.4
Annuities	144	0.2	318	0.1
Nominal gifts (<$1,000)	30	0.0	46	0.0
Gifts to other donees	123	0.2	383	0.1
Art	211	0.3	1,338	0.3
Other/Unknown	1,641	2.3	20,456	4.9
Total	70,503	100.0	420,359	100.0

Source: Computed from gift tax returns filed in 2013 and 2016, which mostly represent gifts made in 2012 and 2015.

reported on tax returns filed in 2013 surged to $420 billion, compared to the $70.5 billion reported in 2016.

In addition to the unprecedented volume of transfers witnessed, and as shown in table 4.9, the composition of assets transferred also changed. Cash, with $132 billion in gifts, continues to represent the largest category of assets transferred. But its share of total gifts declined from 44 to 31 percent. The share of corporate stock in total transfers remained at about 22 percent. But the share of closely held stocks increased from 5 to more than 9 percent, with the share of other stocks declining. The share of all other assets slightly increased, with the most notable being real estate partnerships (5.1 vs. 3.1) and limited partnerships (4.5 vs. 1.2), among others.

Valuations

As with the estate tax, minority discounts are also claimed on gift tax returns. Indeed, claiming such discount on lifetime gifts is often key to enabling estates to claim discounts as well. Overall, taxable gifts were reduced by $5.3 billion in valuation discounts in calculating the gift tax liability, or about 11.4 percent of taxable gifts. Corporate equity, $1.2 billion in closely held and $0.3 billion in other stocks, accounts for about 29 percent of these discounts, real estate for 23 percent, and noncorporate businesses for 32 percent. Farms, limited partnership, and other assets account for the remaining 17 percent.

Once again, comparing the gifts reported in 2016 to those reported in 2013 reveals dramatic differences in valuation discounts claimed. First, the reported discounts of $5.3 billion in 2016 are less than 10 percent of the $54 billion reported in 2013. Also, the composition of assets for which discounts are claimed has changed as well. As shown in the right panel of table 4.10, the share of corporate stocks is lower in 2016 when compared to that in 2013 (28.6 vs. 34.2 percent). Similarly, the shares of real estate (22.5 vs. 25.5), limited partnerships (3.3 vs. 10.9), and farms (7 vs. 9.4) are lower, whereas that of noncorporate assets is higher.

Gifts Reported on Estate Tax Returns

Gifts are not only observed on gift tax returns filed during life. Information on cumulative lifetime gifts are observed on estate tax returns as well, reflecting the unified nature of transfer taxes. Because under the unified transfer tax system gifts are added to the taxable estate, the estate tax provides a tax credit for lifetime gift transfers in order to

Table 4.10
Valuation Discounts Reported on Gift Tax Returns (Amounts in $Millions)

	2016		2013	
Asset Type	Amount	Percent	Amount	Percent
Total	$5,292	100	$54,101	100
Stock	1,515	28.6	18,479	34.2
Real estate	1,189	22.5	13,787	25.5
Limited partnerships	176	3.3	5,905	10.9
Farms	372	7.0	5,100	9.4
Noncorporate business assets	1,673	31.6	7,937	14.7
Other assets	366	6.9	2,893	5.3

Source: Computed from gift tax returns filed in 2013 and 2016, which mostly represent gifts made in 2012 and 2015.

avoid double taxation. Table 4.2 shows that 13 percent of estate tax returns filed for the least wealthy in 2016 reported cumulative lifetime gifts in excess of the annual exclusion, compared to 72 percent for the wealthiest estates. The amount of gifts made as a percentage of wealth is about 3.6 percent, ranging from around 2.5 percent for the least wealthy to 3.8 percent for the wealthiest.

Gifts by States
Table 4.11 provides a geographical breakdown of these gift tax returns. Consistent with the estate tax data, the greatest number of returns with tax liability was filed by residents of the states of California, Florida, New York, and Texas; they account for 32 percent of the taxable returns and 41 percent of the tax liability. Overall, returns with tax liability represent less than 1 percent of all filers, and a much smaller fraction of the population in the U.S.

Summary

About 5,200 individuals left behind taxable estates from a total of 12,411 of estates that were filed in 2016. They reported $192.2 billion in assets, with much of it consisting in stocks ($72 billion), real estate ($45 billion), partnerships and noncorporate assets ($17 billion), cash ($15 billion), and bonds and notes ($11 billion). The value of these assets has been reduced by $9 billion in valuation discounts, which also exclude some $10 billion in life insurance proceeds on the life of the decedents from policies owned by the beneficiaries.

Table 4.11

Geographical Breakdown of Gift Tax Returns Filed in Fiscal Year 2016 (Amounts in $Millions)

State or Area	Returns Filed	Tax Paid	State or Area	Returns Filed	Tax Paid
U.S. total	249,302	2,457	Montana	994	3
Alabama	2,163	10	Nebraska	1,554	4
Alaska	411	0	Nevada	1,604	6
Arizona	3,543	20	New Hampshire	1,550	13
Arkansas	1,099	5	New Jersey	9,989	116
California	26,733	346	New Mexico	1,030	1
Colorado	4,891	26	New York	21,676	345
Connecticut	6,471	48	North Carolina	5,849	50
Delaware	717	1	North Dakota	1,177	0
District of Columbia	861	5	Ohio	7,686	49
Florida	22,846	265	Oklahoma	1,845	2
Georgia	4,955	21	Oregon	3,149	4
Hawaii	1,184	14	Pennsylvania	10,588	116
Idaho	778	4	Rhode Island	897	6
Illinois	9,964	92	South Carolina	2,838	20
Indiana	3,489	8	South Dakota	1,051	0
Iowa	2,100	8	Tennessee	3,473	10
Kansas	2,225	11	Texas	17,454	140
Kentucky	2,483	47	Utah	1,075	3
Louisiana	1,769	4	Vermont	718	1
Maine	1,156	2	Virginia	6,704	47
Maryland	5,243	83	Washington	6,018	83
Massachusetts	9,698	66	West Virginia	732	2
Michigan	5,876	30	Wisconsin	5,154	26
Minnesota	5,733	24	Wyoming	842	36
Mississippi	927	26	Other	2,241	65
Missouri	4,099	139			

Source: *IRS Data Book,* Internal Revenue Service, Washington, DC, 2016.

The reported gross estates are further reduced by debts outstanding ($7.2 billion), state death taxes ($2.7 billion), and estate-related expenses ($1 billion). More important, they are reduced by $74 billion in spousal bequests, or just under 40 percent of gross estates. Charitable bequests of $18.5 billion further reduce the gross estate by close to 10 percent. The resulting taxable estates are augmented with cumulative lifetime taxable gifts of $19.5 billion. After applying the tax rate schedule, the computed tentative tax is reduced by the unified credit and other credits to yield a tax liability of $18.3 billion.

In addition to the estate tax, the unified transfer tax also extends to lifetime transfers. Reflecting on the filing requirements, a large number of gift tax returns are filed in 2016. More specifically, 243,000 gift tax returns are filed but with only 2,700 donors reporting tax liability. Total gifts of $70.5 billion are reported, which are reduced by $1.8 billion and $12.6 billion in spousal and charitable transfers, respectively. The value of these reported gifts is also reduced by $5.3 billion in valuation discounts. Cash is the largest asset category transferred, accounting for $31 billion or 44 percent of all gifts. This is followed stocks (22 percent), and real estate (15 percent).

Residents of California, Florida, New York, and Texas, account for about 49 percent of all taxable estates and pay 55 percent of the tax liabilities. In the case of the gift tax, these residents account for 35 percent of all gift tax returns and close to 45 percent of the tax liability. There is considerable variation in the share of the taxes attributed to these four states. As an example, California residents account for 21 percent of the estate tax liability but only 14 percent of the gift tax. In contrast, New York residents account for 11 percent of the estate tax liability and 14 percent of the gift tax, as with California residents.

5 The Beneficiaries

Chapter 4 addressed the profile of estate tax payers, namely the decedents. They are important because they are the ones who accumulated wealth during their lifetimes, decided on the composition of assets to hold in their portfolios, engaged in tax planning, and decided how many children or heirs to have. They also planned for succession and how their wealth is to be divided among the heirs and beneficiaries of their estates. Ultimately, they bear the statutory burden of the estate tax.

Equally important is the profile of the beneficiaries and their relationship to the deceased. Also important, with regard to succession planning, is the extent to which bequests are made available to the beneficiaries and whether they can be accessed at their will. These issues are of interest to policymakers but are equally interesting in their own right. Charities represent a specific class of beneficiaries with their own set of important questions, including: how many charities benefit from an estate, what types of charitable organizations receive bequests, and how much do they receive?

The Heirs

Estate tax returns not only provide information on the size of an estate and its composition, but also on how the estate is disposed of and distributed among beneficiaries. More specifically, estate tax returns report the name of each beneficiary, the relationship to the deceased, and the amount of transfers to each. They also provide information on whether the transfers are made directly to a beneficiary or through a trust. All of these details are reported on Federal Estate Tax Form 706, page 2, part 4, box 5.

With this information, we can identify how bequest division varies with the size of estates, among other estate and decedent attributes of interest. Equally important, by linking the beneficiaries' information to their respective income tax returns, we can obtain a vast amount of information on the heirs to study their attributes.

Such data sources and matches across tax systems are conducted by the Statistics of Income (SOI) Program of the Internal Revenue Service. Studies that link the income tax returns of heirs to the estate tax returns of decedents have been undertaken in 1976, 1982, 1989, and 1992. The 1982 data provides the most reliable figures on the pattern of bequests as estates of $1 million or more are sampled with certainty. The studies for 1989 and 1992 employ much smaller samples and may not necessarily be representative of the beneficiaries and all their attributes.

In preparing the data, which are documented in my 1994 paper, "The Distribution and Division of Bequests," I employ the 1982 Collation Data that consists of a sample of 8,509 estate tax returns drawn from a population of close to 60,000 estates, each with assets in excess of $300,000.[1] These estate tax returns are then matched or rather linked to the income tax returns of the heirs going back to 1980 (and forward to 1985).

These estate-income matches are often referred to as Collation Studies. Summary statistics from the 1982 Collation are reported in tables 5.1a through 5.1c. As noted earlier, for each of the heirs, the amount of inheritance and the relationship to the decedent is reported on the estate tax return. The data classifies the heirs along eleven categories of relationships: (1) spouse, (2) son, (3) daughter, (4) grandchild, (5) sibling, (6) niece or nephew, (7) aunt or uncle, (8) parent, (9) other, (10) estate or trust, and (11) not ascertainable. Category 9 includes sons-in-law and daughters-in-law, great grandchildren, and cousins, as well as unrelated individuals. Category 10 includes bequests not immediately distributed to heirs. Spousal trusts are classified under spousal bequests.

Tables 5.1a and 5.1b provide a breakdown of bequests by number of heirs or amount of inheritance, by relationship to the decedent and size of the estate. The total number of beneficiaries is estimated to be 237,064, or roughly four to each estate. Among them, they receive $34.2 billion in total bequests, after payment of estate taxes and charitable bequests. About one-half of this distributable estate (net worth less estate expenses, estate taxes, and charitable bequests), or $16.7 billion, is bequeathed to surviving spouses, 24 percent to children, 3.8 percent

Table 5.1a
Number of Heirs by Type of Relation and Size of Estate, 1982

Gross Estate	(1) Spouse	(2) Son	(3) Daughter	(4) Grandchild	(5) Sibling	(6) Niece/ Nephew
$300,000 < 500,000	15,941	18,234	17,798	12,666	7,862	18,671
500,000 < 1,000,000	9,143	9,856	11,162	13,893	4,275	5,106
1,000,000 < 2,500,000	3,758	3,693	3,778	4,139	1,387	4,342
2,500,000 < 10,000,000	1,088	1,083	1,148	1,532	455	1,303
10,000,000 and over	130	144	135	248	33	154
Total	30,061	33,010	34,020	32,478	14,012	29,576

Gross Estate	(7) Aunt/ Uncle	(8) Parent	(9) Other	(10) Estate or Trust	(11) N.A.	Total
$300,000 < $500,000	0	546	16,815	4,695	2,839	116,067
500,000 < 1,000,000	0	237	11,755	7,006	1,187	73,620
1,000,000 < 2,500,000	32	87	8,582	3,155	717	33,673
2,500,000 < 10,000,000	9	11	3,546	1,405	176	11,756
10,000,000 and over	1	3	801	239	60	1,948
Total	42	885	41,500	16,499	4,981	237,064

Source: David Joulfaian, "The Distribution and Division of Bequests," OTA Working Paper 71 (U.S. Department of the Treasury, Washington, DC, 1994).

Table 5.1b
Amount of Inheritance by Type of Relation and Size of Estate, 1982

Gross Estate	(1) Spouse	(2) Son	(3) Daughter	(4) Grandchild	(5) Sibling	(6) Niece/ Nephew
$300,000 < $500,000	3,926,071	1,529,153	1,735,046	323,263	589,332	592,828
500,000 < 1,000,000	4,120,104	995,438	1,461,548	354,223	468,199	353,115
1,000,000 < 2,500,000	3,405,539	742,180	763,310	200,969	157,741	292,655
2,500,000 < 10,000,000	2,745,338	394,187	384,516	155,674	63,560	141,172
10,000,000 and over	2,511,222	99,240	86,438	50,751	5,338	9,774
Total	16,708,274	3,760,200	4,430,857	1,084,880	1,284,169	1,389,544

Gross Estate	(7) Aunt/ Uncle	(8) Parent	(9) Other	(10) Estate or Trust	(11) NA	Total
$300,000 < $500,000	0	31,668	360,467	777,818	92,173	9,957,835
500,000 < 1,000,000	0	77,069	418,150	1,293,393	21,770	9,563,011
1,000,000 < 2,500,000	2,392	12,760	304,867	955,033	29,815	6,867,253
2,500,000 < 10,000,000	176	4,192	153,543	685,974	8,782	4,737,113
10,000,000 and over	57	1,892	61,501	235,048	1,838	3,063,100
Total	2,625	127,581	1,298,527	3,947,266	154,379	34,188,313

Source: David Joulfaian, "The Distribution and Division of Bequests," OTA Working Paper 71 (U.S. Department of the Treasury, Washington, DC, 1994).

Table 5.1c
Average Inheritance by Type of Relation and Size of Estate, 1982

Gross Estate	(1) Spouse	(2) Son	(3) Daughter	(4) Grandchild	(5) Sibling	(6) Niece/ Nephew
$300,000 < $500,000	$246,281	$83,861	$97,487	$25,523	$74,964	$31,751
500,000 < 1,000,000	450,623	101,003	130,943	25,497	109,528	69,158
1,000,000 < 2,500,000	906,096	200,951	202,022	48,551	113,688	67,395
2,500,000 < 10,000,000	2,524,249	363,965	334,979	101,588	139,675	108,377
10,000,000 and over	19,299,988	690,073	641,803	204,910	161,279	63,436
Total	555,817	113,910	130,242	33,404	91,649	46,982

Gross Estate	(7) Aunt/ Uncle	(8) Parent	(9) Other	(10) Estate or Trust	(11) NA	Total
$300,000 < $500,000	$0	$58,006	$21,437	$165,667	$32,468	$85,794
500,000 < 1,000,000	0	324,521	35,571	184,618	18,334	129,897
1,000,000 < 2,500,000	74,738	146,331	35,523	302,734	41,556	203,940
2,500,000 < 10,000,000	19,342	368,505	43,300	488,242	49,803	402,939
10,000,000 and over	57,000	552,699	76,757	985,342	30,385	1,572,188
Total	62,138	144,090	31,290	239,242	30,996	144,215

Source: David Joulfaian, "The Distribution and Division of Bequests," OTA Working Paper 71 (U.S. Department of the Treasury, Washington, DC, 1994).

to siblings, 4.1 percent to nieces and nephews, and 3.2 percent to grandchildren, with 4.6 percent distributed to parents, aunts and uncles, and others; the remaining 11.5 percent are bequeathed to trusts with the ultimate beneficiary not identified or captured.

Table 5.1c shows that the surviving spouse receives the largest inheritance, with a mean value of $556,000 (1982 dollars). On average, a child received an inheritance equal to 22 percent of that received by the surviving spouse, or about $122,000 ($113,910 for sons and $130,242 for daughters). There are 33,010 sons and 34,020 daughters with total inheritances of $3.8 billion and $4.43 billion, respectively. Perhaps not surprisingly, the average inheritance received rises with the size of the gross estate.

Grandchildren were the third-largest recipients. There were 32,478 grandchildren with $1.1 billion total in inheritances received in the data. They received much smaller inheritances, an average of $33,400 or about 25 percent of the average inheritance received by a child.

Siblings, comprising 14,012 heirs, received $1.3 billion in inheritances, with an average inheritance of $91,649 or about 75 percent of that of the average child. Nieces and nephews accounted for 29,576 beneficiaries, inheriting $1.4 billion total for an average of $46,982. Bequests to older generations seldom occur. Only 42 aunts and uncles were reported with an average inheritance of $62,138. There were 885 parent beneficiaries who inherited much more. Their average inheritance was $127,581, slightly higher than that of the average child.

Of the "other" category, heirs not included elsewhere, there were 41,500 beneficiaries with $1.3 billion in inheritances and an average of $31,290. This category includes great grandchildren, in-laws, and friends, among others. There were 16,499 bequests to trusts and estates totaling $3.5 billion for an average transfer of $239,242.

A Profile of the Children

Once again, I resort to the 1982 Collation Study to gain insights into the profile of children. The key variables of interest here are how inheritances vary with the size and circumstances of the children, as well as how the children's income varies with the size of parental wealth. Using the matched beneficiary income tax records and decedents estate tax returns, tables 5.2a and 5.2b provide statistics on the distribution of inheritance received by size of the pre-inheritance income of the children and the parents' gross estate.

Tables 5.2a and 5.2b provide summary statistics on the adjusted gross income (AGI) of the children in 1981 along with the inheritance received. The figures reported in table 5.2a show that 54,237 children received inheritances from estate tax decedents in 1982. Their total AGI in 1981 is about $2.6 billion and the inheritance received is $8.3 billion, or about three times their income. The top panel shows that wealthy parents are more likely to have high-income children. Less than 1 percent of the children of the least wealthy, or 220 out of 28,483 individuals, have incomes in excess of $200,000. In contrast, 34.9 percent of the children of the wealthiest parents, or 84 out of 241 observations, have incomes in excess of $200,000. The reverse pattern is observed for children with positive AGI under $10,000. About 12 percent (3,409 out of 28,483) of the children of the least wealthy compared to 5 percent of those of the wealthiest fall in this income group.

The top two panels of table 5.2b report mean values for AGI and inheritance received. The average AGI is $47,433, and ranges from a positive mean AGI of $5,376 to a high of $352,427. In addition, the average income of children increases with the wealth of the parent. The average income of children of the least wealthy group of parents is

Table 5.2a
Number of Children, Total Income, and Inheritance Received, 1982

Number of Children by Parent's Gross Estate and Child's Adjusted Gross Income (AGI)

Gross Estate	No AGI	$1 < $10,000	$10,000 < $20,000	$20,000 < $30,000	$30,000 < $50,000	$50,000 < $75,000	$75,000 < $100,000	$100,000 < $200,000	$200,000 and over	Total
$300,000 < $500,000	1,100	3,409	4,729	6,708	5,938	3,739	1,100	1,540	220	28,483
500,000 < 1,000,000	251	1,506	2,134	3,138	5,147	1,632	1,130	1,757	251	16,946
1,000,000 < 2,500,000	191	614	731	816	1,263	933	605	1,025	431	6,609
2,500,000 < 10,000,000	61	127	165	181	302	231	196	362	333	1,958
10,000,000 and over	8	13	14	11	23	19	26	44	84	241
Total	1,610	5,670	7,772	10,855	12,673	6,554	3,056	4,728	1,320	54,237

Total AGI by Parent's Gross Estate and Child's AGI ($000)

Gross Estate	NO AGI	$1 < $10,000	$10,000 < $20,000	$20,000 < $30,000	$30,000 < $50,000	$50,000 < $75,000	$75,000 < $100,000	$100,000 < $200,000	$200,000 and over	TOTAL
$300,000 < $500,000	-50,187	$19,260	$72,992	$164,152	$226,528	$227,916	$93,492	$193,720	$47,888	$995,760
500,000 < 1,000,000	-7,203	7,126	30,310	78,292	193,633	99,298	99,054	230,026	66,270	796,806
1,000,000 < 2,500,000	-13,345	3,324	10,979	20,620	49,415	57,099	52,413	140,279	152,150	472,933
2,500,000 < 10,000,000	-5,372	692	2,450	4,508	11,946	14,211	17,181	52,196	143,926	241,739
10,000,000 and over	-491	76	198	279	867	1,113	2,289	6,259	54,800	65,390
Total	-76,597	30,478	116,929	267,850	482,389	399,636	264,430	622,479	465,034	2,572,628

Total Inheritance by Parent's Gross Estate and Child's AGI ($000)

Gross Estate	No AGI	$1 < $10,000	$10,000 < $20,000	$20,000 < $30,000	$30,000 < $50,000	$50,000 < $75,000	$75,000 < $100,000	$100,000 < $200,000	$200,000 and over	Total
$300,000 < $500,000	$122,837	$367,531	$421,454	$739,337	$1,189,707	$507,011	$103,254	$259,654	$13,012	$3,723,794
500,000 < 1,000,000	66,547	144,845	188,604	450,243	659,454	378,175	136,201	263,232	47,692	2,334,993
1,000,000 < 2,500,000	38,500	99,436	137,598	142,637	260,291	228,667	141,807	253,678	108,281	1,410,889
2,500,000 < 10,000,000	15,331	32,849	49,469	49,512	100,288	84,843	76,288	137,504	125,844	671,929
10,000,000 and over	2,407	4,910	8,237	4,703	11,242	12,378	17,723	35,353	54,853	151,807
Total	245,623	649,571	805,362	1,386,432	2,220,983	1,211,074	475,274	949,421	349,682	8,293,413

Average Income and Inheritance Received by the Children, 1982

Average Child AGI in 1981 by Parent's Gross Estate and Child's AGI

Gross Estate	No AGI	$1 < $10,000	$10,000 < $20,000	$20,000 < $30,000	$30,000 < $50,000	$50,000 < $75,000	$75,000 < $100,000	$100,000 < $200,000	$200,000 and over	Total
$300,000 < $500,000	-46,000	$5,650	$15,436	$24,470	$38,146	$60,956	$85,015	$125,825	$217,729	$34,960
500,000 < 1,000,000	-29,000	4,731	14,203	24,948	37,623	60,849	87,677	130,890	263,966	47,019
1,000,000 < 2,500,000	-70,000	5,409	15,029	25,276	39,115	61,199	86,629	136,811	353,038	71,555
2,500,000 < 10,000,000	-88,000	5,438	14,856	24,847	39,608	61,539	87,848	144,305	431,660	123,452
10,000,000 and over	-61,000	6,042	14,347	24,657	38,374	59,088	86,827	142,431	651,429	271,254
Total	-48,000	5,376	15,045	24,675	38,065	60,979	86,516	131,658	352,427	47,433

Average Inheritance by Parent's Gross Estate and Child's AGI

Gross Estate	No AGI	$1 < $10,000	$10,000 < $20,000	$20,000 < $30,000	$30,000 < $50,000	$50,000 < $75,000	$75,000 < $100,000	$100,000 < $200,000	$200,000 and over	Total
$300,000 < $500,000	112,000	$107,809	$89,126	$110,213	$200,340	$135,600	$93,892	$168,651	$59,161	$130,740
500,000 < 1,000,000	265,000	96,157	88,381	143,471	128,132	231,743	120,558	149,785	189,965	137,787
1,000,000 < 2,500,000	202,000	161,817	188,354	174,848	206,037	245,089	234,384	247,406	251,247	213,468
2,500,000 < 10,000,000	251,000	258,155	299,913	272,883	332,504	367,407	390,066	380,159	377,426	343,142
10,000,000 and over	301,000	391,045	596,416	416,221	497,441	657,237	672,188	804,497	652,065	629,733
Total	153,000	114,568	103,623	127,723	175,258	184,794	155,499	200,809	265,007	152,909

Average Inheritance as Percentage of Average AGI by Parent's Gross Estate and Child's AGI (%)

Gross Estate	No AGI	$1 < $10,000	$10,000 < $20,000	$20,000 < $30,000	$30,000 < $50,000	$50,000 < $75,000	$75,000 < $100,000	$100,000 < $200,000	$200,000 and over	Total
$300,000 < $500,000	-	1,908	577	450	525	222	110	134	27	374
500,000 < 1,000,000	-	2,033	622	575	341	381	138	114	72	293
1,000,000 < 2,500,000	-	2,992	1,253	692	527	400	271	181	71	298
2,500,000 < 10,000,000	-	4,747	2,019	1,098	839	597	444	263	87	278
10,000,000 and over	-	6,472	4,157	1,688	1,296	1,112	774	565	100	232
Total	-	2,131	689	518	460	303	180	153	75	322

Source: David Joulfaian, "The Distribution and Division of Bequests," OTA Working Paper 71 (U.S. Department of the Treasury, Washington, DC, 1994).

$34,960, compared to $271,254 for the average income of children of the wealthiest group.

In contrast to AGI, the mean inheritance received seems to be invariant to the size of income of the heirs. The average inheritance ranges from about $115,000 in the lowest positive AGI class to $265,000 in the top AGI class, and from $131,000 for the heirs of the least wealthy to about $630,000 for the heirs of the wealthiest. On average, the inheritance received is about three times the average income. This inheritance-income multiple ranges from a high of 21 in the lowest positive AGI class to a low of 0.75 in the top bracket, potentially reflecting on a weak relationship between inheritance received and the income of the recipients.

Recent Evidence on Bequest Divisions

While estate-income tax match studies have not been undertaken since 1992, recent estate tax studies have captured information on beneficiaries and the amounts received in inheritances. We do not have the income tax returns of the beneficiaries to study the pattern of bequests and how it may vary with the attributes of the children and other heirs. Another limitation is that the filing threshold has expanded dramatically, thereby limiting the scope of the studies to an increasingly richer segment of society.

Notwithstanding the limitations, it may be useful to explore who are the beneficiaries of recent estates and the amount they receive in inheritances. For estate tax returns filed in 2016, and more specifically from estate tax Form 706, page 2, part 4, box 5, we have information on the amounts of inheritances by type of relationship. And, technically, these should exclude bequests to spouses and charities. Table 5.3 provides a summary of the information gleaned from the filed returns. Children represent the largest beneficiaries, receiving some 43 percent of the estimated total inheritances of $75 billion. Another 39 percent is for the most part transferred to trusts. Grandchildren, at a distant third, account for 3 percent. The average inheritance is about $3.5 million for trusts, but with an unknown number of beneficiaries. This is followed by children with $1.6 million, and $1.4 million for parents.

Lifetime Recipients

As with bequests, lifetime gifts are made to benefit recipients with different relationships to the donor. In the previous chapter, we learned

Table 5.3
Inheritances by Type of Relation (Amounts in $Millions)

Relation	Number	Amount
Son or daughter	19,790	$31,917
Grandchild	8,186	2,035
Sister or brother	1,730	1,401
Niece, nephew, great niece, or great nephew	5,813	3,221
Aunt or uncle	23	2
Mother or father	134	186
Cousins	1,191	278
Divorced/partner	134	91
Other individuals	10,101	6,499
Trusts and unknowns	8,452	29,375
All	55,554	75,003

Source: Computed from a sample of estate tax returns filed in 2016.

Table 5.4
Gifts Reported in 2016 by Type of Relation (Amounts in $Millions)

Relationship	Number	Gifts
Spouse/ex-spouse	11,086	$2,230
Children, including in-law	432,880	33,249
Grandchildren	210,995	3,810
Parents, including in-law	9,090	576
Siblings	31,145	1,395
Nieces, uncles, aunts, cousins ...	23,497	1,075
Noncharitable trusts	46,626	10,985
Charitable trusts	1,112	1,935
Charities	33,054	10,792
Other/unknown	76,389	4,457
Total	875,875	70,503

Source: Computed from a sample of gift tax returns filed in 2016.
Notes: Children include adopted and stepchildren; grandchildren include great grand-children and in-law; parents include grandparents; siblings include in-law; nieces include cousins and in-law.

that 242,585 gift tax returns were filed in 2016, reporting gross gifts of $70.5 billion. These transfers were received by 875,875 recipients. Unlike the evidence from estate tax returns where spousal transfers make up about one-half of all bequests, only $1.2 billion in spousal gifts, less than 2 percent of total gifts, are reported. Not surprisingly, children represent the largest beneficiaries as shown in table 5.4. About one-half of the recipients are children who also received slightly less than one-half of all gifts, a total of $33 billion. These include adopted children and stepchildren, as well as children-in-law.

They were followed by grandchildren who make up slightly less
than a quarter of all recipients, but received slightly more than 10
percent of the amounts received by the children, a total of $3.8 billion.
This group includes grandchildren-in-law, and great grandchildren.
Siblings, on one hand, and nieces and nephews, plus cousins, uncles,
and aunts, account for a sizeable number of recipients, 31,145 and
33,497 respectively. But they receive disproportionately smaller
amounts than the children, with each group receiving $1.4 and $1.1
billion in gifts, respectively. Not surprisingly, only about 9,100 parents
receive gifts.

Some $11 billion is transferred through 46,626 trusts where the ulti-
mate beneficiary relationship cannot be easily identified. About $1.1 is
transferred through charitable trusts, and another $10.8 is transferred
to charitable organizations directly. About $4.5 billion is transferred to
some 76,000 other recipients.

Approximately $47 billion, or 67 percent of total gifts, is transferred
directly to the recipients with $23.5 billion transferred through trusts.
Of the latter, $4.5 billion are made to simple trusts, $2.2 billion to family
or unified credit trusts, $0.5 billion to generation-skipping trusts, $1
billion to life insurance trusts, $0.4 billion to education 529 trusts,
among others.

Some of the gifts do not go directly to the recipients, at least not in
the most direct way possible. To qualify for the annual exclusion, a gift
must represent a transfer of present interest in a property. In other
words, the beneficiary has immediate and unrestricted access to the
funds to be used in any way he or she wishes. When parents set up
trusts with funds to be available to beneficiaries at a certain date in the
future, then transfers of such future interests to the trusts do not benefit
from the annual exclusion. Nevertheless, such transfers to a trust with
Crummey powers will qualify for the exclusion. These Crummey
trusts, so named after D. Clifford Crummey, provide a short window,
say thirty to sixty days, for beneficiaries to access funds.[2] If they don't,
then the funds remain in the trust until distributed to beneficiaries at
some future set date. However, it is very well understood that if beneficiaries were to withdraw the funds during the short window, then they
can very well expect to not receive any additional funds from the
donor. This implicit threat usually provides adequate incentives for the
strategy to work and the exclusions to be claimed.

A total of $3.8 billion in transfers to Crummey trusts is reported on
gift tax returns filed in 2016. These transfers took place over 152,642

donor-donee-asset type transfers. As an example, there are 142,503 observations where donors transferred a total of $2.1 billion in cash. These are the largest transfers of this category, representing 55 percent of all Crummey transfers. This is followed at a distant second by gifts of stock, with a total of about $450 million. These are followed real estate, noncorporate businesses, and municipal bonds, among others. Life insurance transfers account for $110 million with a frequency of 1,595. These are summarized in table 5.5.

Transfers to Crummey trusts surged in 2012. As gleaned from gift tax returns filed in 2013, $29.5 billion in such transfers were made, close to eight times the volume reported in 2016. While gifts of all types of assets surged, the composition of assets transferred also shifted between the two periods. As suggested by the figures in the right panel of figure 5.5, the share of stocks, real estate, noncorporate assets, and farms was much higer on the 2013 returns, while the share of cash was much lower, accounting for 34 percent in 2013 compared to 56 percent in 2016.

Charities

In addition to the number of relations of heirs to the decedent, estate tax returns also provide information on bequests to another category

Table 5.5
Crummey Trusts by Type of Gift (Amounts in $Millions)

Type of Gift	Reported in 2016		Reported in 2013	
	Frequency	Amount	Frequency	Amount
Cash	142,503	$2,148	168,082	$10,061
Closely held stock	4,849	293	4,947	2,060
Other stock	6,423	248	8,932	3,422
Real estate partnership	1,205	225	4,332	2,270
Other real estate	540	164	6,923	1,793
Other noncorporate	468	199	4,684	2,095
Limited partnership	1,087	56	4,927	2,184
Family limited partnership	152	76	1,380	38
State and local bonds	312	197	3,195	690
Life insurance	1,595	110	2,115	128
Farm	354	19	3,956	1,334
Depletables/intangibles	97	25	426	24
Total	152,642	3,840	197,187	29,474

Source: Computed from samples of gift tax returns filed in 2013 and 2016.
Notes: There are about $80 million in gifts of other assets reflected in the total but not identified separately.

of unrelated beneficiaries, namely charitable organizations. Such information includes the size of bequests to each charity, the type of recipient (e.g., educational institution vs. religion), as well as the number of
charitable beneficiaries. This provides us with a window on the type
of charities the wealthy give to. And when contrasted with the size of
wealth also reported on estate tax returns, we are able to gauge the
generosity of donors.

Table 5.6 captures the trend in reported bequests to charities over
thirty-two years, from 1982 through 2014. The table also provides information on the number of donors, as well as information on the number
of estates along with information on the size of wealth in these estates.
Using these figures, the relative frequency of giving as well as the share
of wealth bequeathed are generated and reported in the table.

Much of the statistics reported thus far employ information obtained
from estate tax returns filed in 2016. Given the delay in filing, and as
was stated earlier, much of this information is primarily for decedents
in 2015, with some for decedents in 2016, as well as 2014 and earlier
years. As a departure from these tabulations, the figures reported in
tables 5.4 through 5.7 are constructed to reflect information on decedents in a particular year. The purpose of this is to present consistent
times series data on giving that stretches from 1982 through 2014 and
correlates well with law changes taking effect in every year. This should
enhance the readers' use of the data in any analytical framework they
envision, and help in the study of time-varying factors that may have
shaped giving.

Charitable bequests grew from about $3 billion in 1982 to close
to $22 billion in 2014, peaking at $28 billion for the estates of decedents in 2007. During this period wealth reported on estate tax returns
expanded from $44.6 billion to $162.3 billion.[3] Some of this expansion
can be explained by the growth in the economy and the appreciation
of assets in the portfolios of estates. This trend is also influenced by
the structure and administration of the estate tax. Raising the filing
threshold, for instance, reduces the number of estates required to file,
thus reducing the value of reported wealth and bequests. Alternatively,
when the filing threshold is not indexed for inflation, the decline in
the real value of the threshold increases the pool of estates required
to file.

The figures reported for 2010 are noteworthy as the estate tax expired
this year. But in mid-December, the law was changed to allow estates
to choose between basis carryover—which taxes the heirs on future

Table 5.6
Charitable Bequests Reported on Estate Tax Returns (Amounts in $Millions)

Year of Death	Wealth Returns	Amount	Charitable Bequests Returns	Amount	Wealth Share	Fraction Giving	Maximum Tax Rate
1982	61,006	44,653	9,931	2,907	6.5%	16.3%	65
1983	65,901	50,595	9,293	3,111	6.1%	14.1%	60
1984	66,397	56,189	11,633	4,156	7.4%	17.5%	55
1985	42,892	53,425	7,998	3,595	6.7%	18.6%	55
1986	46,306	61,180	9,189	4,121	6.7%	19.8%	55
1987	44,245	67,868	8,555	5,033	7.4%	19.3%	55
1988	46,976	71,633	8,338	4,812	6.7%	17.7%	55
1989	53,195	82,803	9,977	5,644	6.8%	18.8%	55
1990	57,297	87,431	10,736	6,762	7.7%	18.7%	55
1991	58,008	89,479	10,641	5,877	6.6%	18.3%	55
1992	60,454	97,012	11,317	7,982	8.2%	18.7%	55
1993	69,085	112,720	11,872	10,536	9.3%	17.2%	55
1994	71,479	110,176	13,271	7,903	7.2%	18.6%	55
1995	78,481	126,856	14,291	9,657	7.6%	18.2%	55
1996	87,833	147,468	14,811	14,009	9.5%	16.9%	55
1997	98,198	166,189	17,189	11,786	7.1%	17.5%	55
1998	105,900	185,407	17,618	13,614	7.3%	16.6%	55
1999	111,278	209,047	18,631	16,692	8.0%	16.7%	55
2000	107,726	204,091	18,577	15,589	7.6%	17.2%	55
2001	111,359	218,855	18,339	19,763	9.0%	16.5%	55
2002	65,528	177,451	12,345	15,479	8.7%	18.8%	50
2003	69,479	190,121	12,497	16,588	8.7%	18.0%	49
2004	43,392	177,384	8,828	17,413	9.8%	20.3%	48
2005	50,087	206,044	9,637	19,138	9.3%	19.2%	47
2006	34,141	185,418	6,973	18,542	10.0%	20.4%	46
2007	37,996	215,125	7,283	28,027	13.0%	19.2%	45
2008	33,670	178,438	6,386	15,865	8.9%	19.0%	45
2009	14,057	130,322	3,077	14,826	11.4%	21.9%	45
2010	2,853	25,684	691	4,582	17.8%	24.2%	0 or 35
2011	9,440	131,536	2,469	14,809	11.3%	26.2%	35
2012	10,365	130,605	2,445	13,386	10.2%	23.6%	35
2013	11,125	148,416	2,621	17,970	12.1%	23.6%	40
2014	11,885	162,320	2,644	21,772	13.4%	22.2%	40

Note: Computed from samples of tax returns filed 1982 through 2017; 1983–1985 figures are not very reliable given sample size and design. Figures for 2014 are likely to be slightly understated as they do not include returns filed late in 2018 and beyond. The estate tax was optional in 2010, with basis carryover as the alternative choice.

capital gains realizations—or the 2011 estate tax laws enacted. And so
the figures observed reflect the outcome of a tax-minimization strategy
by the executors and potentially heirs of the estates. As it turns out,
estate tax returns filed for 2010 decedents represent some 20 percent of
those who filed in the previous year. And these estates are, otherwise,
more generous in giving to charity, carry more debt, and have decedents more likely to have been married.[4]

Because the values of the underlying assets also change over time,
bequests measured as a fraction of the reported wealth may be a better
gauge of generosity. Using this measure, and with wealth defined as
net worth less estate expenses, bequests increased from 6.5 percent of
wealth in 1982 to about 13 percent in 2014, but fluctuated considerably
in the intervening years. A similar pattern is observed for the fraction
of estates giving to charities, where 16 percent of the estates provided
for bequests in 1982 compared to 22 percent in 2014, but again with
varying relative frequencies of giving between the two years.

As the estate tax filing threshold has expanded over the years, by
virtue of the expanding size of exempted estate, the concentration of
wealthier estates unavoidably also expanded. Because wealthier estates
typically provide for larger bequests to charities, estate tax data, such
as those reflected in table 5.3, can create the illusion that the wealthy
have become more generous over time despite the reduction in tax
rates. As an alternative, studying the trend in giving by those with
wealth above the filing thresholds in all years may provide a better way
of exploring the generosity of the rich.

Accordingly, table 5.7 replicates table 5.6, but restricts the figures to
those estates with wealth in excess of $10 million, adjusted for inflation
and stated in 2014 dollars using the consumer price index.[5] As can be
seen, these estates account for more than half of the bequests when
compared to the figures in the early years in table 5.6. By 2014, these
estates account for close to 90 percent of all reported bequests.

Reported wealth for this high-wealth group expanded from $8.5
billion in 1982 to $111.3 billion in 2014, with some ups and downs
reflecting the state of the economy, in particular the Great Recession
of 2008. Bequests also expanded from $1.5 billion to $19.2 billion over
this period. The share of wealth transferred to charities stood at 17.6
percent in 1982, and, as with the figures in table 5.3, fluctuated considerably over the years before converging to a wealth share of 17.3
percent transferred in 2014. Similarly, the fraction of estates giving also

Table 5.7
Charitable Bequests Reported on Estate Tax Returns
Returns with Wealth over $10 million, in $2014

Year of Death	Wealth Amount	Wealth Returns	Charitable Bequests Amount	Charitable Bequests Returns	Wealth Share	Fraction Giving	Maximum Tax Rate
1982	8,511	785	1,498	329	17.6%	41.9%	65
1983	10,139	981	1,809	439	17.8%	44.8%	60
1984	11,536	927	1,872	385	16.2%	41.5%	55
1985	14,005	1,308	1,907	463	13.6%	35.4%	55
1986	15,901	1,441	1,930	549	12.1%	38.1%	55
1987	19,979	1,476	2,696	559	13.5%	37.9%	55
1988	19,898	1,549	2,470	557	12.4%	36.0%	55
1989	24,073	1,734	3,138	646	13.0%	37.3%	55
1990	24,720	1,589	3,778	603	15.3%	37.9%	55
1991	22,825	1,539	2,873	597	12.6%	38.8%	55
1992	26,784	1,607	4,862	637	18.2%	39.6%	55
1993	31,844	1,673	7,062	646	22.2%	38.6%	55
1994	28,038	1,719	3,999	659	14.3%	38.3%	55
1995	34,014	1,778	5,524	666	16.2%	37.5%	55
1996	43,011	2,106	9,467	772	22.0%	36.7%	55
1997	45,862	2,349	6,483	922	14.1%	39.3%	55
1998	51,534	2,687	7,836	1,000	15.2%	37.2%	55
1999	61,652	2,924	10,001	1,189	16.2%	40.7%	55
2000	56,009	2,981	8,501	1,086	15.2%	36.4%	55
2001	66,062	2,885	12,724	1,086	19.3%	37.6%	55
2002	59,307	2,615	9,316	995	15.7%	38.0%	50
2003	64,531	2,824	10,740	1,016	16.6%	36.0%	49
2004	72,237	2,920	12,001	1,046	16.6%	35.8%	48
2005	82,591	3,282	13,287	1,114	16.1%	33.9%	47
2006	84,889	3,373	13,628	1,092	16.1%	32.4%	46
2007	102,592	3,713	22,835	1,240	22.3%	33.4%	45
2008	76,933	2,926	11,113	983	14.4%	33.6%	45
2009	76,472	2,750	12,090	909	15.8%	33.1%	45
2010	12,218	532	3,633	199	29.7%	37.4%	0 or 35
2011	92,068	2,961	12,544	1,006	13.6%	34.0%	35
2012	86,408	3,176	11,667	1,036	13.5%	32.6%	35
2013	101,195	3,140	15,401	1,027	15.2%	32.7%	40
2014	111,315	3,531	19,244	1,081	17.3%	30.6%	40

Note: Computed from samples of tax returns filed 1982 through 2017; 1983–1985 figures are not very reliable given sample size and design. Figures for 2014 are likely to be slightly understated as they do not include returns filed late in 2018 and beyond. The estate tax was optional in 2010, with basis carryover as the alternative choice.

fluctuated over the years, dropping from 44 percent in 1982 to about 31 percent in 2014.

Table 5.8 provides statistics on the pattern of charitable bequests for decedents in 2014. About 22.2 percent (2,644) of the returns reported charitable bequests, with 54 percent (92) of the wealthiest estates choosing to give to charities. Total charitable bequests were $21.8 billion, or about 13.4 percent of total wealth, with the wealthiest giving about 26 percent of their wealth. Over all, bequests benefited 11,506 charities representing some 6,267 unique categories; bequests to two charities engaged in the same line of charitable work (e.g., schools) would be treated as giving to one category.

Table 5.9 provides a breakdown of giving by type of charitable organization as classified according to the National Taxonomy of Exempt Entities (NTEE) codes, and as reported by the estates of decedents in 2014. Of the $21.8 billion in bequests, over one-half, or some $12.8 billion, is bequeathed to philanthropies and voluntary organizations. These primarily represent private foundations and their purpose may overlap with those of the other types of charities listed in table 5.8.

About 22 percent of the estates of decedents in 2014 provided for charitable bequests, and these donors gave away about 37.3 percent of their wealth. But this tells us little about the heterogeneity of this generosity. Do most estates give close to the 37.3 percent share of wealth, or is there a wide distribution around this mean? Indeed, the data

Table 5.8
Charitable Bequests Reported on Estate Tax Returns of Decedents in 2014 (Amounts in $Millions)

Gross Estate ($1,000s)	Estates	Wealth	Charitable Bequests Estates	Amount	Number of Charities	Categories
< 5,000	1,278	$3,963	198	$100	641	422
5,000 < 10,000	6,786	44,543	1,302	2,298	5,068	3,172
10,000 < 20,000	2,420	30,911	618	2,179	2,656	1,532
20,000 < 50,000	992	27,698	326	2,882	2,349	708
50,000 < 100,000	242	15,552	107	1,964	377	233
100,000 and over	169	39,652	92	12,349	415	200
All	11,885	162,320	2,644	21,772	11,506	6,267

Source: Computed from samples of estate tax returns of decedents in 2014 filed during 2014–2017.

suggest that these donors exhibit considerable diversity in their pattern of generosity, with some leaving much of their estates to charity. As shown in table 5.10, the bulk of bequests, 70 percent of the total, are reported by estates that transfer over 70 percent of their wealth to charities. And close to one-half of these charitable transfers are made by estates that gave away over 90 percent of their wealth.

Not surprisingly, these donor estates pay little in estate taxes as they provide little in inheritances, or otherwise taxable bequests, to their heirs. As an example, those who donate 90 to 99 percent of their wealth bequeathed $6.9 billion to philanthropies and paid only $49 million in estate tax; their heirs received only $180 million in inheritances, or about 2.5 percent of what charities received. When combined with the next class of donors, those giving more than 99 percent of their wealth,

Table 5.9
Charitable Bequests in 2014 Decedents (Amounts in $Millions)

Type	Estates	Amount	Percent of All
Arts, culture, humanities	436	1,047	4.8
Educational institutes	1,148	2,576	11.8
Environmental quality, protection	192	287	1.3
Animal-related activities	218	416	1.9
Health—general and rehabilitative	505	506	2.3
Mental health, crisis intervention	46	17	0.1
Disease/disorder/medical disciplines	249	221	1.0
Medical research	79	115	0.5
Public protections/legal services	38	13	0.1
Employment/jobs	28	8	0.0
Food, nutrition, agriculture	72	18	0.1
Housing/shelter	55	19	0.1
Public safety/disaster relief, preparation	28	6	0.0
Recreation/leisure/sports, athletics	62	25	0.1
Youth development	96	15	0.1
Other human services	613	828	3.8
International	84	48	0.2
Civil rights/civil liberties	68	39	0.2
Community improvement/development	72	44	0.2
Philanthropy and voluntarism	920	12,757	58.6
Science	11	6	0.0
Social sciences	9	3	0.0
Public affairs/societal benefit	49	60	0.3
Religion/spiritual development	960	758	3.5
Mutual membership benefit organizations	43	3	0.0
Unknown	182	1,914	8.8
Total	2,644	21,772	100.0

Source: Calculated from estate tax returns of decedents in 2004 filed during 2004–2006.

Table 5.10
Pattern of Giving Reported on Estate Tax Returns of Decedents in 2014

Share of Wealth (%)	Number of Estates	Wealth ($Millions)	Charitable Bequests ($Millions)	Tax ($Millions)	Inheritance ($Millions)
0	9,223	104,069	0	11,201	45,588
0–10	1,407	23,661	634	4,461	10,596
10–20	305	5,564	797	1,047	2,374
20–30	129	3,881	918	857	1,451
30–40	94	1,850	636	298	729
40–50	94	3,045	1,344	507	911
50–60	78	2,244	1,259	162	459
60–70	57	1,397	888	91	297
70–80	96	1,484	1,130	62	273
80–90	111	4,329	3,672	146	415
90–99	174	7,284	6,908	49	180
99–100	98	3,591	3,586	3	3
All	11,866	162,399	21,771	18,884	63,275
Donors only	2,643	58,331	21,771	7,683	17,687

Source: Computed from estate tax returns of 2014 decedents filed in 2014–2017.
Note: Unlike previous tables, negative wealth returns are excluded here. Tax is defined as the sum of the federal estate tax and the deduction for state death taxes. Spousal bequests, not reported, represent the difference between wealth and the sum of charitable bequests, taxes, and inheritances. Figures may not add up due to rounding.

these two groups account for one-half of all bequests, even though they only account for less than 3 percent of all estates.

Because the figures in table 5.10 are reported by estates at a time when the size of exempted estate is $5.34 million, table 5.11 replicates these figures for 2001 using data on decedents at a time when the exemption and filing thresholds were only $675,000. Notwithstanding the difference in the wealth of the estates covered, the pattern of giving over the two periods is very similar. Those who give bequeath a substantial fraction of their wealth to charity. And those who give at least 90 percent of their wealth bequeath more than 55 percent of the total of charitable bequests.

Summary

Spouses continue to represent the largest number of recipients of bequests, accounting for close to 40 percent of the reported gross estates. Net of spousal and charitable bequests, as well as taxes, children receive 43 percent of inheritances, and grandchildren receive 3

Table 5.11
Pattern of Giving Reported on Estate Tax Returns of Decedents in 2001

Share of Wealth (%)	Number of Estates	Wealth ($Millions)	Charitable Bequests ($Millions)	Tax ($Millions)	Inheritance ($Millions)
0	92,750	158,073	0	19,328	74,371
0–10	11,020	30,070	747	7,455	14,097
10–20	1,344	5,322	799	1,328	2,000
20–30	1,035	2,858	698	674	1,235
30–40	715	2,128	741	437	804
40–50	511	1,876	848	282	551
50–60	507	1,970	1,063	273	533
60–70	313	916	587	71	223
70–80	561	1,821	1,351	120	331
80–90	591	2,309	1,959	68	241
90–99	1,112	4,737	4,507	46	175
99–100	619	6,487	6,448	2	5
All	111,078	218,567	19,748	30,084	94,566
Donors only	18,328	60,494	19,748	10,756	20,195

Source: David Joulfaian, "On Estate Tax Repeal and Charitable Bequests," *Tax Notes* 123, no. 10 (June 2009): 1221–1229. Computed from estate tax returns of 2001 decedents filed in 2001–2007.

percent. Bequests through trusts are sizeable and account for 39 percent of inheritances.

Charities also represent recipients of sizeable bequests that may rival amounts received by some of the beneficiaries. And among the latter, private foundations, with NTEE-designation philanthropy and voluntarism, account for close to 60 percent of giving, followed by educational institutions (11.8 percent), and the arts (4.8 percent), among others. More than 75 percent of charitable bequests are made by those who give more than half of their wealth to charity.

In contrast to the estate tax filers, spousal transfers account for a small fraction of lifetime transfers, representing 2 percent of all gifts. Children are the largest recipients (47 percent), followed by grandchildren as a distant second (5.4 percent). Charitable gifts are also sizeable, accounting for 18 percent of total gifts.

6 Fiscal Contribution

Federal estate and gift tax revenues fluctuated over the years, reflecting changes in tax law, the economy's business cycles, as well as the performance of financial markets. They generated about $21.3 billion in revenues, or less than 1 percent of federal revenues in fiscal year 2016. When first enacted estate tax receipts were $6.1 million, or 0.8 percent of total receipts in fiscal year 1917. The share of estate and gift taxes in total federal revenues peaked at 9.7 percent, or at $379 million, in fiscal year 1936. Table 6.1 and figure 6.1 summarize the historical trend of estate and gift tax revenues and their contribution to total government receipts for the fiscal years 1917 through 2016.

The contribution of estate and gift tax revenues to federal receipts grew rapidly in the first decade of the inception of the transfer tax. As its scope narrowed, with attempts to repeal the tax altogether in the 1920s, tax revenues from this source decreased. This trend was reversed in the 1930s when estate and gift taxes contributed nearly 10 percent of total receipts. However, it should be noted that the latter share is in part explained by the acceleration of gifts in anticipation of pending higher gift tax rates, as shown in table 6.2. During World War II, the income tax base was expanded, and with it the relative contribution of estate and gift taxes greatly diminished.

The contribution of the tax to federal receipts may also reflect changes in income tax laws. Terminal wealth can be defined as the difference between cumulative lifetime after-tax income and personal expenditures. If income taxes are increased, then accumulated wealth will decrease, other things being equal, thereby shrinking the estate tax base. It may also reflect the increased use of aggressive tax-avoidance technology, at times sanctioned by the courts, with Congress unwilling to address the issue, which raises the risk that a sizeable

Table 6.1
Estate and Gift Tax Revenues, Nominal and Real in 2016 Prices

Fiscal Year	Amount ($Millions)	Real ($Millions)	Share of Total Receipts	Fiscal Year	Amount ($Millions)	Real ($Millions)	Share of Total Receipts
1917	6	134	0.55%	1967	2,978	22,060	2.00%
1918	48	891	1.30%	1968	3,051	21,924	1.99%
1919	82	1,303	1.60%	1969	3,491	24,077	1.87%
1920	104	1,437	1.56%	1970	3,644	23,831	1.89%
1921	154	1,848	2.76%	1971	3,735	23,104	2.00%
1922	139	1,869	3.46%	1972	5,436	32,215	2.62%
1923	127	1,810	3.29%	1973	4,917	28,233	2.13%
1924	103	1,446	2.66%	1974	5,035	27,217	1.91%
1925	108	1,521	2.98%	1975	4,611	22,448	1.65%
1926	109	1,495	2.87%	1976	5,216	23,269	1.75%
1927	100	1,360	2.50%	1977	7,327	30,906	2.06%
1928	60	829	1.54%	1978	5,285	20,931	1.32%
1929	62	869	1.60%	1979	5,411	19,919	1.17%
1930	65	910	1.60%	1980	6,389	21,121	1.24%
1931	48	691	1.55%	1981	6,787	19,769	1.13%
1932	47	748	2.46%	1982	7,991	21,099	1.29%
1933	34	601	1.72%	1983	6,053	15,055	1.01%
1934	113	2,089	3.77%	1984	6,010	14,482	0.90%
1935	212	3,798	5.89%	1985	6,422	14,835	0.87%
1936	379	6,637	9.71%	1986	6,958	15,520	0.90%
1937	306	5,275	5.66%	1987	7,493	16,409	0.88%
1938	417	6,949	6.13%	1988	7,594	16,044	0.84%
1939	361	6,140	5.73%	1989	8,745	17,742	0.88%
1940	353	6,095	5.43%	1990	11,500	22,259	1.11%
1941	403	6,909	4.63%	1991	11,139	20,455	1.06%
1942	420	6,857	2.88%	1992	11,143	19,636	1.02%
1943	441	6,493	1.84%	1993	12,577	21,515	1.09%
1944	507	7,034	1.16%	1994	15,225	25,288	1.21%
1945	637	8,687	1.41%	1995	14,763	23,909	1.09%
1946	668	8,907	1.70%	1996	17,189	27,070	1.18%
1947	771	9,490	2.00%	1997	19,845	30,357	1.26%
1948	890	9,579	2.14%	1998	24,076	36,003	1.40%
1949	780	7,768	1.98%	1999	27,782	40,908	1.52%
1950	698	7,039	1.77%	2000	28,949	41,709	1.43%
1951	708	7,051	1.37%	2001	28,324	39,479	1.42%
1952	818	7,551	1.24%	2002	26,439	35,842	1.43%
1953	881	7,979	1.27%	2003	21,882	29,199	1.23%
1954	934	8,396	1.34%	2004	24,797	32,345	1.32%
1955	924	8,244	1.41%	2005	24,794	31,501	1.15%
1956	1,161	10,397	1.56%	2006	27,836	34,215	1.16%
1957	1,365	12,045	1.71%	2007	26,009	30,971	1.01%
1958	1,393	11,898	1.75%	2008	28,844	33,388	1.14%
1959	1,333	11,070	1.68%	2009	23,429	26,123	1.11%
1960	1,606	13,246	1.74%	2010	18,843	21,077	0.87%
1961	1,896	15,374	2.01%	2011	7,301	8,036	0.32%
1962	2,016	16,183	2.02%	2012	13,946	14,881	0.57%
1963	2,167	17,222	2.03%	2013	18,783	19,636	0.68%
1964	2,394	18,777	2.13%	2014	19,275	19,859	0.64%
1965	2,716	21,028	2.33%	2015	19,119	19,386	0.59%
1966	3,066	23,361	2.34%	2016	21,337	21,609	0.65%

Source: Treasury Department and Office of Management and Budget, various years.

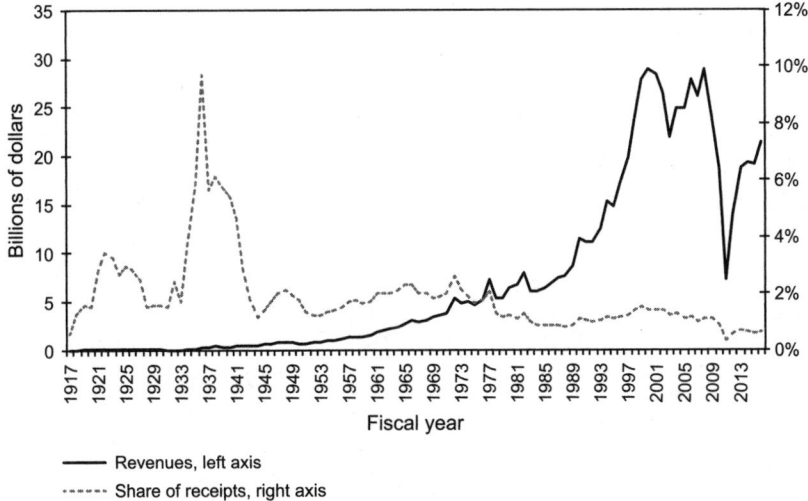

Figure 6.1
Estate and gift tax revenues ($billions).

share of the wealth may disappear from the tax system. This reduction in reported wealth may be caused by valuation discounts as well as the use of certain trusts as means to dramatically reduce the tax on transfers to heirs.

Not only has the combined contribution of estate and gift taxes varied over time, but the contribution of each has varied as well. Table 6.2, which provides a breakdown of revenues by source, shows that on average, gift tax receipts account for about 9 percent of the combined estate and gift tax revenues. Often, however, the share of gift tax receipts diverged from its historical mean, especially in anticipation of changes in the tax laws. Examples of the gift tax share surging include the mid-1930s as well as fiscal years 1977 and 2013 when gift tax rates were expected to increase as documented in tables 2.2 and 2.6, and when the estate tax expired in 2010 (2011 fiscal year effect).

Trend in Estate Tax Revenues

Revenues from the estate tax reflect the tax structure, the performance of the economy, and the specific attributes of decedents in a given year, including the manner in which their estates are settled. Table 6.2

Table 6.2
Estate and Gift Tax Revenues by Source ($Millions)

Fiscal Year	Estate Tax	Gift Tax	Gift Share	Gift* Share	Fiscal Year	Estate Tax	Gift Tax	Gift Share	Gift* Share
1917	6	0	0.00	0.00	1967	2,692	286	0.10	0.12
1918	48	0	0.00	0.00	1968	2,679	372	0.12	0.16
1919	82	0	0.00	0.00	1969	3,098	393	0.11	0.14
1920	104	0	0.00	0.00	1970	3,205	439	0.12	0.15
1921	154	0	0.00	0.00	1971	3,303	432	0.12	0.15
1922	139	0	0.00	0.00	1972	5,073	363	0.07	0.09
1923	127	0	0.00	0.00	1973	4,280	637	0.13	0.17
1924	103	0	0.00	0.00	1974	4,594	441	0.09	0.11
1925	101	8	0.07	0.09	1975	4,236	375	0.08	0.11
1926	106	3	0.03	0.04	1976	4,784	432	0.08	0.11
1927	100	0	0.00	0.00	1977	5,551	1,776	0.24	0.30
1928	60	0	0.00	0.00	1978	5,146	139	0.03	0.03
1929	62	0	0.00	0.00	1979	5,236	175	0.03	0.03
1930	65	0	0.00	0.00	1980	6,173	216	0.03	0.03
1931	48	0	0.00	0.00	1981	6,571	216	0.03	0.03
1932	47	0	0.00	0.00	1982	7,883	108	0.01	0.01
1933	30	5	0.13	0.17	1983	5,904	149	0.02	0.02
1934	104	9	0.08	0.10	1984	5,858	152	0.03	0.03
1935	140	72	0.34	0.40	1985	6,146	276	0.04	0.04
1936	219	160	0.42	0.49	1986	6,577	381	0.05	0.05
1937	282	24	0.08	0.10	1987	6,990	503	0.07	0.07
1938	382	35	0.08	0.11	1988	7,168	426	0.06	0.06
1939	332	28	0.08	0.10	1989	7,916	829	0.09	0.09
1940	324	29	0.08	0.11	1990	9,372	2,128	0.19	0.19
1941	351	52	0.13	0.16	1991	9,903	1,236	0.11	0.11
1942	328	92	0.22	0.27	1992	10,099	1,044	0.09	0.09
1943	408	33	0.07	0.10	1993	11,141	1,436	0.11	0.11
1944	469	38	0.07	0.10	1994	13,136	2,089	0.14	0.14
1945	590	47	0.07	0.10	1995	12,965	1,792	0.12	0.12
1946	621	47	0.07	0.09	1996	14,975	2,191	0.13	0.13
1947	701	70	0.09	0.12	1997	17,136	2,709	0.14	0.14
1948	813	77	0.09	0.11	1998	20,801	3,289	0.14	0.14
1949	719	61	0.08	0.10	1999	23,047	4,646	0.17	0.17
1950	649	49	0.07	0.09	2000	24,926	4,023	0.14	0.14
1951	617	91	0.13	0.16	2001	24,441	3,883	0.14	0.14
1952	735	83	0.10	0.13	2002	24,813	1,626	0.06	0.06
1953	774	107	0.12	0.16	2003	19,990	1,892	0.09	0.09
1954	862	72	0.08	0.10	2004	23,397	1,400	0.06	0.06
1955	836	88	0.09	0.12	2005	22,813	1,981	0.08	0.08
1956	1,048	113	0.10	0.13	2006	25,916	1,921	0.07	0.07
1957	1,240	125	0.09	0.12	2007	23,636	2,373	0.09	0.09
1958	1,259	134	0.10	0.12	2008	25,611	3,233	0.11	0.11
1959	1,216	117	0.09	0.11	2009	20,433	2,996	0.13	0.13
1960	1,419	187	0.12	0.15	2010	16,116	2,727	0.14	0.14
1961	1,725	171	0.09	0.12	2011	805	6,496	0.89	0.89

Table 6.2 (continued)

Fiscal Year	Estate Tax	Gift Tax	Gift Share	Gift* Share	Fiscal Year	Estate Tax	Gift Tax	Gift Share	Gift* Share
1962	1,777	239	0.12	0.15	2012	11,934	2,011	0.14	0.14
1963	1,951	216	0.10	0.13	2013	13,089	5,694	0.30	0.30
1964	2,089	305	0.13	0.16	2014	16,842	2,433	0.13	0.13
1965	2,425	291	0.11	0.14	2015	17,067	2,052	0.11	0.11
1966	2,619	447	0.15	0.19	2016	19,042	2,296	0.11	0.11

Source: David Joulfaian, "The Federal Estate and Gift Tax: Description, Profile of Taxpayers, and Economic Consequences," OTA Working Paper 80 (U.S. Department of the Treasury, Washington, DC, 1998); *IRS Data Book*, Internal Revenue Service, Washington, DC, various years; and other sources.
* Adjusts for the gift tax rate that was set at 75 percent of the estate tax rates before calendar year 1977.

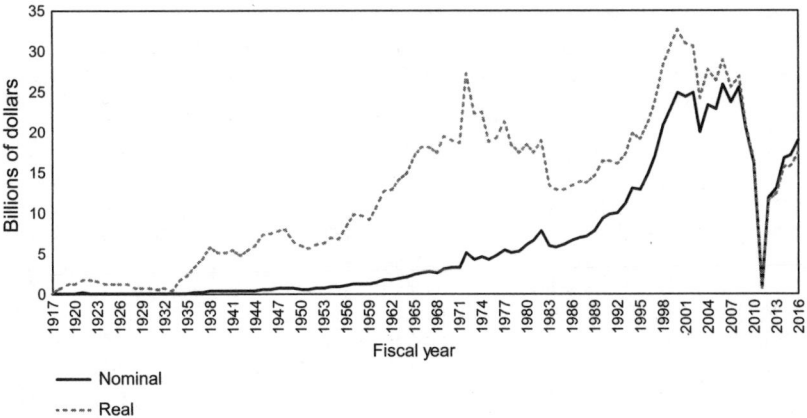

Figure 6.2
Estate tax revenues ($billions).

and figure 6.2 show the trend of estate tax revenues from inception of the estate tax in fiscal year 1917 to 2016. The decline in revenues in the late 1920s reflects the dramatically lower estate tax rates introduced by the Revenue Act of 1926 as well as the onset of the Great Depression.

Despite the absence of any major tax increase, estate tax revenues grew rapidly in the post–World War II period through the middle of the 1970s. The emerging pattern is even more dramatic when revenues are adjusted for inflation. Strong economic growth in this period is certainly a major contributor to the revenue yield. Another major

90

Chapter 6

contributor is the inflationary expansion in wealth. As inflation eroded the value of the exemption, as shown in table 6.3 and figure 6.3, more estates became subject to the estate tax. When compared to its value in 1955, for example, the exemption remained unchanged at $60,000 but lost half of its value in real terms by 1976.

Reductions in revenues in the late 1970s reflect lower tax rates, an expanded exemption (unified credit) brought about by the TRA76, and

Table 6.3
Estate Tax Exemption or Equivalent; Real Amounts in 2016 Prices

Year	Amount	Real	Year	Amount	Real	Year	Amount	Real
1916	50,000	1,100,959	1950	60,000	597,533	1984	325,000	750,750
1917	50,000	937,535	1951	60,000	553,867	1985	400,000	892,227
1918	50,000	794,732	1952	60,000	543,417	1986	500,000	1,094,932
1919	50,000	693,668	1953	60,000	539,346	1987	600,000	1,267,653
1920	50,000	600,023	1954	60,000	535,336	1988	600,000	1,217,290
1921	50,000	670,416	1955	60,000	537,334	1989	600,000	1,161,334
1922	50,000	714,313	1956	60,000	529,432	1990	600,000	1,101,801
1923	50,000	701,781	1957	60,000	512,475	1991	600,000	1,057,308
1924	50,000	701,781	1958	60,000	498,289	1992	600,000	1,026,411
1925	50,000	685,740	1959	60,000	494,864	1993	600,000	996,577
1926	100,000	1,355,983	1960	60,000	486,505	1994	600,000	971,696
1927	100,000	1,379,362	1961	60,000	481,623	1995	600,000	944,917
1928	100,000	1,403,561	1962	60,000	476,839	1996	600,000	917,816
1929	100,000	1,403,561	1963	60,000	470,606	1997	600,000	897,230
1930	100,000	1,437,180	1964	60,000	464,534	1998	625,000	920,280
1931	100,000	1,579,007	1965	60,000	457,160	1999	650,000	936,505
1932	50,000	875,945	1966	60,000	444,461	2000	675,000	940,846
1933	50,000	923,112	1967	60,000	431,154	2001	675,000	915,071
1934	50,000	895,556	1968	60,000	413,809	2002	1,000,000	1,334,369
1935	40,000	700,756	1969	60,000	392,385	2003	1,000,000	1,304,397
1936	40,000	690,673	1970	60,000	371,148	2004	1,500,000	1,905,761
1937	40,000	666,692	1971	60,000	355,569	2005	1,500,000	1,843,699
1938	40,000	680,877	1972	60,000	344,511	2006	2,000,000	2,381,538
1939	40,000	690,673	1973	60,000	324,336	2007	2,000,000	2,315,080
1940	40,000	685,740	1974	60,000	292,100	2008	2,000,000	2,230,007
1941	40,000	653,086	1975	60,000	267,668	2009	3,500,000	3,915,044
1942	60,000	883,469	1976	60,000	253,085	2010*	5,000,000	5,502,875
1943	60,000	832,401	1977	120,667	477,907	2011	5,000,000	5,335,359
1944	60,000	818,213	1978	134,000	493,270	2012	5,120,000	5,352,443
1945	60,000	800,030	1979	147,333	487,070	2013	5,250,000	5,409,112
1946	60,000	738,489	1980	161,563	470,589	2014	5,340,000	5,414,560
1947	60,000	645,764	1981	175,625	463,714	2015	5,430,000	5,499,242
1948	60,000	597,533	1982	225,000	559,606	2016	5,450,000	5,450,000
1949	60,000	605,065	1983	275,000	662,675	2017	5,490,000	5,450,000

* Estate tax was temporarily repealed in 2010; retroactively, estates may choose between basis carryover and 2011 estate tax law.

a slowdown in the economy. The maximum tax rate was reduced from 77 percent to 70 percent, and the size of the exempted estate was effectively tripled in nominal terms (and doubled in real terms) between 1976 and 1981.

Reductions in revenues in the early 1980s reflect the tax rate reductions, the increase in the unified credit, and, most important, the unlimited marital deduction brought about by ERTA81. The maximum tax rate was gradually reduced from 70 to 55 percent. Similarly, the unified credit was gradually increased from $47,000 to $192,800, with equivalent exemptions of $175,625 and $600,000, respectively. The unlimited marital deduction took effect in 1982, up from one-half of the estate.

Increases in revenues in the late 1980s and early 1990s in part reflect the deferral of estate taxes in the early 1980s after the introduction of the unlimited marital deduction in 1981. The timing of these increases, of course, reflects the surviving spouse's life expectancy and the respective filing of her estate tax return.[1] Through the early 1980s, estate tax returns for women, usually the surviving spouse, represented about one-third of the returns filed for estates in excess of $600,000; this fraction increased to about 44 percent beginning in the late 1980s. This increase in revenues is also explained by the strong economic growth and the booming stock market in the late 1990s.

Reductions in revenues in fiscal years 2000–2002 reflect the 2001 recession and a downturn in the stock market. For the remainder of the decade, however, the reduction in revenues can be explained by the scale back in the tax introduced by EGTRRA in 2001 to take effect in tax years 2002 through 2010. The expansion in the unified credit, intended to raise the size of the exempted estate to $3.5 million by 2009, is the largest source of revenue loss.

Estate tax revenues all but disappeared in fiscal year 2011, following temporary repeal in 2010. Revenues picked up in subsequent years, but at a slower pace as the size of the exempted estate increased to $5 million (indexed). The doubling of the exemption to $10 million (indexed) in 2018 is likely to slow revenue receipts in fiscal years 2019 and beyond.

Trend in Gift Tax Revenues

As with the estate tax, revenues from the gift tax reflect the tax structure in effect and the performance of the economy. In addition, gift tax

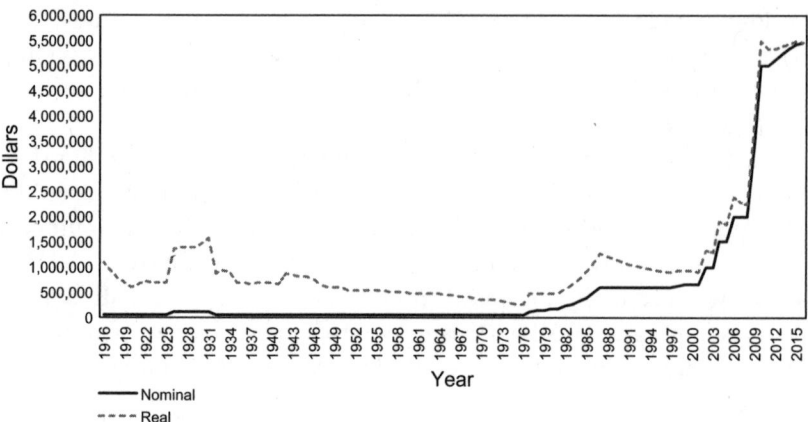

Figure 6.3
Estate tax exemption: nominal and real.

revenues depend on expectations of tax law changes. Table 6.2 and figure 6.3 provide figures on the gift tax yield since its inception. In fiscal year 1925, its first year in effect and before its repeal the following year, gift tax receipts were $8 million. In fiscal year 2016 they stood at $2.3 billion; they peaked in 2011 at $6.5 billion.

At the time of its reenactment in 1932, Congress deliberately set the gift tax's rates below those of the estate tax. The intent was to create incentives for lifetime wealth transfers and accelerate the flow of tax revenues to Treasury. True to expectations, gift tax receipts seem to fluctuate widely in response to changes in estate and gift tax rates.

In fiscal year 1977, which reflects calendar year 1976 transfers, gift tax receipts soared to $2 billion, about five times the receipts in the previous year and an all-time high in real terms. Gift taxes accounted for 24 percent of the combined yield of estate and gift tax revenues, well above its historic mean. This surge in receipts reflects the acceleration in gifts made in anticipation of the higher gift tax rates to take effect in 1977, brought about by TRA76. This surge may have resulted in lower gift tax receipts in the late 1970s when perhaps these transfers would have taken place absent the changes made by TRA76.

This is not the first time that top wealth holders have accelerated inter vivos transfers. In 1935, estate tax rates were increased mid-year, while corresponding gift tax increases were delayed to the end of the calendar year. The maximum estate tax rate, for instance, was increased from 60 to 70 percent on August 31, 1935. The same legislation, however,

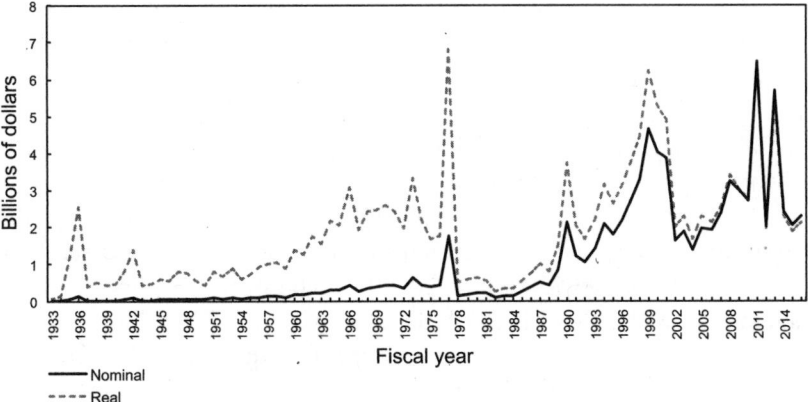

Figure 6.4
Gift tax revenues ($billions).

increased the maximum gift tax rate from 45 to 52.5 percent (75 percent of the applicable estate tax rate), effective January 1, 1936, four months later. In both fiscal years 1935 and 1936, gift tax receipts stood well above the trend. A similar pattern is also observed in fiscal year 1942, as gift tax rate increases lagged behind estate tax rate increases; the maximum gift tax rate increased from 52.5 percent to 57.75 percent.

The strong growth in gift tax receipts in the late 1980s may reflect the stability of the tax system compared to the early 1980s when tax rates were scheduled to decline gradually from 70 percent down to 50 percent. Increases in revenues in fiscal year 1990 (calendar year 1989 gifts) may also reflect the expiration of the $2 million GSTT exemption per donee at the end of calendar year 1989; transfers accelerated to take advantage of the exemption are fully taxable under the gift tax. The overall increase in gift taxes may also be explained by the unlimited marital deduction which, by expanding spousal bequests, may have delayed transfers to heirs.

Gift tax receipts declined sharply in anticipation of the reduction in estate and gift tax rates and the expansion in exemptions following changes ushered by EGTRRA. This trend in tax receipts reversed course in fiscal year 2007 to peak at $6.5 billion in 2011 (calendar year 2010), an all-time high in nominal terms, as well as in real terms when adjusted for the lower tax rate of 35 percent and inflation. The wealthy seem to have bet on continued wealth transfer taxes if not future higher tax rates; in 2011 the maximum tax rate was set to revert to 55 percent. This pattern is repeated once again in fiscal year 2013 (gifts made in 2012) as the temporary $5 million exemption and the maximum tax rate of 35 percent were set to expire and revert to an exemption of $1 million with a maximum tax rate of 55 percent. Gift tax receipts rose to $5.7 billion before declining.

Table 6.4 provides another look at what transpired in 2010 and 2012. Taxable gifts in excess of $5 million surged in 2010 and once again in 2012 as the tax rates were expected to rise from 35 percent to 55 percent (reset to 2001 law levels). What table 6.4 further reveals is the acceleration of gifts under $5 million in 2012. These gifts surged from an average of $20 billion to $30 billion per year to $370 billion in 2012. While these transfers have little revenue consequence in 2012, because they are sheltered by the $5 million exemption, they are likely to depress future revenues to the extent that they are borrowed from gifts and bequests likely to have been made in the future.

Enforcement and Tax Evasion

Not all revenues collected over the years are voluntary in nature. What is reported on tax returns should reflect applicable provisions of the tax code as well as the underlying assets held by an estate reduced by allowable deductions for expenses and bequests to spouses and

Table 6.4
Trend in Taxable Gifts ($Billion)

Year Gift Made	Gifts≤$1M	$1M<Gifts≤5M*	Gifts>$5M	All
1997	14.4	3	2.3	19.7
2002	22.7	1.9	1.4	26.0
2003	17.8	1.5	1.0	20.3
2004	20.5	2.2	1.2	24.0
2005	21.7	1.7	1.5	24.9
2006	21.4	2.1	2.1	25.6
2007	22.0	2.8	3.3	28.1
2008	20.0	2.5	2.8	25.2
2009	18.9	2.2	2.7	23.8
2010	18.9	4.3	13.2	36.3
2011	26.9	85.9	7.8	120.7
2012	48.4	380.7	22.4	451.5
2013	20.4	16.0	1.9	38.3
2014	20.8	15.1	3.9	39.8
2015	21.6	18.0	4.2	43.8
2016	21.8	20.8	4.1	46.7

Source: David Joulfaian, "Intergenerational Transfers under an Uncertain Estate Tax," mimeo, August 2014, U.S. Department of the Treasury, Washington, DC; updated using data through 2016.
* Includes gifts over $5 million made after 2011 when the value, adjusted for inflation, is under $5 million.

charities. But at times, taxpayers, or perhaps more correctly their legal representatives, underreport the size of taxable estates, and consequently underreport their tax liabilities.

Over the past three decades, and on average, about $1 billion dollars a year in additional estate taxes have been assessed following audits by the Internal Revenue Service, as shown in table 6.5. These assessments have been relatively stable over the past two decades despite the reduction in the number of returns examined and audit coverage; assessments grew rapidly over the past two years. These tax audits,

Table 6.5
Estate Tax Returns Examined and Additional Tax Assessed

Fiscal Year	Returns Filed*	Returns Examined	Percent Examined	Additional Tax Assessed ($1,000s)	Assessment per Return
1988	67,600	15,117	22.36	963,000	63,697
1989	52,000	12,463	23.97	746,000	60,346
1990	55,800	11,798	21.14	1,832,000	15,525
1991	60,800	10,930	17.98	820,000	75,023
1992	64,600	12,013	18.60	1,211,000	101,791
1993	70,000	11,829	16.90	1,050,476	90,208
1994	73,000	11,077	15.17	1,252,296	115,187
1995	80,400	11,419	14.20	890,933	79,373
1996	81,500	11,794	14.47	958,064	82,472
1997	90,600	11,686	12.90	1,400,907	122,775
1998	102,300	10,451	10.22	1,432,624	141,769
1999	110,100	9,319	8.46	1,055,631	166,993
2000	116,500	8,024	6.89	1,044,678	133,240
2001	123,500	7,707	6.24	829,154	109,454
2002	122,412	7,151	5.84	1,432,090	200,229
2003	113,959	7,265	6.38	1,181,955	162,677
2004	87,114	6,455	7.41	972,575	150,634
2005	74,172	6,081	8.20	970,091	160,655
2006	54,851	5,299	9.66	1,436,268	271,199
2007	59,978	4,616	7.70	1,147,801	248,657
2008	47,298	3,852	8.14	834,285	216,697
2009	48,274	4,468	9.26	1,622,548	363,149
2010	42,366	4,288	10.12	1,405,415	327,755
2011	23,014	4,195	18.23	1,539,617	367,012
2012	12,582	3,762	29.90	1,145,640	304,530
2013	28,061	3,250	11.58	3,295,992	1,014,151
2014	33,719	2,853	8.46	774,489	271,465
2015	35,619	2,770	7.78	428,109	154,552
2016	36,130	3,187	8.82	789,805	247,821
2017	35,042	2,876	8.21	798,898	277,781

Source: *IRS Data Book*, Internal Revenue Service, Washington, DC, various years.
* Previous calendar year. In contrast, returns examined can be from several years in the past.

while raising tax revenues directly, also serve the greater purpose of encouraging compliance and deterring tax evasion.

Not filing an estate tax return usually is not a very effective form of noncompliance. There is no statute of limitations for returns not filed, and the books remain open indefinitely. In addition, and because ownership of assets held by third parties (e.g., banks, brokerage houses) needs to be verified, not filing can become an obstacle to the proper transfer of the underlying assets from the decedent to the beneficiaries. Of course this third-party information may be shared with the IRS. Also, and especially in the case of the very well off, noncompliance is more likely to take the form of understating the value of assets as well as aggressive tax planning that is manifested in the form of smaller estates reported for tax purposes.

As with the estate tax, some of the gift tax revenue was also involuntarily collected, as shown in table 6.6. The additional tax assessed fluctuated over the years, but more significantly in fiscal years 2013 and 2014 with over $1.2 billion in assessments. The average assessed tax was over $400,000 per return, despite the lower tax rates and expanded exemptions. The number of returns examined also fluctuated over the years. The implied audit rate, or the number of returns examined as a fraction of all returns filed, also fluctuated over the years. It appears to be under 1 percent in recent years. But this low audit rate can be misleading or at the very least difficult to interpret. Because of the rising size of the exempted estates over the years, the number of audited returns suggests a much higher coverage rate. As an example, fewer than one thousand tax returns with taxable gifts in excess of $5 million were filed in 2016, or about one-half the number of returns audited. However, individuals may underreport the value of gifts below this threshold and potentially expand the pool of tax returns that should be audited. This would suggest a much broader universe of tax returns to consider in measuring the audit ratio.

The statute of limitations for filed estate tax returns is typically three years, which requires an audit to take place within this period. This limitation originally applied only to filed estate tax returns, and not to filed gift tax returns. Because of the cumulative nature of estate and gift taxes, gift tax audits often took place at the same time as those of the estate tax, with cumulative transfers reconciled at the same time. All of this changed when Congress extended the three-year statute of limitation to the gift tax as part of the changes introduced by the Tax Relief Act of 1997. Rather than keeping the status of gift tax returns

Table 6.6
Gift Tax Returns Examined and Additional Tax Assessed

Fiscal Year	Returns Filed*	Returns Examined	Percent Examined	Additional Tax Assessed ($1,000s)	Assessment per Return
1988	101,300	1,669	1.65	227,000	135,913
1989	104,000	1,276	1.23	409,437	321,288
1990	123,500	1,640	1.33	246,775	150,526
1991	147,700	1,704	1.15	140,902	82,746
1992	156,800	2,071	1.32	193,849	93,737
1993	170,500	2,120	1.24	202,009	93,834
1994	217,800	1,853	0.85	212,144	114,487
1995	215,700	1,893	0.88	201,603	85,784
1996	216,200	1,934	0.89	350,680	121,741
1997	232,000	2,085	0.90	375,004	129,708
1998	255,600	2,010	0.79	367,035	182,695
1999	261,200	2,369	0.91	346,061	146,208
2000	291,900	2,097	0.72	459,785	219,888
2001	308,600	2,005	0.65	343,279	171,382
2002	303,800	1,899	0.63	405,047	213,369
2003	282,625	1,855	0.66	488,923	263,855
2004	284,852	1,979	0.69	546,442	276,257
2005	262,164	2,125	0.81	670,901	319,833
2006	265,455	2,051	0.77	504,731	246,090
2007	264,315	1,490	0.56	230,833	154,921
2008	255,123	1,071	0.42	223,537	208,718
2009	257,010	1,569	0.61	294,977	188,003
2010	238,851	1,777	0.74	203,403	114,464
2011	226,241	2,623	1.16	301,423	114,915
2012	223,090	3,164	1.41	351,167	110,988
2013	260,426	2,775	1.07	1,228,034	442,535
2014	371,747	3,098	0.83	1,332,885	430,240
2015	267,600	2,539	0.95	286,026	112,653
2016	238,324	1,843	0.77	302,836	164,317
2017	244,974	1,886	0.77	439,458	233,011

Source: *IRS Data Book,* Internal Revenue Service, Washington, DC, various years.
* Previous calendar year. In contrast, returns examined can be from several years in the past.

open until an estate tax return is filed, now tax examiners have to real-locate resources to examine gift tax returns within three years of the return's filing. They are no longer able to wait over the life expectancy of the donor or wealth holder for joint audits of estate tax returns and the associated gifts made during the life of the decedent.

In addition to the pressure from the time constraints due to the limit-ing nature of the statute of limitations, the budget allocated to auditing the tax returns may have been declining as well. As reported by David Cay Johnston, the audit staff was reduced from 345 to 157, plus an additional reduction of seventeen support personnel, in 2006.[2] The subsequent decline in the number of estate and gift tax returns examined through 2008 should therefore not be surprising.

Tax Administration

Receipts from the estate and gift taxes should be adjusted for the cost of their administration in order to arrive at their net fiscal contributions. These costs include the processing of tax returns, compliance and enforcement personnel, legal staff to draft regulation, and office space, among others. Isolating the cost of the administration of the estate tax from that of the entire tax system is a difficult undertaking in the presence of task sharing and the joint use of resources. The cost of office space and computer facilities, for instance, is difficult to allocate to the various taxes in place.

One approach, albeit imperfect, is to allocate the cost of administering the tax by apportioning the entire IRS budget based on the share of estate tax-related activities. The IRS budget for fiscal year 2017 was $11.5 billion, as reported in table 6.7, a figure that has not really changed since 2008. It processed a total of 195 million tax returns and examined slightly over 1.5 million returns, not including excise tax returns and other returns related to pension and tax-exempt bond issuance. Estate and gift tax returns represent less than two-tenths of

Table 6.7
Cost of Tax Administration Cost

	2008	2017
Cost incurred by IRS, $millions	11,307	11,526
Total returns filed	183,529,945	195,614,161
Estate tax returns filed	47,298	35,042
Percent of all returns filed	0.026%	0.018%
Gift tax returns filed	255,123	244,976
Percent of all returns filed	0.139%	0.125%
Returns examined	1,540,771	1,059,924
Estate tax returns examined	3,852	2,876
Percent of all returns examined	0.250%	0.271%
Gift tax returns examined	1,071	1,886
Percent of all returns examined	0.070%	0.178%

Source: *IRS Data Book*, Internal Revenue Service, Washington, DC, various years.

1 percent of all returns filed, and less than one-third of 1 percent of all returns examined. The latter suggest that administration cost is likely to be very small in particular when measured relative to the revenue collected.

Of course there are private costs to consider as well and these can be sizeable depending on how they are measured. In a 1999 paper, Charles Davenport and Jay Soled report estimates of the cost of tax planning.[3] More specifically, they conduct a survey among tax professionals focusing on the charges for typical estate planning in six different estate-size classes. They then apply the reported estimates to the number of estate tax returns filed in 1996. This generates an estimated cost for typical estate planning of $290 million. Applying some adjustments for tax planning and estate administration costs brings their total estimate to about $1.7 billion in 1999, or some 6.4 percent of receipts. With the expanded size of exempted estates from $600,000 to $5 million in 2013 and $10 million in 2018 (both indexed), their reported estimate should be adjusted downward, as there are fewer estates to be impacted by the tax.

Absent the estate tax, private costs will continue to be incurred. These may include expenses related to succession planning and probate. Wills will continue to be drawn, and estates will continue to be probated. As an alternative, individuals may create trusts and transfer some if not all of their assets to them during life and avoid probate. Some of the tax planning will also continue to take place in order to avoid the income tax, including capital gains taxes. Indeed, the current estate tax-avoidance technology also involves income tax avoidance, making it rather difficult to quantify the relative cost of compliance. But while this will make it difficult to quantify the compliance cost of the estate tax, it should not be dismissed.

Summary

Estate tax revenue grew over the years as the scope of the tax expanded, and erosion in the size of exempted estate was unchecked due to inflation. With reductions in tax rates and expansions in the size of exemption to $5 million in 2011, estate tax revenues declined over the years to less than 1 percent of total federal receipts.

The gift tax also followed a similar pattern albeit along a more turbulent path. Donors seemed to aggressively react to pending tax increases and accelerated their transfers, as experienced in the early

1930s, 1976, 2010, and 2013 in particular. And with these surges in gifts, the share of the gift tax in the combined estate and gift tax revenues also fluctuated over time. It is about 11 percent for recent filers.

Not all revenues collected are voluntary in nature. Direct revenues from enforcement over the years peaked at $3.3 billion in 2013 for the estate tax and about $1.3 billion for the gift tax in 2014; a combined $1.2 billion was generated for estate and gift taxes in 2017. Overall, direct enforcement revenues have been influenced by the evolving estate tax structure and changing tax rates and exemptions. Of course, enforcement also has an indirect effect on revenues through improved compliance.

7 Behavioral Effects Related to Saving and Labor Decisions

With its many features, the estate tax is likely to influence a number of economic activities. Its architects deliberately shaped its structure to elicit a change in behavior. Indeed, the early proponents of the estate tax lobbied for its enactment in order to discourage certain behavior. Examples of the latter include Andrew Carnegie, a staunch supporter of progressive estate taxation and one of the richest men of his time, who argued a century ago that "the parent who leaves his son an enormous wealth generally deadens the talents and energies of the son, and tempts him to a lead a less useful and worthy life than he otherwise would."[1]

In addition to the labor supply considerations voiced by Carnegie, the estate tax may also influence saving decisions and shape the observed wealth accumulations. Of course, the estate tax may have other unintended consequences that, like any other tax, may induce and distort behavior in ways that may blur the measurement of saving. A primary—and universal—concern when inheritance taxes are levied is the potential for lifetime gifts to be used as means for skirting taxes levied at death. Higher estate tax rates, without a concomitant increase in gift tax rates, can accelerate transfers during life. And these lifetime transfers will certainly complicate the measurement of saving given that wealth may have changed hands from parents to children, without necessarily changing overall saving. The omission of tax-induced lifetime transfers along with other avoidance schemes will very likely bias estimates of saving and wealth accumulation.

Saving and Wealth Accumulation

In its simplest form, the estate tax is a tax on saving by parents, or donors in general. This leads to both income and substitution effects and therefore a gross ambiguity in the total effect on wealth accumulation. The substitution effect leads individuals to consume more as the tax may discourage some of them from saving, while the income effect leads individuals to save more in order to offset the reduction of wealth to be transferred to the heirs caused by the estate tax.

In addition to its effects on donor saving, the estate tax may also influence the saving behavior of the heirs as well. The receipt of an inheritance may lead the recipient to increase consumption. As the estate tax has the potential to shape inheritances, it may also undercut some of the effects of the transfers received.

Saving by Donors
At the outset, the effects of the tax on saving by donors are likely to depend on the underlying bequest motive. As an example, bequests can be accidental in nature and will not be responsive to estate taxation. Individuals may have precautionary savings in case of unforeseen shocks to income (e.g., stock market crash) and expenditures (e.g., major health event). And given the uncertainty of lifetime length, they may leave behind unplanned bequests of wealth not consumed during life.[2]

Alternatively, individuals may have altruistic bequest motives toward their children. They may care about the welfare of their children and attempt to compensate for the lower-earning children.[3] Because parents derive utility from their children's consumption and well-being, they will care about the after-tax bequests they leave behind to them. Accordingly, in preparation for eventual estate taxes, these parents may save more to offset the tax-induced reduction in inheritances received by their heirs.

The joy of giving is one bequest motive that may also be present. Here, parents may derive joy or a "warm glow" from giving to their children (and other beneficiaries).[4] Parents derive utility from the bequests they leave behind for their children and are less concerned about compensating them for any income differences. As with the altruistic bequest-motivated savers, parents are likely to respond to estate taxes that will reduce inheritances received by their heirs.

In addition, strategic or exchange-related motives may be at play as well.[5] Under these motives, parents provide for bequests to their children in exchange for receiving services in their old age or to gain attention, such as frequent visits, from them. Because transfers are positively related to the value of services they obtain, increases in estate taxes imply that parents may have to save more to benefit from the same level of services and care provided by the children.

Another saving motive to consider is the wealth in utility or "capitalist spirit."[6] Here, parents enjoy being wealthy or successful with little consideration to leaving bequests to their heirs. Consequently, increases in estate taxes should not impact individual savings. Examples of these may include Warren Buffett with his billions in accumulated wealth, or his counterpart Andrew Carnegie from a century ago. While amassing massive amounts of wealth, very little of this was and is destined to benefit their heirs. Now that he is in his eighties, Warren Buffett has been donating billions to charity. And Andrew Carnegie donated much of his wealth at a late age before his death in 1919 as well. Indeed, Carnegie had donated some $350 million, leaving him only $30 million on his death in 1919.[7]

And last, some of these motives may be present as different individuals may face different bequest motives as well as different relationships and social settings. At the outset, however, there is no consensus among economists on the existence of a bequest motive.

At the theoretical level, a number of attempts have been made to simulate the effects of the estate tax on saving using varying assumptions about bequest motives, often integrating the saving response of the heirs with that of donors. In his 2001 chapter "Simulating the Effects on Inequality and Wealth Accumulation of Eliminating the Federal Gift and Estate Tax," John Laitner developed a steady-state simulation model in which parents exhibit altruistic preferences toward their children. He finds that estate taxes reduce wealth accumulation among the top percentile of wealthy households.[8] Similarly, and in the same volume as Laitner's chapter, William Gale and Maria Perozek evaluate the potential effects of estate taxation under various bequest motives. They conclude that the effects on savings (by donors and beneficiaries) depend on the underlying bequest motive.[9] More recently, Cagetti and De Nardi also use a steady-state simulation model, but focus on the saving and investment decisions of firms. They conclude that the estate tax would significantly increase savings and capital accumulation; the estate tax's ability to distort economic decision making is much more pronounced in larger firms.[10] Wojciech Kopczuk provides a brief overview of the literature.[11]

Moving to the empirical findings, Douglas Holtz-Eakin and Donald Marples attempt to identify the impact of transfer taxes on households' wealth accumulation in their 2001 paper, "Distortion Costs of Taxing

Wealth Accumulation: Income Versus Estate Taxes."[12] They employ
data from the 1992 *Health and Retirement Study* (HRS), which is a nation-
ally representative, random sample of the older working-age population. It began in 1992 with a random sample of non-institutionalized
men and women aged 51 to 61 and their families, and follow-up interviews have occurred every two years (wave). At the time of their
writing, four waves, or two-year periods, of information were available
in public release, and this paper makes use of wave 1. The baseline
survey contains 12,652 respondents from 7,607 households.

Augmenting the publicly available data with nonpublic information that identifies the state of residence of respondents, Holtz-Eakin
and Marples attempt to exploit variations in cross-state estate and
inheritance tax rates in their analysis. They conclude that the estate
tax has depressing effects on wealth, but concede that the individuals
in the data panel employed are not sufficiently wealthy to be subject
to the federal estate tax. And so clearly, the paper is unable to speak
on the effects of the federal tax.

At about the same time, Wojciech Kopczuk and Joel Slemrod employ
aggregate time-series estate-tax data for 1916 to 1945, 1962, 1965, 1969,
1972, 1976, and for each year from 1982 to 1996. In their 2001 paper
"The Impact of the Estate Tax on the Wealth Accumulation and Avoidance Behavior of Donors," they examine the effects of the estate tax
on reported wealth.[13] They find that reported net worth of the top
estates, measured relative to national wealth, are negatively correlated
with estate tax rates. These results are robust in a multiple regres-
sion framework that controls for a number of relevant explanatory
variables.

Next, moving away from aggregated data and turning to individual-
level tax return data, the authors utilize both time-series variations in
the tax rate structure and cross-sectional variation in observable individual characteristics. They estimate a positive elasticity of the reported
sizes of estates with respect to the net of tax rate (i.e., negative with
respect to the tax rate itself) and statistically significant.

Their result also holds for older decedents, suggesting that a behavioral response is likely present for the wealthy with a bequest motive.
The estimated negative behavioral response is even more pronounced
when tax rate measures that prevailed over the course of one's lifetime
were investigated. In particular, and the innovation introduced in this
study, the marginal tax rate is computed using the law individuals
faced at the age of 45. This measure proved to be both economically

and statistically significant, dominating all other measures in the analysis. The findings suggest that an estate tax rate of 50 percent would reduce the reported net worth of the richest half percent of the population by 10.5 percent when its effect is realized after many years. The authors conclude that it is not clear whether this reflects a marginal choice not to save or tax avoidance.

I also explore the effects of the estate tax on wealth accumulation in my 2006 paper, "The Behavioral Response of Wealth Accumulation to Estate Taxation: Time Series Evidence."[14] In this study, I employ time-series data consisting of a stream of federal estate tax revenues collected over a period of fifty years to examine the effects of estate taxation on bequests. Because the key variable of interest is wealth held at death, I first convert the tax revenue collection stream to aggregate wealth held at death each year, or more appropriately, taxable estates. This is accomplished by dividing the revenue collected by a representative estate tax rate.

Next, and rather than gauge how accumulated wealth varies with the estate tax rate, I convert the representative estate tax rate (e) to an equivalent income tax rate (τ) that would be levied annually during the donor's lifetime and one that would keep the heirs equally well off. In other words, the beneficiaries should be indifferent between having an estate tax apply to the donor's wealth at death, and a specific income tax rate that applies to the return on these assets that is taxed annually during life. This equivalent income tax rate is defined as:

$$\tau = \frac{(1+r)-(1+r)(1-e)^{1/n}}{r}$$

where r is the return on the underlying asset and n is the life expectancy of the donor. For a given estate tax rate, the above equation implies that the equivalent income tax rate declines with life expectancy of the donor; the longer the donor is expected to live the lower the tax rate. It also declines with the expected rate of return. Alternatively stated, older individuals face a higher equivalent income tax rate while those expecting high rates of return face low tax rates. In many ways, this can be viewed as my extension of Poterba's analysis of the effects of the estate tax on after-tax rates of return.[15]

The implications of the estate-income tax-equivalent tax rates are captured in figure 7.1. It shows how the measured equivalent income tax rate varies with age and rate of return. As an illustration, consider a male individual subject to an estate tax rate of 40 percent. For an individual age 21, with a rate of return of 10 percent on assets and life expectancy of 54.6 years (using general mortality tables), the equivalent income tax rate on annual earnings is 10 percent. This declines to 6 percent when a rate of return of 20 percent is expected. The respective tax rates become 68 percent and 31 percent in the case of a 71-year-old with a much shorter life expectancy of 12.5 years. For older wealth holders, where life expectancies are short, the equivalent income tax rate is likely to exceed 100 percent of the rate of return as the estate tax applies to principle as well as the return to an asset.

In a multivariate setting, the size of the taxable estate is regressed on the equivalent income tax rate. Using a number of specifications, the findings in this study suggest that the estate tax results in taxable estates that are about 10 percent smaller than if there were no estate tax. As with the findings in the 2001 paper by Wojciech Kopczuk and Joel Slemrod, these results may either reflect the effects of estate taxation on saving and wealth accumulation or simply tax avoidance and aggressive tax planning. Of course, the aggregate nature of the data is a major limitation of the findings as it may introduce errors in measuring wealth and the appropriate measure for the representative estate tax rate.[16]

In an earlier paper in 1996, Kenneth Chapman, Govind Hariharan, and Lawrence Southwick Jr. explore how estate tax rates shape estate

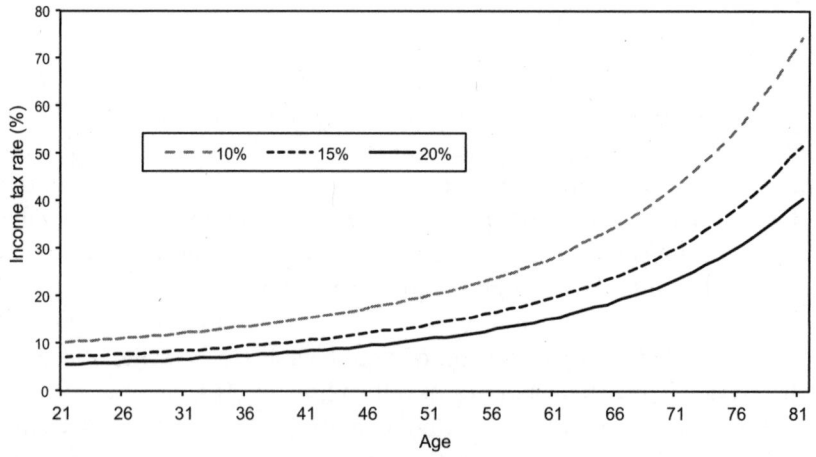

Figure 7.1
Estate equivalent income tax rates (by age and rate of return).

tax revenues.[17] The authors employ a time series of annual data on federal estate and gift tax revenues for fiscal years 1958 through 1994. They regress these annual fiscal year revenues collected on a measure of the estate tax rate to gauge how revenues change in reaction to a contemporaneous change in tax rates. They report a negative relationship between estate and gift revenues and the tax rates. Unfortunately, the dependent variable they employ is the combined sum of estate and gift taxes, two variables that do not always move in tandem and are at times governed by different tax regimes. Indeed, the sharp increase in revenues reported by the authors in fiscal year 1977 is explained by the acceleration in gift tax revenues documented in table 6.2 and figure 6.3 caused by the pending increases in the gift tax rate in 1977, and have little to do with estate tax rates.

Wealth Accumulation and Timing of Transfers   As suggested by the preceding findings, care should be taken to not necessarily interpret reductions in wealth accumulated by parents and other donors as reductions in overall saving, given that some of the wealth reported by the estates may be underreported for a variety of reasons other than tax-induced dissaving. This is particularly the case in the presence of tax avoidance when wealth is transferred to children and other beneficiaries during life in response to differences in the tax treatment of gifts and bequests, or to exploit temporary changes in tax law to accelerate transfers in a bid to minimize taxes.

Indeed, attempts to compare trends in wealth accumulation over different periods is quite challenging, in particular during periods when estate and gift tax rates diverge or when changes in tax rates have been enacted. The easiest way to avoid estate and inheritance taxes is through tax-free lifetime gifts, unless this is checked by the imposition of gift taxes. It is noteworthy that during the congressional deliberations in 1932 to increase the maximum estate tax rate from 20 to 45 percent, and the introduction of a gift tax regime, one individual is reported to have made about $100 million in gifts, and another to have made gifts of about $50 million as reported by President Roosevelt.[18] Considering that the entire yield of the estate tax in 1932 was $400 million, the tax-free inter vivos transfers of $150 million by these two individuals alone, not to mention likely gifts by scores of others, demonstrate the sizeable leakages from the estate tax in the absence of the gift tax, particularly at a time when estate-tax-rate increases are being considered.

History repeats itself, and the pattern noted for 1932 is repeated over the years. Table 6.2 and figure 6.4 in chapter 6 document additional episodes of spikes in gift tax receipts as individuals accelerate gifts in the face of pending higher estate taxes. Another more recent example is the spike in gifts in 2012 documented earlier in table 6.4, where gifts of $450 billion were made. This amount is nearly twenty times the amount of gifts reported in each of prior years over the past decade. And for the first time, this is also more than twice the value of the gross estates reported at death on estate tax returns, but with little of it subject to the gift tax because many of the gifts are sheltered by the $5 million exemption.

There is little doubt that these flows of transfers are generally reflective of changes in ownership and result in smaller wealth accumulated by the donor. Empirical studies that focus exclusively on the wealth of the donor will invariably conclude that the tax has led to dissaving or wealth de-accumulation in the face of higher tax rates. But these transfers should have little effect on national saving as assets have simply changed hands from one generation to another. These also make intertemporal comparisons of accumulated wealth by parents a challenging undertaking, and may, as noted earlier, produce biased behavioral estimates when periods with and without gift tax regimes are included in the same sample. There is a preponderance of evidence both from estate tax records and gift tax records to document the timing of transfers.

Choosing between Lifetime Gifts and Bequests As alluded to already, one of the earliest concerns commonly acknowledged in taxing bequests at death is how lifetime gifts may be employed in preempting bequest taxation. Reflecting on this concern, the gift tax was introduced to harmonize the tax treatment of transfers, whether during life or at death. But as we have seen in chapter 3, a wedge between the two tax rates continues to this date, albeit much narrower than when exempting gifts altogether.

While the estate and gift taxes were unified in 1976, with a common tax rate schedule, lifetime gifts and bequests continue to be treated differently by the tax code. And this treatment differential may influence how donors allocate their transfers between these two modes of transfers. In the case of bequests, the tax is computed on the wealth left behind in the estate; some of this wealth is paid in taxes and what is left passes on to the heirs. In the case of gifts, however, the tax is levied on what the beneficiary receives, which is by default exclusive of the tax. Because gifts are taxed on a tax-exclusive basis, this reduces the effective tax rate on gifts relative to the estate tax rate on bequests, and generally creates incentives for making lifetime gifts.

More specifically, the price or out-of-pocket cost of making a gift of cash, denoted as P_G, can be defined as $1 + g$, where g is the gift tax rate. Whereas, with e as the estate tax rate, the price of a bequest of cash is $1 / (1 - e)$, denoted as P_B, ignoring asset appreciation and discounting. As an example, consider a parent wishing to transfer \$1 to her children. At an estate tax rate (e) of 0.55, the parent would have to save and forgo \$2.22 to transfer \$1 to her heirs and pay \$1.22 in taxes. In contrast, and at a gift tax rate (g) of 0.55, the parent would have to give up \$1.55 for every \$1 in gifts received by the recipient. In other words, the cost of transferring \$1 to children is \$2.2 in the case of bequests compared to \$1.55 in the case of gifts, making gifts some 30 percent less costly than bequests. Alternatively stated, the price of gifts relative to that of bequests is $(1 + g)(1 - e)$; at a tax rate of 0.55, the relative price of gifts is 1.55×0.45 or 0.6975.

The treatment of transfers of appreciated assets is a bit more complicated, as the income tax accords a step-up in basis for bequests and, in contrast, basis carryover for gifts. Under step-up in basis, all past accrued gains by the donor are extinguished and no longer taxable when the underlying assets are sold in the future. While under the basis carryover regime, the recipient of gifts is subjected to future capital gains taxes on gains accumulated by the donor. Also, when gifts are made within three years of the date of death, the gift tax itself becomes subject to the estate tax. Combined, these may offset the benefit of the tax-exclusive nature of the gift tax, and may even make gifts less attractive.

With capital gains tax rate c, accrued gains share in assets transferred β, asset appreciation rate of π, discount rate of also π for simplicity, and probability of death within three years of making a gift ρ, the price of gifts takes on the following more complicated form:[19]

$$P_G = \frac{\left(1 + g + \dfrac{c\beta g}{1 - c\beta}\right)(1 + \delta)^n}{(1 + \pi)^n - c\beta(1 - g) - c\left[(1 + \pi)^n - 1\right] - \rho e g}$$

This equation is derived in my 2005 paper, "Choosing between Gifts and Bequests: How Taxes Affect the Timing of Wealth Transfers," which also provides evidence of the effects that capital gains, estate, and gift taxes have on the timing of transfers.[20]

To empirically gauge how the wealthy respond to taxes in the timing of transfers, and the choice between giving during life vs. at death, in my 2005 paper I employ data drawn from the estate tax returns of decedents in 1989. Estate tax returns provide information on wealth and its composition. Information is available on assets held at death, debts, and expenses related to settling the estate. More important, they also provide information on the cumulative amount of lifetime taxable gifts made through 1989. These gifts are transfers in excess of the annual exclusion of $10,000, and do not include payments for tuition and medical expenses, all of which are tax free. Demographic information is available on age of the decedent, marital status, gender, and state of residency.

This dataset is a subset of a larger sample for returns filed in 1989 prepared by the SOI program and for which we observed the number and relationship of beneficiaries to decedents. I restrict the sample to the estates of parents only with total assets in excess of $600,000, the filing threshold in 1989. The number of observations used in my analysis is 2,361, of which only 928 reported to have made taxable gifts during their lifetime.

For each of the fifty states and the District of Columbia, I compute the estate tax rate net of the federal credit for state death taxes. Federal tax rates are augmented with state estate, gift, and capital gains tax rates. Individual annuitant mortality tables are then employed in determining life expectancies and the probability of dying within three years of the date of the gift. Assets are assumed to appreciate at the rate of 8 percent, and the share of accrued gains of noncash assets is set at 0.5.[21]

The findings in this paper suggest that taxes are an important consideration in choosing between gifts and bequests. The relative frequency or probability of making gifts tends to rise with wealth. In addition, both the amount and the fraction of wealth transferred during life rise with wealth as well. In the absence of estate and gift taxes, lifetime gifts may decline substantially by an estimated 64 percent. And this will certainly impact the observed wealth held by the donor.

Timing of Gifts   Even when parents, or donors in general, plan to make their transfers only during life, without any consideration of bequests, they may time their gifts to take advantage of low tax regimes. Changes in the gift tax laws may create incentives for them to alter the timing of their gifts. Indeed, gift tax revenue collections, documented in table 6.2 and figure 6.4, clearly indicate that the wealthy are very responsive to changes in tax regimes and act decisively to take advantage of tax rate differentials. For instance, and in anticipation of an increase in the federal gift-tax rates in 1977, individuals accelerated their transfers into 1976 (fiscal year 1977) as illustrated in figure 6.4. In another recent example, and as documented in table 6.4, total reported gifts increased some twenty-fold in 2012 in anticipation of lowering the exemption from $5 to $1 million and the increase in the maximum tax rate from 35 to 55 percent in 2013. Qualitatively, this was not unlike that observed in 1934, 1936, 1942, and the past decade.

A similar pattern of behavior was also observed in the state of New York, which repealed its gift tax effective in 2000. In 1999, the maximum state gift tax rate was 21 percent, and the maximum combined state and federal gift tax rate was 71 percent (55 percent federal and 16 percent for the state). With repeal of the state gift tax, the combined tax rate declined to 55 percent. In anticipation of this change, gift tax receipts in fiscal year 2000 (most likely from transfers made in calendar year 1999) declined by 60 percent when compared to prior year receipts.

Evidence from Gift Tax Revenues   In my 2004 paper, Gift Taxes and Lifetime Transfers: Time Series Evidence, I examine how taxes affect the timing of lifetime transfers.[22] I employ time series data on gift tax collections over the years 1933 through 1998, a period when significant changes in gift tax rates are observed. The study illustrates how trends in gifts by the wealthy dramatically shift in response to changes in gift tax rates, particularly in the short run.

Tax data are usually reported on a fiscal year basis reflecting the flow of revenues to the government. Hence, I first convert the stream of revenues to calendar year basis. This is simply done by using the lead value of reported data; fiscal year 1995, for instance, becomes calendar year 1994. For each year I first employ the maximum current and future expected gift and estate tax rates in calculating the tax prices, assuming all wealth is held in cash. Because some of the legislated rate changes were to take place over a number of years, I set the expected rate to the fully phased-in rate. As an example, the maximum gift and estate tax rates were set to decrease in 5 percentage point increments from 70 percent in 1981 to 50 percent in 1985. While the rate in 1982 was set at

65 percent, 60 percent in 1983, and so on, I set the expected future rate in 1981 to 50 percent, the fully phased-in law. I extend a similar treatment to capital gains taxes as well. I exclude the 1932 observation because the gift tax was enacted in the middle of the year.

The use of the maximum tax rates to gauge incentive effects on giving may not be totally satisfactory, and indeed can lead to misleading results. Consider the case where the top tax rates do not change, but rates for those in lower wealth brackets change significantly. As an example, the maximum gift tax rate in the early part of 1941 was 57.75 percent and applied to transfers in excess of $50 million. The changes introduced in the latter part of that year also set the maximum rate at 57.75 percent on such transfers, suggesting no change in tax rates. But in the case of transfers slightly in excess of $500,000, the marginal tax rate increased from 18.98 percent to 26.25 percent. For the less wealthy, this is a much bigger change than that observed for those in the maximum tax bracket.

Thus, as an alternative to the maximum tax rate, in the paper I derive a measure of the tax price using the marginal tax rate on a hypothetical fixed amount of gifts. Based on information reported on estate tax returns of decedents in 1995, the conditional average amount of gifts reported by donors was $6 million. I calculate the representative marginal tax rate using this amount, after adjusting it for growth in real GDP and available exemptions.

As we have seen in table 4.9, not all gifts take the form of cash. Some of the gifts are transfers of stock or real estate ownership, among other assets that change in value over time. Because the recipients carryover the basis of such assets, they may become subject to capital gains taxes on gains accrued by the donor if and when the assets received are sold in the future. Of course capital gains taxes are irrelevant in the case of bequests, as assets are stepped up in value at death.

For gifts made in the form of corporate equity, or appreciable property in general, the price of gifts is modified to account for the capital gains tax as in the previous section. Four critical assumptions are made in measuring the tax price. First, assets are assumed to appreciate at the rate of 7 percent (π). Second, donor life expectancies are set at 20 years (n = 20). Third, and in order to allow for consistent comparisons between gifts and bequests, donees are assumed to sell assets in period $t + n$. Fourth, assets are assumed to appreciate at the donor's discount rate, i.e., δ, with share of accrued gains of $\beta = 0.5$.[23] Finally, I assume that assets held by the wealthy are 30 percent cash, or equivalent, and 70 percent noncash, which reflects the average portfolio reported on estate tax returns. This allocation is then applied in constructing a weighted price for gifts (P_G).

During the period under study, the tax treatment of generation-skipping transfer also changed, in addition to the treatment of gifts and bequests. To account for the expiration of the $2 million-per-donee exemption in 1989 under the GSTT introduced in 1986, I set a dichoto-mous variable equal to one in 1989. Ideally, the GSTT should be reflected in the gift price to grandchildren and other generation-skipping benefi-ciaries. Unfortunately, and given the aggregate nature of the data, we do not observe the size of generation-skipping transfers. This, and the temporary nature of the per donee exemption, makes it rather difficult to use a separate price measure for grandchildren.

The gift tax revenue collections are modified to make them as com-parable as possible over time regardless of tax rate changes. This is done by dividing gift tax collections by the representative effective gift tax rate $g / (1 + g)$, with g as the gift tax rate, which yields a proxy measure for taxable gifts. This taxable gifts measure is then adjusted for inflation using the consumer price index (CPI) to remove any infla-tionary component of the emerging trend. The resulting trend is similar to that reported in figure 6.4, but with the spikes more amplified to reflect the lower tax rate when gifts seem to have been accelerated.

The inflation-adjusted measure of taxable gifts is then regressed on past, current, and future expected gift tax price, with tax rates com-puted using a predicted level of gifts as noted earlier. More specifically, all these variables are specified in natural logarithm and differenced. In other words, it is the real growth rate in gifts regressed on the percent change in tax prices. Control variables include real GDP growth rate, to control for the business cycle, and real Standard & Poors 500 (S&P 500) index growth rate to control for fluctuations in the stock market. Two different specifications are considered, with one including and the second excluding the estate tax rates. The estimated short-term response of gifts to tax rate changes, or transitory elasticity, is quite large, sug-gesting a very robust response to changes in gift tax rates. On the other hand, the long-term response, or permanent elasticity, is not statisti-cally different from zero, suggesting little in permanent effects.

In an alternative set of estimates, the predicted gift tax rate using a hypothetical constant amount of gifts is replaced with the maximum gift tax rate. Similar qualitative results are obtained. The transitory price elasticity is quite large, again pointing to a very robust response to changes in gift tax rates. Similarly, the permanent elasticity is imprecisely measured.

In short, using data on gift tax collections made in the years 1933 through 1998, the findings suggest that the wealthy are quite responsive to taxes in the timing of their gifts, particularly in the short run. The transitory price elasticity is very high, in absolute value, seemingly large but very consistent with the observed pattern over the past six decades. Perhaps not surprisingly, the permanent response is much smaller.

Evidence from Matched Estate and Gift Tax Returns   Rather than focus on aggregate time-series data, an alternative approach could employ data on decedents for a particular year and track the gifts they had made in every year during life. In my 2004 paper with Kathleen McGarry, "Estate and Gift Tax Incentives and Inter Vivos Giving," we employ such data using estate tax returns of decedents in 1992.[24] While estate tax returns typically provide information on cumulative lifetime gifts, the returns at hand were also linked to all individual lifetime gift tax returns ever filed. The results suggest that gifts are highly elastic with respect to gift tax rates, and provide further support for tax minimization as an important consideration in the timing of intergenerational transfers.

More specifically, our data from estate tax returns filed with the IRS consist of a sample of returns for decedents in 1992. It represents a subset of the 1992 sample prepared by SOI, and for which we observed beneficiary information. For this subsample, the estate records are matched to gift tax records dating back some fifty-six years, to the 1930s. As noted earlier, the applicable estate-tax-filing threshold in 1992 was $600,000, including both bequests and lifetime gifts in excess of the annual exemption. The tax filing requirement for inter vivos gifts varied with the size of the annual exclusion over the period for which we have gift tax returns, as shown in table 2.2.

By law, estate and gift taxes affect a tiny fraction of the population and, not surprisingly, our sample of tax returns represents about 0.2 percent of all decedents in 1992. The estate tax returns provide information and the size and composition of terminal wealth while gift tax records capture annual inter vivos transfers that are above the relevant exemption. We also employ the Health and Retirement Study (HRS) which is representative of the population and necessarily contains fewer well-off individuals, but is much richer in providing information on gifts below the exclusion amount and other demographic information typically not available on tax returns.

The HRS consists of samples of several elderly and close-to-retirement age cohorts. The original HRS cohort consists of those born between 1931 and 1941, and a second sample, the Asset and Health Dynamics study (AHEAD), consists of those born in 1923 or earlier. The HRS cohort was first interviewed in 1992 and has been interviewed biennially ever since with the most recent data available for 2000. Interviews for the AHEAD cohort were begun in 1993 with follow-up surveys in 1995, 1998, and biennially thereafter. Other than the difference in age, the two studies are nearly identical. Our sample, therefore, consists of five waves of data for the original HRS cohort (1992, 1994, 1996, 1998, and 2000) and four waves of data for AHEAD (1992, 1995, 1998, and 2000).

With both sets of data at hand, one obtained from administrative records and others from survey data, we are able examine the extent to which the wealthy exploit the potential for tax-free gifts as a means of spending down their estates. To provide some consistency with the HRS, we restrict this administrative sample to those decedents who were either 70-years-old or older (to correspond with the AHEAD cohort), or between the ages of 51 and 61 (to correspond with the original HRS cohort).

And with these restrictions in place we have a total of 2,830 observations from estate tax returns and 13,357 families from the HRS. The pattern of gifts observed in the HRS makes it clear that lifetime gifts are not fully exploited up to the annual exclusion amount to reduce the size of the taxable estate and minimize taxes to the fullest extent. Similarly, estate tax data also show that gifts in excess of the exclusion represent a small share of the observed terminal wealth with a considerable number of estates not reporting gifts at all. But the gifts observed suggest a pattern that is highly responsive to changes in tax rates. And using the estate–gift tax-matched data, we examine how the gift tax influences the probability of making gifts, the amount of gifts made in every year of the sample, as well as how lifetime gifts are allocated over time.

The estates in our sample are large with mean wealth of approximately $8 million and mean age at death of 77. Slightly over half of the sample were married at the time of death and 37 percent widowed, with the remainder either never-married single or divorced. The sample is predominately male, with men representing 62 percent of it. We calculate total lifetime gifts to be $335,000 in nominal dollars. Because these gifts are made over a span of many years, the real value of the transfers varies. To correct for economic growth and asset appreciation over the years in the sample, we inflate the value of gifts to 1992 dollars using the S&P 500 index. With this correction, the average amount transferred rises to $763,000.

First, we focus on the probability of making gifts using the linked estate–gift tax records. Controlling for the S&P 500 index, year, and age, we explore the determinants of the probability of giving during life with a particular emphasis on the role of current and future gift tax rates. The findings point to a very strong transitory effect of tax rates on making gifts, but with a smaller permanent effect. In other words, the immediate response to changes in tax rates is much stronger than the response in the long run.

Conditional on the probability of making a gift, we next examine the determinants of the amount of gifts made annually. Similar explanatory variables are considered as in the case of estimates for the probability of making gift, including current and future tax rates. The findings once again suggest that the gift tax has a large effect on the size of gifts in the short run, with a permanent effect close to zero.

In an alternative specification, we examine the determinants of the share of wealth transferred in gifts made in each year and not the actual amount of the gifts as estimated earlier. The estimates again suggest a very strong transitory response to tax rate changes, but a permanent response not statistically different from zero. In addition to the tax effects, gifts are also shown to rise over time as donors get older, with succession planning perhaps more at play.

Overall, the findings in my 2004 paper using time series data on gift tax revenues over fiscal years 1933 through 1998, and in my 2004 paper with Kathleen McGarry, which employs linked estate and gift tax records of decedents in 1992, point to a very high transitory response to gift taxation, but with much weaker permanent response. Both papers confirm that gifts are primarily accelerated in immediate response to a regime change with minimal effects observed in later periods.

Saving by Heirs
In addition to the parents, or donors in general, the effect of the estate tax on heirs is of interest too. Indeed, the estate tax, by reducing

inheritances, may also affect the savings of beneficiaries. Accordingly, it is necessary to consider the effects of the estate tax on the savings of the donor and the recipients as well. But as with the uncertainty of the effects of the tax on donors, a similar uncertainty may also exist in gauging the effects on the saving behavior of the heirs.

At the outset, the timing of inheritances should not have a material effect on the behavior of beneficiaries in generationally linked families, where all generations are assumed to operate under a common intertemporal budget constraint.[25] However, the degree of uncertainty surrounding the size and timing of the receipt of inheritances may influence the pattern of life-cycle saving.[26] Even when fully anticipated, bequests may influence the pattern of consumption in the presence of precautionary saving and liquidity constraints. Indeed, some households may not be able to borrow against and collateralize their future inheritances. Thus, both in terms of magnitude and sign, what the effects of inheritances are on saving remains an open empirical question.

In my 2006 paper "Inheritance and Saving," I explore how inheritances influence the saving behavior of recipients.[27] More specifically, I examine the wealth of heirs before and after the receipt of inheritances. I employ administrative data that consists of a sample of matched estate tax returns of donors and income tax returns of heirs. The starting point is a sample of estate tax returns for decedents in 1989, where the wealthy are overrepresented because they are oversampled. This sample of estate tax returns is then linked to the income tax returns of the heirs for the years before and after the receipt of an inheritance. More specifically, the linked income tax returns are for the years 1988 through 1991, with inheritances received from the estates of decedents in 1989.

From estate tax returns we obtain information on the relationship of the heirs to the deceased, as well as the amount of bequests to heirs. Using beneficiary information reported on the estate tax return, the income tax returns of heirs are obtained. The latter provide information on the various sources of labor and capital income. I exclude heirs under the age of 21 in 1989 or over the age of 61 in 1991 from the sample to control for the effects of normal labor force entry and retirement decisions. Similarly, individuals with partnership income and losses are excluded from the sample to simplify the analysis. The resulting sample consists of 819 observations of matched estate and income tax returns pairing decedents and beneficiaries.

Income and estate tax returns, among other administrative records, have many advantages over survey data, in particular as they contain more top wealth holders and do not suffer from sampling nonresponses. But their primary shortcoming is that consumption and wealth information are not reported on income tax returns to help gauge how they change with receipt of inheritances. What is typically available is information on the flow of income or the return to capital assets. More specifically, and in addition to wages, information is available on self-employment income, interest, and dividends. As such, wealth is constructed as the capitalized value of interest and dividend income. Interest income is capitalized using prevailing interest rates for 1988 through 1991. Similarly, dividends are capitalized using the dividend yield in 1988 through 1991. Wealth is then defined as the sum of these capitalized values. Because inheritances are stated in 1989 levels, the wealth measures are adjusted to reflect 1989 prices.

Roughly a third of the observations received inheritances of less than $25,000. Another third received inheritances of between $25,000 and $150,000, and the remainder received transfers in excess of $150,000. I examine the wealth mobility in the sample, as individuals move from one wealth group in 1989 to another in 1991, and contrast the observed pattern for the three inheritance groups. For each inheritance group, the sample is further divided into three wealth classes: (1) under $25,000 for the low-wealth group, (2) $25,000 to $150,000, (3) and over $150,000 for the high-wealth group. For period two, year 1991, post-inheritance wealth is reduced by the amount of inheritance received to allow for comparisons over 1988 and 1991.

Transition matrices are constructed to study the wealth mobility over the periods. The goal here is to examine what fraction of the individuals in a particular wealth group remained in the same group or move up or down to another group, depending on the size of the inheritance received. The greatest mobility is observed for those in the high-inheritance group receiving over $150,000. Only 58 percent of the wealthiest group maintained its position, down from 96 percent for those receiving inheritances under $25,000. Some 31 percent migrated to the least wealthy group of under $25,000, and 10 percent transitioned to the middle wealth group falling between $25,000 and $150,000 wealth groups.

The simple transition matrices suggest that large-inheritance recipients are likely to experience a reduction in wealth (net of inheritances). The findings from multivariate analysis further suggest that the wealth of heirs declined after the receipt of transfers. For every dollar received in inheritances, the results suggest that wealth increases by only $0.60.

It should be noted, however, that a major limitation of the findings in my study is that income tax records represent a poor source of information on wealth, and capitalizing the flow of interest and dividend incomes is likely to miss other component of wealth (e.g., business assets). Notwithstanding these concerns, I also explored whether inheritances lead heirs to exit from the labor force and into early retirement as a way to validate the findings on the effects on savings. It turns out that they do, which is consistent with the findings of inheritances leading to dissaving. A longer discussion of labor supply effects will be provided in the next section.

In an earlier study with Mark Wilhelm in 1994, "Inheritance and Labor Supply," we use data from the panel survey of income dynamics (PSID) to examine how inheritances affect saving.[28] More specifically, we attempt to gauge how household expenditures change before and after receiving or expecting the receipt of an inheritance. This is unlike tax records, which provide information only on the actual and not the expected inheritances. The PSID data we employ is from the 1984 wave. We limit the sample to only heads of household who were between the ages of 25 and 60 in that year so that the estimates of the inheritance effects are not confounded with those related to education and retirement choices. Dollars are converted to 1989 levels using the implicit GNP price deflator for personal consumption expenditures.

There are 2,067 individual observations in our sample with about 21 percent receiving an inheritance, or with 439 heirs and 1,628 non-heirs. The average inheritance is $64,906 for heirs who have received at least one inheritance, an amount discounted over the years received. Nearly 28 percent expect to receive an inheritance, and these heirs are more likely to expect future inheritances. In addition, they are also more likely to expect much larger inheritances, an average over $120,000. Because the PSID surveys provide information on expected inheritances, we use this information on additional future inheritances to test for any delayed responses.

The only measure of consumption in the PSID is for expenditures on food. And not surprisingly, in our multivariate analysis we find a positive relationship between consumption and inheritances. As an example, estimated regressions of expenditures on inheritances show that an additional inheritance of $10,000 raises consumption by $1.80

only. When unexpected inheritances are considered, the estimated effect rises to $14. Unexpected inheritances have a larger effect consistent with what economic theory suggests, but still continue to be small overall. We estimate alternative specifications, but the estimated effects remain small.

Overall, our findings suggest that consumption increases after the receipt of inheritances. But such effects are small and economically insignificant. The findings are also limited by the nature of the data, which limits expenditures to expenditures on food only.

In his 1994 paper "The Saving of the Elderly in Micro and Macro Data," David Weil also addresses the effects of receipt of inheritances, expected or otherwise, on household consumption.[29] As in my 1994 paper with Mark Wilhelm, he also employs the PSID, using the 1984 wave. His sample consists of 6,736 observations, or 2,458 individuals, with 963 having received an inheritance, 1,241 expecting to receive an inheritance, and 254 having both already received an inheritance and expecting to receive an additional inheritance or more.

As I have noted, the PSID data on consumption is only limited to food consumption, and not total expenditures. But following the methodology developed by Jonathan Skinner in 1987, Weil uses a proxy for total consumption.[30] It turns out that similar results are produced when food consumption is used in place of the proxy measure for total consumption.

To capture the effect of bequests on consumption, Weil estimates a number of equations that regress consumption on measures of inheritances. He estimates a variety of specifications, to gauge the effects of receiving as well as expecting to receive inheritances, controlling for income, age, and education, among other factors. And his findings show that previously received inheritances or anticipated receipt of an inheritance may increase consumption by 4 to 10 percent.

In a more recent paper, "Do People Save or Spend Their Inheritances? Understanding What Happens to Inherited Wealth," Jay Zagorsky employs the National Longitudinal Survey of Youth 1979 (NLSY79) to address how heirs respond to inheritances.[31] The NLSY79, conducted by Ohio State's Center for Human Resource Research for the U.S. Bureau of Labor Statistics, is a longitudinal study, with surveys of individuals in their 20s, 30s, and then 40s. The author uses observations on 7,514 people participating in the NLSY79, and for whom expenditures, income, and inheritance received are reported. About 11 percent of the participants received an inheritance, with a median inheritance of $11,340. The results reported by the author suggest that on average a participant in the panel survey spent about half of the inheritance he or she received. Of more relevance to the debate on the effects of the estate tax: for those who received $100,000 or more, about 19 percent spent their entire inheritance.

Work Effort and Labor Supply of the Heirs

In addition to their potential effect on the saving of donors, estate taxes may have a related effect on work effort and labor supply. For example, by reducing the size of inheritances, estate taxes may also affect the heirs' work effort. Conceptually, individuals choose between work and leisure subject to a budget constraint. By expanding or rather relaxing household budget constraints, receipt of inheritances may lead to a reduction in labor supply and an expansion in leisure. Of course, what the effect of the estate tax is, and by proxy inheritances, is an empirical question that requires data on labor supply before and after the receipt of inheritances. Are recipients of large inheritances more likely to exit the labor force and quit working or take early retirement if they are close to age 62? Would they work fewer hours after receiving significant inheritances, or would they become self-employed? Ultimately, these among others are empirical questions to answer.

Labor Force Exit
A key variable of interest is whether the heirs exit the labor force after receipt of inheritance, in particular well before the early retirement age of 62. To address this question one needs data on heirs before and after they receive their inheritances, along with the amount received. In a 1993 study with Douglas Holtz-Eakin and Harvey Rosen, "The Carnegie Conjecture: Some Empirical Evidence," we employ a sample of estate tax returns of decedents in 1982 matched to the heirs' income tax returns for the years 1982 through 1985.[32] The estate tax returns are restricted to estates with assets in excess of $300,000, the sampling threshold, and range well into the hundreds of millions of dollars. These returns provide information on the relationship of the beneficiaries and the amount of inheritances received by each. From the income tax returns we observe the employment status of the heirs in 1982 and in 1985, three years after the passing of the estate holder. Consequently, we are able to identify whether any of the beneficiaries exited the labor force, meaning, stopped working, and are generally able to observe

whether employment status changed from what it was before receipt of inheritance to what it was after receipt.

In order to avoid confounding the effects of inheritances with those of retirement, we limit the sample of beneficiaries to those age 19 through 58 in 1982. This way, all the retained beneficiaries are under the age of 62 in 1985, before they are able to retire early and receive Social Security benefits. With these omissions, along with the inability to match some beneficiary records on the estate tax returns with their respective income tax returns, we have a usable sample of 4,332 beneficiaries. Of these, 2,700 represent married individuals, and 1,662 are single individuals, including widowed and divorced.

We split the sample by marital status, and for each of the single and married individuals we compare their labor income (and its presence) in 1982 to that in 1985, and examine how employment status has varied with the amount of inheritance received. As an example, and in the case of single individuals, those who dropped out from the labor force by 1985 had received greater inheritances than those who remained employed. Indeed, of those employed in 1982, about 9 percent dropped out. They inherited an average of $167,060 compared to $83,846 in inheritances for the others who remained in wage employment.

To gain further insights and better gauge the effects of inheritances, we examine individuals in each of the three inheritance-size categories: those who have received inheritances of less than $25,000, those received between $25,000 and $150,000, and those who received over $150,000. We compare the labor force participation across the three groups and check for any changes as we move from one group to another. We find that those with larger inheritances are more likely to exit from the labor force. Individuals in the highest category, those receiving over $150,000, are about four times more likely to drop out of the labor force when compared to those in the lowest inheritance group, or 18.2 percent vs. 4.6 percent as shown in figure 7.2 for single individuals.

We replicate the same exercise for married individuals filing joint income tax returns. This is a slightly more complicated exercise as there are likely to be dual-earner families. Here the questions of interest become whether one, two, or none of the dual-earner families exit the labor force. Whereas the transition for singles is between employment and exodus from the labor market between 1982 and 1985, in the case of married individuals there are potentially nine outcomes. Each couple may transition from having zero, one, or two people employed in 1982

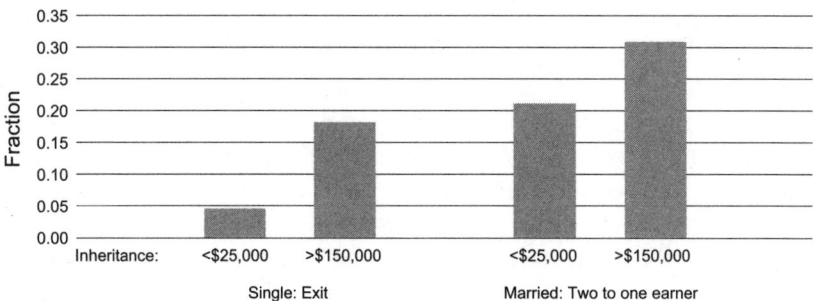

Figure 7.2
Percent exiting labor force after inheritance receipt.
Source: Douglas Holtz-Eakin, David Joulfaian, and Harvey S. Rosen, "The Carnegie Conjecture: Some Empirical Evidence," *Quarterly Journal of Economics* 108, no. 2 (1993): 413–436.

to zero, one, or two employed in 1985. As an example, a couple with two employed in 1982 may have zero, one, or two employed in 1985.

The examination of joint filers reveals a qualitatively similar result to that observed for singles. For two-earner households receiving inheritances in excess of $150,000, 30.9 percent become single earners by 1985 compared to 21.2 percent for those receiving less than $25,000; a factor of 1.5 to 1 for employed husband or wife to drop out. For single-earner households, 6.65 percent of the top inheritance group exit the labor force compared to 2.16 percent for those in the lowest inheritance group, a factor of 3 to 1 as shown in figure 7.2 for married individuals.

Multivariate analyses was next employed to better control for other factors that may drive labor force transitions. As an example, large inheritance recipients are typically older than those receiving smaller inheritances. Or it could be that those who exit the labor force have smaller earnings, and thus have a smaller opportunity cost if they were to drop out and stop working. Similarly, recipients of large inheritances may have independently accumulated a large amount of wealth that would have shaped their exit decisions regardless of how much they received in inheritances. For all these reasons, we first estimate a Logit equation for the odds of dropping out for first singles. A set of equations were estimated where the control variables included the age of the beneficiary, their employment status before receiving an inheritance, pre-inheritance earnings, the sum of interest and dividends as proxy for financial wealth, and the number of dependents. For joint filers, we estimate the odds of having zero, one, or two employed post-inheritance receipt. The findings from these multivariate analyses confirm the findings from the pattern observed in the earlier transition matrices. Larger inheritances lead to greater exit from the labor force.

These findings are replicated in my 2006 paper "Inheritance and Saving," using data from the estates of decedents in 1989.[33] As was noted earlier on the effects on saving, the purpose of this exercise was to validate the findings on the effects of inheritances on the saving behavior of heirs. But in the process, the findings from the 1989 estates confirm those from the 1982 estate tax data reported in my 1993 paper "The Carnegie Conjecture" with Holtz-Eakin and Rosen. Using a sample of 458 single individuals, I find that an additional inheritance of $100,000 has the effect of increasing the probability of exiting the labor force by 3.5 percentage points.

Inheritance and the Retirement Decisions of the Heirs
In our 1993 paper, Holtz-Eakin, Rosen, and I restricted our data to earners under the age of 62, at three years after the receipt of inheritances. An interesting question, not completely addressed in our paper, is what happens to those who are close to the retirement age and receive an inheritance. This is a group, being close to the age of 62, that is much older than those we have examined whose mean age is around 40.

Addressing this question, and using the HRS, Jeffrey Brown, Courtney Coile, and Scott J. Weisbenner set out to investigate how retirement decisions are shaped by the size of inheritances received.[34] Their sample consists of individuals age 52–62 in 1994, a group close to retirement. And these are followed at two-year intervals (or waves) until 2002. As was noted earlier, the HRS began in 1992 as a survey of people who were ages 51–61 and their spouses, with re-interviews of these individuals every two years. The authors employ data only from waves 2 through 6 (1994–2002) of the survey in their analysis as information on inheritance expectations was not available in the earlier wave. Unlike administrative records, the HRS is rich with detailed information on demographics, labor supply, health, and education, as well as finances. They employ 4,508 individuals, who represent 17,801 person-wave observations, with about 20 percent having received inheritances.

The HRS data provides information on receipt of inheritances in each wave, making note of any receipt of inheritances since the last wave, the amount received, the reported probability of receiving an inheritance over the next ten years, and—conditional on expecting an inheritance—the amount to be received. Individuals unable to provide a conditional value for expected inheritances are asked to check one of the following brackets: $0 to $10,000; $10,000 to $50,000; $50,000 to $250,000; $250,000 to $1 million; or over $1 million. Because of the panel feature of the HRS, individuals are observed over time and the authors are able to study how beneficiaries change behavior following inheritance receipt.

With this long panel data spanning the years 1994 through 2002, and using data on individuals older than those we had employed in our paper, the authors set out to examine labor force exits and retirements over a much longer time interval than our study. Also, in addition to actual amounts of inheritances received, HRS also contains measures of expected-inheritances information that naturally is not available on tax returns. In addition, and unlike our 1993 study, not all individuals received an inheritance during the period studied. Indeed, only about 20 percent of the individuals in the survey inherited during this time, with median inheritance of $28,343.

The specification employed by these authors is similar to the one Douglas Holtz-Eakin, Harvey Rosen, and I used in our 1993 paper. Perhaps not very surprisingly, their results are also quite similar. Their estimated Probit marginal effects suggest that receipt of an additional inheritance of $100,000 may increase the probability of retiring by 2 percentage points over a two-year period.

Given the ten-year length of their panel data spanning the years 1994 and 2002, the authors next address whether inheritances received may lead to retirement any time in this period. They report that the receipt of an additional $100,000 in inheritance leads to an increase of 3.8 percentage points in the probability of retiring, at any time during the ten-year period.

And last they consider the effects of both expected and unexpected inheritances on the probability of retiring earlier than planned. The planned retirement information was available in the first wave of the panel, but was only available for 2,499 observations. They report that an unexpected inheritance of $100,000 leads to a 10.3 percentage-point increase in the probability of retiring earlier than planned. In the case of an expected inheritance, they estimate only a 4.3 percentage-point increase. Inheritances seem to accelerate retirement, and more so when they are unexpected.

Notwithstanding the findings, a caveat on distinguishing between expected and actual inheritances is in order. Of those who predicted that they would not receive inheritances between 1994 and 2002, the authors report that close to 10 percent did so by 2002. And of those who expected to inherit with certainty during the same period, 40 percent did not receive an inheritance by 2002. Even the expected amount of inheritances at times diverged quite a bit from what recipients actually inherited as documented in the 2006 version of their paper.[35]

Heirs' Hours of Work

Even for those who stay in the labor force after receiving large inheritances, there remains the question of whether individuals adjust their hours of work and not necessarily quit working altogether. In my 1993 paper "The Carnegie Conjecture," with Holtz-Eakin and Rosen, discussed earlier, we could not study the effects on the number of hours worked. Tax return data typically contains earnings that in effect represent the number of hours worked multiplied by a wage rate. Assuming that the real wage rate does not change during the period under study, the findings should then be a good proxy for the effects on hours worked. With this caveat in mind, we regress wages on inheritances received to gauge its effects on earnings. This is in addition to exploring the inheritance-induced exodus from the labor force reviewed earlier.

While inheritances are found to have a depressing effect on wages, such effects are estimated to be very small. And we can conclude, holding wage rates constant, that labor supply reductions are generally small, despite the absence of information on hours of work. Of course, we should note the possibility that after receiving large inheritances some individuals may switch to a lower-paying yet more satisfying job.

In my earlier 1994 paper coauthored with Mark Wilhelm, we employed the panel survey of income dynamics (PSID) to examine how inheritances affect saving. In the very same paper, and using the same data, we also examined how inheritances shape labor supply decisions as the number of hours worked are captured in the data. To enrich the study, we also examined the matched estate and income tax data alongside the PSID. For both datasets, we exclude observations with extreme values.

Starting with the PSID data, we estimate equations where earnings are regressed on inheritances and a set of control variables. The findings show that the elasticity for the number of hours of work with respect to inheritance is negative but economically very small. When we interact the inheritance received with a variable indicating whether additional inheritances are expected, the estimated elasticity increases, suggesting that the labor supply response by those expecting future inheritances is larger. For those who do not expect future inheritances, the estimates imply no change in hours of work.

The larger response we observed when additional inheritances are expected in the future suggests that beneficiaries do not delay reductions in the number of hours worked as they await these receipts. And the results obtained further imply that the heirs may have incorporated the knowledge about these future inheritances into their labor supply decisions as they respond to amounts already received.

We experimented with a number of different specifications. And we conclude that our work using PSID data provides evidence on the effect of inheritance receipt on the number of hours worked, with the results showing a small reduction. In general, the findings, with variations among different specifications, suggest that annual hours worked decline by about twenty-four hours from receiving $100,000 in inheritances. The estate- and income tax match data, which contains much larger inheritances that the PSID survey data, produces similar results. We find earnings change little due to receipt of inheritances. Despite the modifications employed here (e.g., dropping outliers), these findings are similar to those we report in my 1993 paper with Douglas Holtz-Eakin and Harvey Rosen, showing a small reduction in earnings.[36]

In a related paper, "The Impact of Inheritances on Heirs' Labor and Capital Income," Mikael Elinder, Oscar Erixson, and Henry Ohlsson extend the analysis to Sweden.[37] More specifically, they employ data from the Swedish Tax Authority's Inheritance Tax Register limited to deaths in 2004 registered in the city of Stockholm. They link these inheritance tax returns to the income tax returns of the heirs obtained from the Tax Authority's Register of Final Tax on Income for the years 2000 through 2008.

Like the earlier studies reviewed thus far, the authors examine the effects of receipt of inheritances in 2004 using this Swedish data on heirs spanning the years 2000 to 2008. But unlike the preceding papers, their study is of interest because a key distinction between the United States and Sweden is that under Swedish laws children cannot be disinherited. This may have the potential the blur the distinction between expected and unanticipated inheritances.

The authors limit their sample to direct heirs age 21 to 59 in 2004. The resulting sample consists of 374 direct heirs, or 3,310 observations when followed over nine years (2000–2008). These heirs received an average of SEK 300,000 in inheritances, and report SEK 310,000 in mean earnings in 2003; around the sample period, the exchange rate was 7SEK = $1.

Their findings are similar to our findings in that the larger the inheritance the lower the labor income becomes. The reduction in labor income appears years after the inheritance was received and indicate that such effects are stronger for older heirs than for young ones. These effects are persistent over the four years after the donor's year of death. Interestingly, the authors also find evidence of anticipation effects whereby labor earnings decline before the receipt of inheritance.

The Working Elderly Heir

Some individuals may continue to work well beyond the retirement age. An interesting question is how such a group of individuals would react to receiving an inheritance. In a 1999 paper I co-wrote, again with Douglas Holtz-Eakin and Harvey Rosen, "Estimating the Income Effect on Retirement," we extend the investigation of the effects of inheritances to the working elderly.[38] This exercise is similar to our 1993 paper that focused on those who were under the age of 62 three years after receiving an inheritance. But because of our focus on retirement issues, we examine only the tax returns of heirs who were aged 62 or older in 1985, the last year in our panel.

In our sample of the elderly, we again focus on labor market transitions between 1982 and 1985. After dropping the young, the number of tax returns with useable data for these two years is 1,751. Of these returns, 1,048 are for married couples filing joint tax returns, and 703 are for single returns or individuals otherwise not claiming to be married. Overall, the mean age of recipients in the sample is 66.6 years, well over 20 years older than individuals we have analyzed in our earlier paper.

We replicate the analysis we had undertaken for the younger group in our earlier paper. The results from basic statistics using transitions matrices and logit estimates for the odds of retiring suggest that the inheritance effects are generally weak. There is no statistically significant difference in the retirement decisions of singles receiving large inheritances and those receiving small inheritances. For married individuals, the effects of inheritances are sometimes significant but always economically small. In addition, for those who chose to remain in the labor force and not retire, the effects of inheritances on the change in earnings are small.

Effects on Self-Employment

Entry by the Heir
We have observed thus far that inheritances have labor-supply disincentive effects. But by stimulating the transition to self-employment, these transfers may have a positive effect as well. And rather than exiting the labor force, an individual may switch from wage employment and transition into self-employment after the receipt of an inheritance. And because estate taxes reduce the size of wealth transfers to beneficiaries, they also have the potential to shape entrepreneurship.

Inheritances may matter for transitioning into self-employment and starting a business if the recipient was liquidity constraints. Some individuals with the talent and desire to become self-employed may opt to remain wage earners if they are unable to access capital markets and raise funds to start their business. For such individuals, receipt of inheritances may relax liquidity constraints and enable them to transition into self-employment.

In my 1994 study with Douglas Holtz-Eakin and Harvey Rosen, "Entrepreneurial Decisions and Liquidity Constraints," we examine how wage earners transitioned into self-employment between 1981 and 1985 after receiving inheritances from the estate of decedents in 1982.[39] The data employed consists of estate tax returns matched to beneficiary income tax records, and represents a subset of the larger data source employed in our earlier "Carnegie Conjecture" study in 1993. And rather than focus on exits from the labor force, our purpose in this paper was to gauge the relationship between inheritances received and the probability of becoming a sole proprietor a few years later.

In particular, the subset of the data we employ is for the matched income tax returns of the heirs that allow us to focus on the transition from wage employment in 1981 to self-employment in 1985. We define self-employment as filing Schedule C or becoming a sole proprietor. Our matched sample consists of 3,620 individuals in 1981; 3,023 of them are wage earners who did not file a Schedule C on their income tax returns. We follow the latter group of wage earners and examine whether some of them had become self-employed, and if so whether such transitions are associated with the receipt of greater inheritances.

The mean age of these wage earners in 1981 is 36.3 years, with 56 percent married. Their mean wage earnings is $24,200, and they have received $84,900 in inheritances sometime in 1982 and 1983. They have $64,700 in estimated liquid assets in 1981, prior to the transition to self-employment and receiving inheritances. Because tax returns do not provide information on wealth holdings, we construct a measure of liquid assets by capitalizing interest and dividend income. Equally important for our exercise, 12 percent of the parents or donors were themselves Schedule C filers. The latter observation is important, as it is entirely possible that the heirs may become self-employed because they inherited a business and not necessarily because inheritances relaxed the liquidity-constraint barrier to entry.

Basic tabulations show that about 20 percent of the sample transitioned from wage employment to proprietorship, filing Schedule C on their income tax returns. But only 8.2 percent of the wage earners transitioned into self-employment and had depreciable assets. The latter group reports such investment assets with an estimated mean value of $14,930. We estimate the determinants of the probability of transitioning into self-employment. Furthermore, conditional on this transition, we estimate the determinants of investments in depreciable assets.

The findings suggest that the probability of a beneficiary becoming self-employed between 1981 and 1985 rises with the amount of inheritance received, controlling for individual demographics, earnings, financial assets, and donor's self-employment status. As an example, an additional inheritance of $100,000 increases the probability of becoming self-employed by 3.3 percentage points. As to the effect on investing in depreciable assets, and, of course, conditional on having positive assets, heirs are likely to spend about 7 percent of additional inheritances received.

Survival of the Entrepreneurial Heir

In addition to stimulating the transition into self-employment, a related question is whether inheritances, by injecting cash into the business, may also enhance the survival of existing firms. In simple terms, will the receipt of an inheritance help an entrepreneur stay in business longer? In a 1994 study I undertook with Douglas Holtz-Eakin and

Harvey Rosen, "Sticking It Out: Entrepreneurial Survival and Liquidity Constraints," we examine how sole proprietorships survived between 1981 and 1985 after receiving inheritances sometime in 1982 or 1983.[40]

The data we employ is very much related to those employed in the preceding studies. The starting point is the sample of estate tax returns of decedents in 1982. These are linked to the beneficiaries' personal income tax returns for 1981 and 1985. Because our focus is on the survival probabilities of individuals who were entrepreneurs in 1981, we limit our study to 1,892 individuals who were sole proprietors in 1981, and these observations comprise our basic sample.

The mean age is 40.4 years, with 82 percent married. Mean AGI is $67,770, with Schedule C receipts of $64,550 in 1981. The mean inheritance in the sample is $178,250, with a wide range in the amounts received; some donees received bequests of as little as $100, while the maximum exceeded $3 million. The members of this group are quite wealthy, with a mean value for liquid assets of over $325,000.

The results suggest that the effect of inheritance on the probability of surviving as an entrepreneur is small but noticeable. An inheritance receipt of $150,000 raises the probability of survival by about 1.3 percentage points. But conditional on surviving, inheritances have a substantial impact on entrepreneurial enterprises. The receipt of $150,000 in inheritance, for instance, is associated with an approximately 20 percent increase in a proprietor's gross revenues over the four-year span.

Retirement of the Entrepreneurial Donor

If we were to switch our focus from the heirs to their donors, perhaps an equally relevant question to ask is whether the estate tax leads to the early retirement of an entrepreneur who feels discouraged by the pending estate tax. Of course, conceptually the estate tax may bring about early retirement again depending on the bequest motive. But reflecting on the estate tax structure, we may never be able to observe actual retirement in the data at hand.

This is a difficult question to address given that the estate tax accords a more favorable treatment to businesses. These include valuation discounts and installment payments described in chapter 3. The entrepreneur may make fractional transfers of the business to the heirs during life, but otherwise is very likely to continue to maintain some form of ownership and postpone full retirement. Indeed, it is not unusual for individuals to create businesses with very little economic substance in order to avail themselves to some of the benefits from valuation discounts, and minority discounts in particular, in order to minimize taxes.

Notwithstanding these data limitations, in a 1999 paper entitled "The Death Tax: Investments, Employment and Entrepreneurs," Douglas Holtz-Eakin examined a sample of 400 business owners surveyed in upstate New York.[41] From his survey, the author finds a negative correlation between potential estate tax liability, based on the current level of wealth of owner, and employment growth in those businesses. He concludes that businesses whose owner would be subject to the estate tax if death is imminent reported significantly less employment growth over the previous five years than firms owned by those who did not expect to be touched by the estate tax. And to be more specific, he reports that expecting to pay an estate tax in the future reduced job growth by approximately 2.32 percent in the prior five years. Notwithstanding the findings, the analysis is plagued with a number of data and estimation limitations. As an example, and as pointed out earlier by William Gale and Joel Slemrod, the effect of the owner's age is not controlled for in the analysis, which may be picking up the normal life cycle of businesses.

Summary

There is evidence to suggest that terminal wealth is influenced by the estate tax. The evidence gleaned from estate tax records thus far suggests that the effect is about a 10 percent reduction in the size of estate. But it is not clear whether this is an indicator of dissaving by the donors or a reflection on tax avoidance. As an example, there is strong evidence that lifetime gifts respond to pending tax increases, which is very likely to depress the observed size of donor wealth.

The empirical evidence also suggests that the estate tax may also influence the savings of heirs. This strongly rests on the assumption that taxes, by reducing transfers, lead to smaller inheritances available to recipients and that these inheritances depress beneficiary savings. But this evidence suffers from a lack of adequate data.

The findings in the literature also suggest that large inheritances lead to an exodus from the labor force, and hasten the retirement decisions of older recipients. There is evidence from survey data to suggest that unexpected inheritances have larger effects than those actually received.

But for those who remain in wage employment, inheritances seem to have small effect on the hours of work and wage earnings in general. Unexpected inheritances seem to have larger effect, but still economically small.

In addition, there is sufficient empirical evidence to suggest that inheritance receipt increases the transitions to self-employment by beneficiaries. Factors that may explain this include the presence of liquidity constraints whereby a wage earner is unlikely to switch to self-employment due to limited access to capital. By relaxing this constraint, inheritances may lead to greater transitions.

The presence of liquidity constraints plays a critical role in starting a business or its survival, and inheritances can play a big role in relaxing such constraints. But perhaps there are also other factors at play. As an example, Erik Hurst and Annamaria Lusardi find that both past and expected future inheritances explain business entry.[42] Because future inheritances are unlikely to reduce liquidity constraints, they point out that inheritances may capture more than simply liquidity concerns.

8   Other Behavioral Effects

Because labor and capital income make up the bulk of national income and economic activity, it is important to examine how the estate tax shapes employment and saving decisions. But the estate tax has the potential to shape behavior well beyond the behavioral effects related to saving and work decisions reviewed in chapter 7. As an example, these behavioral effects were well understood when the tax was modified in 1918, just two years after its enactment, to allow for the deductibility of charitable bequests. There are a number of other examples, whether intended by Congress or otherwise, where the tax distorts economic behavior and shapes the behavior of the wealthy. What follows is a review of a number of economic activities that estate taxation critically influences.

Charitable Giving

The nonprofit sector plays an important role in society in providing the public with services that complement the role of the public sector, and reach out to needy individuals otherwise not served by the government. Nonprofits account for over 5 percent of the GDP and some 10 percent of employment. The contributions that nonprofit organizations receive from the public are what enable them to provide their services. According to Giving USA, $390 billion in contributions were made in 2016, and most of these were tax deductible to the donors.[1]

Individuals make the bulk of all contributions, mostly during life and some as bequests at death; in 2016, corporations accounted for 3.5 percent of total giving. Focusing on the wealthy, there are a variety of reasons why they give the charity. But regardless of the underlying motives, the estate tax has the potential to create incentives for giving to charities. It may influence the size of wealth bequeathed to charitable organizations as donors allocate their terminal wealth between their heirs and the nonprofits entities. It may also influence gifts made during donors' lives as they weigh the option of making gifts before death to their children and charities, against leaving bequests to these beneficiaries after death. Michael Boskin summarized these modes of wealth transfers and bequest divisions in his 1976 paper "Estate Taxation and Charitable Bequests."[2]

Bequests at Death

Unlike bequests to children and other heirs, bequests to charities are exempt from the estate tax. Hence, the estate tax makes it costlier, or raises the price of bequests, to leave inheritances to heirs relative to bequests to charitable organizations, which receive a preferential tax treatment. To appreciate the implications of this preferential treatment, consider a donor facing estate tax rate e. Ignoring asset growth and appreciation, the donor will have to forgo $1 / (1 - e)$ in consumption to transfer $1 to the heirs. Using a tax rate of 0.55, the donor will have to save $2.22, or $1 / (1 - 0.55)$, for the beneficiary to receive $1, with $1.22 paid in taxes. In contrast, bequests to charities are free of tax, and the donor gives up $1 dollar and the charity receives $1. Alternatively stated, and calculated relative to transfers to heirs, the price of charitable bequests is $1 - e$, or 0.45; giving to charity is less costly than transferring wealth to heirs.

A number of studies have examined the effects of estate taxation and its preferential treatment on charitable bequests. With rare exceptions, these report large price and wealth elasticities. Examples of these include the works of Charles Clotfelter using data from estate tax returns filed in 1977, Michael Boskin using data from tax returns filed in the period 1957–1959, and Martin Feldstein who used grouped data by size of estate for the years 1948 through 1963.[3] The exception is the 1984 paper "Estate Taxation and Other Determinants of Charitable Bequests" by Thomas Barthold and Robert Plotnick,[4] in which the authors employ data on large Connecticut estates from the 1930s and 1940s. Controlling for demographics, wealth, and religious preferences, they find that higher estate tax rates do not encourage greater levels of bequests.

In my 1991 paper "Estate Taxes and Charitable Bequests by the Wealthy," I examine how the estate tax shapes charitable bequests.[5] More specifically, I employ estate tax returns for decedents in 1986 filed during the years 1986 through 1988, at a time when the filing threshold was over $500,000 (gross estate plus lifetime gifts). The starting point is a sample of 13,710 estate tax returns prepared by SOI. After excluding those who are age 30 and younger, those with net estates, roughly net worth, under $5,000, as well as those who have bequeathed all their assets to charity (50 estates), this leaves me with a usable sample of 13,492 estates.

The estate tax data contain information on the portfolio composition of each estate listing the assets held at death directly and in trusts (labelled as lifetime transfers on estate tax returns), debts, funeral expenses, attorney fees and executor commissions, life insurance policy loans, and other estate administration expenses, among others. It also includes information on jointly owned property, community property, and life insurance owned by others and excluded from the estate. Demographic information is available on age, marital status, sex, state residency, and date of death of first spouse for widowed decedents. Adjusted for inflation, the individuals in this sample are wealthier than those studied in Boskin (1976) and Clotfelter (1985), but comparable to those in Barthold and Plotnick (1984).[6] My paper addresses how bequests are shaped by the estate tax, controlling for wealth, and demographics such as age, marital status, gender, as well as portfolio composition such as shares of business and life insurance in the estate. It also examines how these factors shape bequests to different types of charitable organizations, including the arts and humanities, religious, education and medical research, social welfare, and private foundations. While the estate tax is found to play an important role in shaping bequests, its effects vary when giving to different types of organizations. As an example, bequests to education and medical research and to religious organizations are found to be most sensitive to the tax price, with bequests to the arts, social welfare, and private foundations the least sensitive.

In a follow-up to this paper in 2000, "Estate Taxes and Charitable Bequests by the Wealthy," I revisit the study of the effects of the estate tax on charitable bequests.[7] This time I employ data for estate tax decedents in 1992, with returns filed during the years 1992 through 1994. Unlike the 1991 study, I pay considerably more attention to how the estate tax may shape giving, employing numerous specifications and different subsamples that account for the marital deductions, spousal QTIP trusts, state taxes, and marital status. The sample is limited to estates with gross estate over $600,000 as well as positive net worth, which leaves me with a sample of 11,915 estates. And unlike my 1991 study, it does not exclude those who left everything to charities, which, looking backward, is an obvious oversight that may have biased estimates of the effects of the estate tax.

The average after-tax wealth observed for these estates is $2.9 million. They bequeath $463,100 to charity, or $264,000 after accounting for its tax deductibility; the latter is the amount heirs could have received net of tax. Charitable bequests are reported by about 2,200 estates, or fewer than 18 percent of the sample. The average age is 68, with 17 percent over age 85. Close to 60 percent of the individuals in the sample are married, and 25 percent widowed, with the remainder either single (never married) or divorced. Mean business share of the estates is 8.5 percent, and life insurance proceeds make up 12.7 percent of wealth. The average tax price is 0.76, or one minus the estate tax rate, and changes very little when adjusted for the election of installment payments. Donors are typically wealthier, older, less likely to be married, and own less in business assets than their nondonor counterparts.

I find the estate tax to be an important consideration in determining transfers to charity. Both the price and wealth elasticities are large, and the effects of the increase in the tax price are partially offset with those of an increase in wealth in the absence of an estate tax. The basic estimates suggest that in the absence of the estate tax, charitable bequests may decline by some 12 percent.

I report a somewhat similar finding in my 2006 working paper, "Estate Taxes and Charitable Bequests: Evidence from Two Tax Regimes," which uses pooled 1976 and 1982 estate tax data.[8] These two years witnessed dramatic changes in tax regimes affecting the tax base as well as the tax rate schedules. While considering data from different tax regimes can be helpful in better identifying the effects of taxes, in particular when compared to the use of a single year's cross-section data, changes in tax provisions have the potential to alter the evolution of the wealth of beneficiaries and the timing of certain economic activity. In moving away from the reliance on cross-sectional estate-tax data, the challenge in using longitudinal data is to control for the tax treatment of transfers to various donees as well as the frequently changing tax regimes.

As a consequence of the introduction of the unlimited marital deduction in 1982, spousal bequests have expanded dramatically, virtually eliminating the tax liability of many of the estates of married decedents.

In doing so, married individuals transfer much of their estates to their surviving spouses, leaving relatively little to charities. Of course, it is very likely that a decision has been made to postpone much of the giving to be made by the estate of the surviving spouse, and not necessarily suggesting that married individuals bequeath less, or none at all, to charity as a results of the estate tax law changes. As a consequence, the reported wealth of the surviving spouse beginning with 1982 has become inflated by the expanding spousal transfers. These widowed decedents seem to be wealthier and more likely to leave behind taxable estates, and also give more generously to charities.

The treatment of spousal transfers, and its consequences, is the most problematic and commonly ignored in the scant literature on charitable bequests. One approach to addressing this problem is to simply exclude married decedents since spousal bequests seem to depress giving, albeit temporarily. As eluded to earlier, however, this will continue to overlook the influence of spousal bequests on the observed wealth of the surviving spouse (the second to die), which itself can be determined by past tax regimes and whose wealth is in part enriched by spousal bequests.

The primary reason I resort to estate tax data for decedents in 1976 and 1982, aside from the absence of data for the intervening years, is because these are years when the data on widowed decedents is the least tainted by tax-induced changes in spousal bequests. The tax code in effect in 1976 had been in place virtually unaltered since 1954. The tax rate schedule in effect in 1982 was ushered by ERTA81, enacted on August 13, 1981, and the rates are markedly lower than those in effect in 1976. These rate reductions were in part anticipated as early as November 1980, following the outcome of the presidential election. Equally important, the wealth reported by widowed decedents in the two periods generally reflects the 1976 tax treatment of spousal bequests, with the marital deduction generally limited to one-half the estate (see table 2.1); the full marital deduction took effect for married decedents in 1982. And typically, about 8 percent of widowed decedents pass away within a year of the passing of the first spouse.[9] Thus, we observe the pattern of giving to charity in the presence of exogenous variations in tax rates, as well as wealth measures for widowed decedents that are not influenced by changes in the marital deduction.

The maximum tax rate in effect in 1976 was 77 percent. TRA76 lowered this maximum tax rate to 70 percent in 1977. And ERTA81 further reduced it in steps beginning in 1982 down to 50 percent by 1985. The enabling legislation also introduced a "unified" tax credit that effectively exempted the first $225,000 in taxable estate in 1982, set to gradually increase to $600,000 by 1987, with the tax parameters in effect in the intervening years reported in table 2.1.

Data on estate tax decedents in 1976 is available only for returns filed in 1977; typically 80 percent of returns of estates of decedents in a given year are filed the following year. Returns with gross estates in excess of $500,000 are sampled at 100 percent, and at 20 percent for those under $500,000. In contrast, population data for 1982 decedents is available for returns filed in 1982 through 1984, but only for those with estates in excess of $1 million; the less wealthy are sampled at an average rate of 30 percent. While estate tax returns are required to be filed within nine months of the date of death, some are filed much later. Evidence suggests that late filers are likely to be wealthier.[10] Thus, to enhance the comparability of the two datasets, I limit the data on decedents in 1982 to estate tax returns filed in 1983, and discard those filed in 1982 and 1984. In addition, only estates in both years with assets in excess of $300,000 in 1982 dollars, the SOI sampling threshold for returns filed in 1983, are considered.

The resulting sample consists of 14,051 estates, with about 7,726 for 1976 decedents and 6,325 for 1982. The mean charitable bequest is $287,300, with about one-third giving to charity. Net of the tax savings from its deductibility, the mean after-tax bequest is $114,900, which is the amount that the heirs could have received instead. These estates are large with mean wealth of about $1.5 million, and standard error of $12 million. Stated net of taxes paid, as well as the tax savings from deducting charitable bequests, disposable wealth is $886,500. This represents the maximum amount that can be transferred to the heirs. The average tax price is 0.65. When evaluated using the expected fully phased-in tax law, with lower tax rates and higher exemptions, the after-tax wealth and charitable bequests, as well as the tax price, are not surprisingly higher.

To motivate the analysis, I first restrict the sample to widowed and married decedents. Their pattern of charitable bequests over the two periods is summarized in figure 8.1, which shows that the share of wealth transferred to charities generally rises with wealth. But given the progressive tax rate schedules in both years, this may also suggest that giving rises with tax rates as well. When the patterns for the two periods are contrasted, the share of wealth transferred is generally lower for estates in 1982 than its counterpart in 1976 when tax rates were higher, particularly for the wealthiest of estates. This may lead us to conclude that lower tax rates depressed giving in 1982.

However, and as demonstrated in figure 8.2, much of the trend observed in figure 8.1 is reversed when married decedents are excluded and the focus is restricted to widowed decedents. Indeed, in the case of the wealthiest of estates, those in excess of $20 million, the share of wealth transferred almost doubles. Despite the tax rate reductions, the "generosity" of the very wealthy seems to have increased.

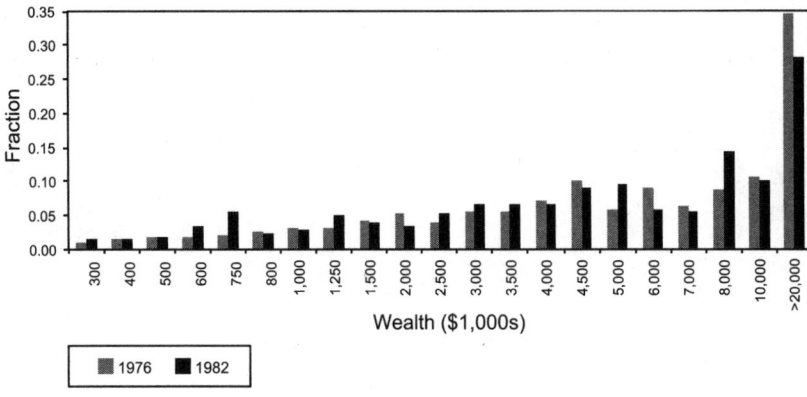

Figure 8.1
Charitable bequests as percent of wealth.
Source: David Joulfaian, "Estate Taxes and Charitable Bequests: Evidence from Two Tax Regimes," mimeo, U.S. Department of the Treasury, Washington, DC, 2006.

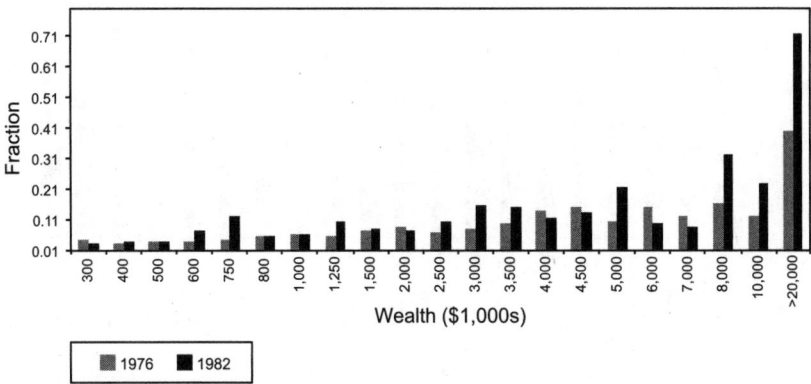

Figure 8.2
Charitable bequests as percent of wealth of widowed decedents: 1976 vs. 1982.
Source: David Joulfaian, "Estate Taxes and Charitable Bequests: Evidence from Two Tax Regimes," mimeo, U.S. Department of the Treasury, Washington, DC, 2006.

Figure 8.3 sheds some light on the diverging trends observed. Married decedents, virtually across all wealth cohorts, seem to leave smaller bequests to charity in 1982 compared to the trend observed for 1976. In contrast, and more interestingly, figure 8.4 exhibits a surge in spousal bequests for all wealth categories, which is very likely to have taken place at the expense of charitable bequests. Figures 8.3 and 8.4, combined, make the case that potential findings from longitudinal data on the effects of estate taxation can be biased if spousal bequests and

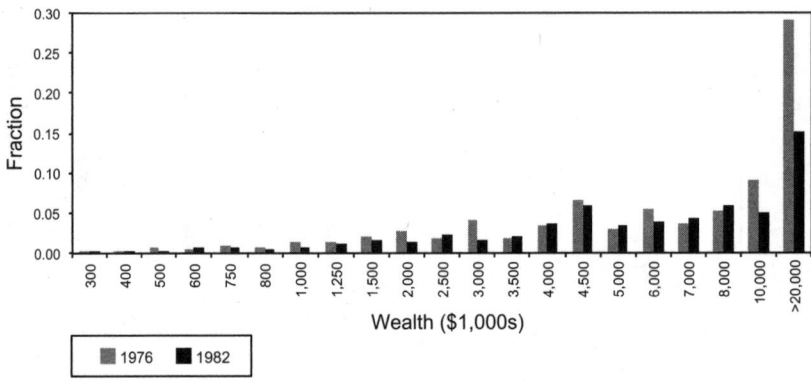

Figure 8.3
Charitable bequests as percent of wealth of married decedents: 1976 vs. 1982.
Source: David Joulfaian, "Estate Taxes and Charitable Bequests: Evidence from Two Tax Regimes," mimeo, U.S. Department of the Treasury, Washington, DC, 2006.

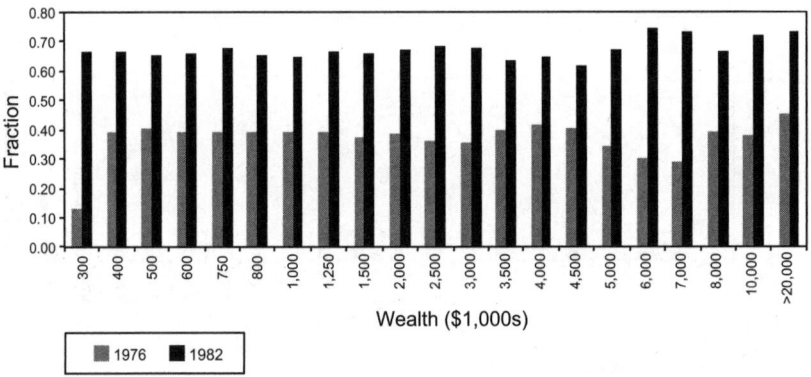

Figure 8.4
Spousal bequests as percent of wealth: 1976 vs. 1982.
Source: David Joulfaian, "Estate Taxes and Charitable Bequests: Evidence from Two Tax Regimes," mimeo, U.S. Department of the Treasury, Washington, DC, 2006.

their consequences for the evolution of wealth are not properly controlled for.

Controlling for the potential shifting of charitable bequests from the first to the second to die and controlling for the influence of spousal bequests in shaping the observed wealth of widowed decedents are difficult tasks, particularly as they require tracing the behavior of married couples and identifying the expected tax regimes they are likely to face. As such, I focus only on widowed individuals, never-married singles, and divorced/separated decedents.

Comparing those who give to those who don't give, I find that the sample of donors are wealthier with mean wealth of $2.6 million compared to $1 million for nondonors. They are also older with mean age of 81 compared to 76 for nondonors, and more likely to have never married. However, there seems to be very little difference in observed tax rates, particularly when the fully phased-in tax law is used.

Next, I rely on multivariate analyses to tease out the price and wealth elasticity estimates and attempt to gauge the effects of taxes on giving. The measures of wealth and price employed reflect the tax regime in place in the year of death, consistent with the convention employed in most studies. These ignore the phased-in reductions in tax rates from 65 in steps to 50 percent over the period 1982 through 1985, as well as the gradual expansion in the effective exemption from $225,000 in 1982 to $600,000 by 1987. Control variables include age, gender, and marital status, as well as after-tax net worth. Holding all else constant, the estimates suggest that charitable bequests would decline by 10 percent in the absence of the estate tax.

Notwithstanding the conventional practice, the calculated tax rates in effect during the year of death may not necessarily reflect the true tax rate shaping decisions to give. Indeed, and unless individuals anticipated dying in 1982, the bequest division and succession plans may very well reflect laws in effect in future years. Of course we don't know what tax regime donors have in mind when they plan for their estate division. Reflecting on the phased-in reduction in tax rates, an expected tax rate is computed as the mortality-weighted sum of tax rates in effect in 1982 and every year beyond, which is employed in reestimating the determinants of giving. In other words, the tax rate is computed as the sum of the rate in 1982 multiplied by the probability of death in 1982, plus the rate in 1983 multiplied by the probability of death in 1983, plus the rate in 1984 multiplied by the probability of death in 1984, and so on. Employing fully anticipated tax law, and using the phased-in tax structure, the revised estimates suggest that charitable bequests would decline by about 5 percent in the absence of the estate tax.

While these estimates are based on two periods, with two very different tax regimes, reported wealth is measured under a single tax regime of spousal bequests so that the wealth of widowed decedents in 1976 and 1982 is not shaped by the acceleration of spousal transfers. To gauge the sensitivity of these estimates to the inclusion of years where the measure of wealth reported by widowed decedents is suspected to be influenced by previous changes in the spousal bequests tax regime, the sample is expanded by adding observations on widowed decedents in 1989 with tax returns filed in 1990. Limiting observations to wealth in excess of $600,000, the filing and taxable thresholds in 1989 yields a sample of 15,483. For this expanded sample, the implied wealth and price elasticity estimates are 0.892 and -0.951, respectively. These suggest that in the absence of the estate tax, charitable bequests would decline by some 25 percent. These simulations highlight the sensitivity of the estimates to the inclusion of periods where the wealth measure is shaped by the expansion in the marital deduction in prior years.

In a 2003 paper, "Charitable Bequests and Taxes on Inheritances and Estates: Aggregate Evidence from across States and Time," Jon Bakija, William Gale, and Joel Slemrod explore the effects of the estate tax on charitable bequests.[11] They employ IRS data for the years 1924 through 1945, 1969, 1976, 1982, and 1985 through 1998. They exclude the estates of married decedents. And next, they group the data into five wealth categories expressed in 1996 dollars; $400,000 to $750,000; $750,000 to $1.25 million; $1.25 million to $2 million; $2 million to $5 million; and $5 million and above. With some adjustments, they group estates into 6,615 cells that they employ in their analysis in place of actual data on individuals.

Using the last year in their sample, the year 1998, the authors estimate that if the estate tax were to be eliminated, this would raise the price of charitable bequests by 77 percent, while raising disposable (after-tax) wealth by an average of only 24 percent. They attribute the difference in the large change in price and smaller change in wealth to a highly progressive tax where the marginal tax rate is much higher than the average tax rate. They then posit that "total repeal will cause charitable bequests to decline among this population unless the wealth elasticity is more than three times as large as the price elasticity, both measured in absolute value."

The authors then regress charitable bequests on the tax price and wealth in an attempt to gauge how the estate tax shapes bequests. They report estimated price and wealth elasticities of -2.1 and 1.55, respectively, in their multivariate analysis. The estimated wealth elasticity is smaller than that of the price in absolute value. It is closer to three-quarters of that of the price elasticity, much smaller than the 3 to 1 ratio criterion the authors had stated earlier. Obviously, their work implies charitable bequest will decline but they do not report any estimates of the effects of the estate tax. They conclude that their "estimates therefore point towards a decline in charitable bequests in response to the abolishing estate and inheritance taxes."

In a 2003 follow-up article, "Effects of Estate Tax Reform on Charitable Giving," published by the Urban–Brookings Tax Policy Center, Jon Bakija and William Gale use elasticity estimates obtained from their coauthored paper with Joel Slemrod to estimate the effects of repealing the estate tax.[12] They employ SOI-published summary statistics from estate tax returns filed in 2001 and not the actual raw data. More specifically, these tabulations show the amount of charitable bequests by size of estate, reproduced in table 1 of their paper. They impute marginal tax rates by using the mean net worth obtained from the tabulations. As an example, those tabulated to be in the largest wealth group face a statutory marginal tax rate of 55 percent. Similarly, they calculate the average tax rates by dividing the reported total tax liability by the total wealth reported for each group. Overall, the average tax rate is 11.3 percent and the marginal tax rate is 45 percent. In their analysis, they use the marginal tax rate to compute the tax price of giving, and the average tax rate to compute the change in after-tax wealth in case of repeal. And then they apply the earlier estimated price and wealth elasticities in their paper with Joel Slemrod. They conclude that the estate tax repeal reduces bequests by 37 percent.

In a 2004 paper for the Congressional Budget Office, "Charitable Bequests and the Repeal of the Estate Tax," Robert McClelland revisits these estimates using data from estate tax returns filed in 1999 and 2000.[13] He replicates the analysis by Jon Bakija and William Gale and arrives at an estimate of a reduction in bequests of 20 percent only and not 37 percent when a "corrected" measure of "wealth" is used, pointing out that the authors had the wrong measure of wealth.[14]

Reflecting on their perception of the progressivity of the tax, Jon Bakija and William Gale are very vocal in making the case for the estate tax to have a large effect on giving, and conclude in their paper that

"Estate tax repeal would have significant deleterious effects on charitable bequests." Notwithstanding the correction to their measure of
wealth described by Robert McClelland, unfortunately, the authors
have misinterpreted the tax law or at the very least incorrectly applied
some of its features, and in particular the credit for state death taxes,
which have led them to overstate the progressivity of the estate tax.
And these measurement errors, and the bias they create, have serious
implications for their reported estimates.

More specifically, the authors advance the progressivity storyline in
their earlier paper with Joel Slemrod, and report a large disparity in
average and marginal tax rates. This disparity in tax rates suggests that
estate tax repeal would raise the tax price disproportionately by more
than it would increase after-tax wealth, and leads to the conclusion that
charitable bequests would dramatically decline in the case of estate tax
repeal. But this disparity in the measured tax rates is primarily an
artifact of computing the marginal tax rate before applying the credit
for state death taxes, which yields a higher tax rate, and the average
tax rate after the credit, which yields a lower tax rate. For example, the
authors set the federal marginal tax rate to 0.55 for the large estates,
and implicitly set the average tax rate to 0.39 by actually dividing
federal tax liability by wealth; tentative federal tax is reduced by state
death tax credit with a maximum rate of 16 percent as shown in table
3.3. Instead, when measured correctly, the two tax rates should be close
to 0.55 (or 0.39 if the 16 percent credit is applied consistently). For a
taxable estate valued at $100 million, estate tax repeal raises the tax
price from 0.45 to one. It should also increase after-tax wealth by the
same proportion from about $45 to $100 million. Both price and wealth
should increase by 122 percent, as estate tax repeal should increase
price and wealth by roughly the same percentage for the very wealthy.
However, in the authors' calculations, wealth increases by only 64
percent, or from $61 to $100 million.[15]

Had these measurement errors been corrected by the authors, their
estimated effect of estate tax repeal on charitable bequests would have
been a fraction of their earlier reported estimates. Another consideration the authors overlook is that reductions in estate taxes and charitable bequests will invariably increase bequests to heirs. With a closer
look at the figures reported in tables 5.10 and 5.11, the estimated reduction in charitable bequests of 37 percent would suggest that the heirs
of the donor estates will likely receive inheritances that are several
multiples larger in the absence of the estate tax.

Survey data has also been employed to address how the estate tax is likely to affect charitable bequests. Using evidence from such survey data on participants with net worth in excess of $5 million, Paul Schervish and John Havens suggest in their 2003 article "Gifts and Bequests: Family or Philanthropic Organizations?" that charitable bequests may increase if estate taxes are reduced.[16] Unfortunately, there is no way to confirm that the intentions reported by the participants in the survey will materialize at death.

Lifetime Contributions
Because donors have the option to give to charity in life and at death, estate taxes may also affect lifetime charitable contributions and not just bequests. Accumulated wealth may be consumed during life, donated to charity, or transferred to the children. In the case of a life- time charitable contribution of, say, $1, the beneficiary charity receives $1. Because it reduces individual taxable income as an itemized deduction, it costs the donor in foregone consumption only $1 less the marginal income tax rate, or 1 − t, or 1 − 0.37 for those facing the maximum federal marginal income tax rate in 2018 as provided for by the Tax Cut and Jobs Act; the donor foregoes only $0.63 in consumption. In contrast, a bequest of $1 to the children costs the parent 1 / (1 − e), ignoring discounting and with e as the estate tax rate. At a tax rate of 0.40, or e = 0.40, the parent foregoes $1.67 (or $2.22 with an estate tax rate of 0.55). An individual compares the price of charitable giving to the price of transfers to his heirs in deciding on the size of contributions to make.

In my 1996 paper with Gerald Auten, "Charitable Contributions and Intergenerational Transfers," we employ estate tax returns for decedents in 1982, a subset of the same dataset employed in the labor supply studies of heirs in chapter 7.[17] But this time, these estate tax returns are matched to the decedents and not beneficiary income tax returns for the years 1980 and 1981.

Using the matched data, we attempt to gauge how charitable contributions reported on income tax returns responded to the estate (and income) tax changes introduced in 1981. After some data cleaning, we have 5,585 observations with a mean age of the primary taxpayer of 76 years, reporting mean contributions of $14,690, disposable income of $96,280, and wealth of $2.7 million. We also experiment with different subsamples where observations are limited to parents only, or when the income of the children is known. We find that estate taxation is an important consideration in determining lifetime contributions.[18] A positive price elasticity of 0.6 is estimated for giving during life with respect to the tax price of bequests. This suggests that in the absence of the estate tax, lifetime contributions may decline by as much as 12 percent. We also find that giving increases as children's income rises.

Pamela Greene and Robert McClelland use survey data in their 2001 paper to measure the effects of the estate tax on lifetime contributions.[19] More specifically, they employ the 1998 Survey of Consumer Finances (SCF). They estimate individual contributions by using the SCF data and supplement it with an SOI sample of income tax returns and Consumer Expenditure (CEX) data. The CEX provides information on contributions of less than $500, the lower limit available in the SCF. Information from the SOI sample about the contributions of the 400 taxpayers with the highest adjusted gross incomes is used as a proxy for the Forbes 400, which are excluded from the SCF.

Greene and McClelland drop from their sample families with negative net wealth or negative net income, those age 30 or less, those with wealth in excess of $4.6 million, as well as those filing as married filing separately or adults who were cohabiting. This reduces their sample size to 2,758. The authors then explore the effects of three hypothetical tax law changes, with estate tax repeal being one. They find that repeal of the estate tax may reduce contributions by up to 6.5 percent.

Giving in Life and at Death
Notwithstanding the preceding discussions, charitable bequests and lifetime contributions may not be independent events as donors are likely to be cognizant of the income and estate tax treatments of giving and their possible interactions. And reflecting on their preferences, and other nontax factors, such as wealth, income, and demographics, individuals may decide how to allocate their giving between contributions during life and those that will take place at death. In other words, giving in life and at death may not be independent choices. Empirically estimating such choice and division over the two periods is rather a challenge given data availability.

I attempt to address the allocation of giving in my 2001 paper "Charitable Giving in Life and at Death." The paper uses a somewhat less representative but much more information-rich sample of estates.[20] In this paper, I compare charitable bequests to lifetime contributions made within ten years (1987–1996) of the date of death. Information on lifetime income, wealth at death, and charitable giving during life and in bequests make this a unique dataset.

More specifically, and in order to examine the pattern of giving and its determinants, I employ data on lifetime contributions obtained from a panel of income tax returns. In 1987, a stratified random sample of some 85,000 income tax returns were selected by the Statistics of Income Program of the Internal Revenue Service. These returns were followed over time through 1996. As individuals in the panel died, their estate tax returns, which provide information on bequests, were obtained. Given the estate tax filing threshold, only estate tax returns reporting assets of $600,000 and over are available.

In my analysis, I follow individuals who filed an income tax return every year for 1987 through 1996. And then I focus on those individuals in the panel who died during the years 1996 through 1998. This yields a sample of 882 individuals with 10-year income tax records matched to their estate tax returns.

To allow for the analysis of the size and the allocation of contributions between life and death, I define "wealth" as the gross estate at death less debts and estate expenses, plus lifetime charitable contributions and inter vivos gifts, and less the tax liability computed in the absence of contributions and bequests to charity. Income is defined as the ten year mean after-tax adjusted gross income (AGI), with taxes computed in the absence of contributions.

For individuals in this balanced panel, the average value of an estate at death is $27 million. The mean income is about $1.8 million averaged over the 10 years, or 6.7 percent of wealth. There are 126 individuals who left behind estates valued under a million, with mean wealth and AGI of $876,000 and $79,000, respectively. There are another 36 individuals with wealth in excess of $100 million, with mean value of $405 million for this top-wealth category. The average income is $15 million for this wealthiest group, which is equivalent to less than 4 percent of their wealth. With mean age of 84, this richest group is eight years older than the sample average of 76 years.

Individuals in this panel of income and estate tax returns seem to express different preferences for the timing of their charitable giving. In the case of the very rich, charitable bequests seem to be the preferred mode of giving. In contrast, lifetime charitable contributions seem to be the preferred mode for the less wealthy. Similarly, married individuals are more likely to give during life, but less so at death. Overall, the findings imply that charitable giving by the individuals in the panel may change very little in the absence of the estate tax. They also suggest that the income tax stimulates lifetime transfers, and that business owners and widowed individuals prefer to delay their transfers until death. When lifetime contributions and charitable bequests are combined into a single variable, the estate tax seems to have little effect on the total amount donated; the reported estate tax price and wealth elasticities are -1.16 and 1.11, respectively.[21]

Capital Gains Realizations

Under the U.S. tax system, appreciation or accrued gains in an asset sold are usually subject to capital gains taxes. If held until death, however, the basis of appreciated assets is stepped up to the market value at death. Thus, when the heirs sell these assets, gains accrued by the decedents are never subject to the capital gains tax. Economists such as Charles Holt and John Shelton, and Joseph Stiglitz, among many others, have long argued that the step-up in basis at death is a major source of the lock-in effect of capital gains taxes, inducing investors to hold on to assets until death to avoid taxation during life.[22] For the wealthy, however, the benefit of the step-up may be partially offset by bequest taxes; accrued gains on assets held at death are potentially subject to the estate tax.

There are a number of reasons for realizing capital gains. An individual, for example, may sell assets and realize capital gains to finance personal expenditures. The amount of gains (G) that can be consumed are reduced by capital gains taxes. In other words, the individual will have to forego the tax on gains at rate ϑ, and is able to consume $1 - \vartheta$ of each dollar of gains realized, in addition to the asset basis. At a tax rate of 0.20, the individual is able to consume only 80 cents on the dollar.

Alternatively, if the individual decides to continue holding the asset for bequests to heirs, estate taxes will have to be paid on the gains at tax rate (e). The combined state and federal maximum capital gains and estate tax rates are approximately 0.25 and 0.55 (at 2001 law).[23] Thus, an individual holding an asset valued at $100 with a zero basis, could elect to realize the gain and consume $75, that is, $100 × (1 − 0.25), or leave an inheritance of only $45, or $100 × (1 − 0.55). Thus, ignoring discounting, bequests are more expensive than the individual's own consumption as long as the estate tax rate exceeds the capital gains tax rate, which should have a direct bearing on the amount of gains realized.

As an alternative to consumption, an individual may realize gains in the process of trading assets and adjusting portfolios. In this case the capital gains tax is typically viewed as a transaction cost; the greater the cost, the less gains are realized. But because capital gains taxes reduce the size of the taxable estate, as in the case of deductible expenses, the true transaction cost has potentially smaller effects on realizations. Unlike the preceding scenario where estate taxes stimulate gains to be consumed, here the effect operates through a reduction in the transaction cost.

In my 2001 paper with Gerald Auten, "Bequest Taxes and Capital Gains Realization," we explore how capital gains realizations vary with the estate tax rate.[24] The literature on capital gains is primarily concerned with how realizations are shaped by capital gains taxes. But because assets held at death, including accrued gains, are touched by the estate tax, these realizations may be influenced by the latter as well.

To investigate how estate taxes influence capital gains realizations, we use data from a special study by the IRS Statistics of Income Program. The dataset consists of the federal estate tax returns and the 1980 and 1981 federal income tax returns for a sample of wealthy individuals who died in 1982. The income tax dataset contains information on capital gains realization and other non-gain income sources, as well as on deductible expenses and demographic information such as marital status and number of dependents. Estate tax records provide information on the size and composition of terminal wealth as well as demographic information such as marital status, age, and the relationship of the beneficiaries to the deceased.

More specifically, we examine capital gains realizations before and after the enactment of changes in capital gains and estate taxes brought about by the Economic Recovery Tax Act of 1981. While our primary objective is to examine the effects of the estate tax on capital gains realizations, we also consider the effects of the capital gains tax rate, wealth, non-gain income, age, and other demographic variables.

ERTA1981 brought about considerable changes to the income tax, in addition to the changes in the estate taxes described earlier. While the estate tax rate was reduced under ERTA81 from a maximum 70 percent in 1981 in 5 percentage points increments between 1982 and 1985, individual income tax rates were reduced, both ordinary and related to capital gains. These changes resulted in a reduction of the maximum rate on capital gains from 28 percent in 1980 to 20 percent in 1981.

Capital gains tax rates are calculated for each of the 1980 and 1981 laws using detailed income tax calculators that incorporate most features of the individual income tax that affect marginal tax rates under each law. Because capital gains and estate tax rates are likely to be endogenous to the size of capital gains realization, one concern here is the potential endogeneity of computed tax rates. This requires measures of tax rates or instruments that are exogenous to realizations but still correlated with capital gains and estate tax rates.

Another concern, or rather challenge, is how to separately identify the effects of estate and capital gains tax rates since both are likely to be determined by other regressors such as wealth and non-gains income. Because our data on realizations straddle major statutory changes in estate and capital gains tax laws, we are able overcome such identification problems.

In calculating the capital gains tax rates, we add $1,000 to realized gains and calculate the effective marginal tax rate over this interval. Because this "last dollar" capital gains tax rate is very likely to be endogenous to the size of gains realized, we also calculate another marginal tax rate designed to be purged of the most important endogenous influences. This alternative tax rate, or the variable that we use to "instrument" the last-dollar capital gains tax rate is computed by first setting capital gains equal to zero, and replacing it with an amount of gains equal to the sample mean ratio of gains applied to wealth, and then calculating the effective tax rate over this range. The interval, which is exogenous to the capital gains tax rate, can be viewed as a proxy for potential permanent realizations.

But augmenting the estate tax returns with income tax returns further complicates matters. For wealthy individuals in our sample, it is very likely that the decision to realize capital gains is very much related to decisions to donate appreciated property to charities as well. As an example, higher capital gains tax rates reduce the price of charitable giving, which may in turn stimulate such contributions. And this may lower reported taxable income and move individuals into lower tax brackets. To address this additional endogeneity problem, a tax rate instrument is created by setting charitable contributions equal to the sample mean of 5.2 percent of non-gain income, where income is computed using predicted rather than actual capital gains.

In addition to the reduction in income tax rates, both ordinary and capital gains, ERTA81 also provided for substantial reductions in estate tax rates. These rates were to be reduced over a period of four years, with the maximum rate scheduled to be reduced from 70 in 1981 to 50 percent between 1982 and 1985. In addition, the unified credit was to rise so as to increase the size of exempted estates from $161,563 in 1980 to $600,000 for 1987 and later years, thereby reducing the tax rate to zero for the affected estates.

The marginal estate tax rate is computed by calculating the effective tax rate over a $1,000 increment to wealth. To account for the enacted changes, the estate tax rates in each year are based on the known or expected tax laws and the probability of death. That is, estate tax rates for 1980 realizations are based on the known 1981 law. The estate tax rate for realizations in 1981 is computed to reflect changes in tax rates in 1982 and expected to take place in future years. More specifically, it is set equal to the probability of dying in 1982 multiplied by the tax rate in effect in 1982, plus the probability of dying in 1983 multiplied by the tax rate in 1983, and so on. Because individuals in our sample represent top wealth holders, we follow Poterba (2000) and employ mortality rates from the Individual Annuitant Mortality Tables.[25]

Because capital gains taxes paid on realizations in 1980 or 1981 lead to smaller estates, the calculated estate tax rate is likely to be endogenous to the amount of gains realized. Another measure of the estate tax rate that is exogenous to realizations is computed as an instrument for the estate tax rate. For 1980, this estate tax rate instrument is computed with any capital gains tax paid in that year or later added back to the estate tax base. For 1981, only taxes paid in that year are added back. Because of the potential endogeneity of lifetime charitable gifts, these gifts, net of the tax saved on the deduction, are also added to the tax base. In general, the estate tax rate and capital gains tax rates are likely to be determined by wealth and income. The changes brought about by ERTA81 introduce variation in tax rates independent of income and wealth, and allow for identifying the tax effects separately from the effects of income and wealth.

After all the adjustments and a string of computations, we are left with a sample of 4,894 estates along with 9,788 matched income tax returns for the two years. Mean wealth is $2.6 million, with mean long-term capital gain realized of $52,611, and average noncapital gains income of $137,661. Slightly over one-half of the sample report realizing long-term capital gains. The mean last-dollar capital gains tax rate is about 19 percent, with a mean marginal estate tax rates of about 32 percent. The average age at death in 1982 is 75, with 24.7 percent of the sample over the age of 85. About 43 percent are married, and 46 percent widowed, with the remainder single, either never married or divorced.

In estimating the factors that shape realizations, we state capital gains realized as a share of wealth and regress it on the estate and capital gains tax rates, while controlling for the effects of non-gain income, age, marital status, and the number of children and dependents. We also control for the censored nature of the data given that close to half of the observations have no gains realized, and correct for the endogeneity of these two tax rates; large gains realized may push individuals into higher capital gains tax rates, and large payments of capital gains taxes reduce the size of taxable estates.

The estimates suggest that the implied elasticity with respect to the estate tax rate is 0.36 evaluated at mean values, and 0.9 with respect to the capital gains tax rate, also evaluated at mean values. Unlike the effects of capital gains taxes, high estate tax rates seem to have an unlocking effect on realizations. Similar estimates are obtained for the estate when a semi-log specification is employed to estimate the behavioral effects. Qualitatively similar effects, but with ranging values, are obtained when we employ different specifications, limit the sample to certain groups (not married, parents only), and control for personal residence, debts, and interactions between estate and capital gains taxes.

In summary, employing tax rate changes between 1980 and 1981 as a natural experiment, we estimate an elasticity coefficient of realizations with respect to the estate tax rate of about 0.4. This implies that in the absence of the estate tax, realizations by those potentially subject to the estate tax may decline by some 30 percent. One noteworthy experiment is that when the analysis is limited to those under the age of 50, the estate tax effect seems to dissipate.

Spousal Bequests and Tax Deferrals

Capital gains taxes also extend their effects to spousal bequests. Assets transferred at death are accorded a step-up in basis under the income tax. Thus, spousal bequests avoid capital gains taxes on past accrued gains. In addition, these bequests also benefit from the unlimited marital deduction, which was ushered in by ERTA81, and avoid estate taxation. These two provisions create incentives for individuals to bequeath much of their wealth to their spouses, thereby avoiding (deferring) estate taxes. At the passing of the surviving spouse, the underlying assets get stepped-up once again as they are transferred to the children.

Prior to ERTA81, and especially in the case of the wealthy, spousal bequests reported on returns filed in 1977 were roughly equal to the deduction limit, or one-half of the estate as gleaned from published figures by SOI. By examining published IRS statistics from the 1980s, Douglas Bernheim concluded in his 1987 paper "Does the Estate Tax Raise Revenue?" that spousal bequests may have increased as a result of the introduction of the unlimited marital deduction by ERTA81.[26] The reported marital deduction seems to have increased so as to absorb much of the taxable estate of married decedents.

This does not truly suggest that ERTA81 somehow enticed the wealthy to transfer additional resources to their spouses, but rather in part reflects tax planning strategies. Indeed, many spousal transfers take the form of QTIP spousal trusts created for the benefit of the children, used as means of deferring estate and income taxes. More specifically, a QTIP, or qualified terminable interest property, is property that passes from the decedent in which the surviving spouse has a lifetime interest but not ownership or control of assets in trust; the spouse receives all the income of the trust during her life, with some restrictions. The remaining assets may pass to the children at the surviving spouse's death.

In my 2000 paper "A Quarter Century of Estate Tax Reforms," I employ data from estate tax returns of decedents in 1995 to simulate the effects of a series of changes in estate tax laws.[27] One feature I examine is the expansion in the treatment of spousal bequests introduced by ERTA81, which expanded the marital deduction from about one-half the gross estate to unlimited as well as allowed the use of QTIPs in facilitating such transfers. These simulations show that 34 percent of spousal bequests would have been denied the deduction under pre-ERTA81 law. And, equally important, on average, QTIPs constituted about 40 percent of the marital deduction claimed. There is a great variation in the use of QTIPS, which rises with the size of estate. For the year studied, 1995, the fraction of spousal bequests using QTIPs peaked at about 86 percent for the largest estates, those with net worth in excess of $50 million.

Even in the absence of QTIPs, and in conjunction with the step-up in basis, the marital deduction may alter the timing of intergenerational transfers in a tax-minimization strategy. The surviving spouse, having avoided estate and capital gains taxes, becomes the parent of choice to make lifetime transfers. In effect, an individual may leave his estate to his surviving spouse free of estate taxes, who shortly afterward gifts the assets to her children. Given that the assets have been stepped up and that the gift tax applies on a tax-exclusive basis, taxes are minimized. In the absence of the estate tax, individuals may bequeath more of their wealth directly to the children.

Interstate Competition

The estate tax credit for state death taxes discourages interstate competition for the wealthy as it equalizes or at least reduces the gap in the death taxes levied by states. Around the time of its enactment, in November 1924, Florida amended its constitution to forbid the enactment of an inheritance tax in addition to the income tax.[28] This was an obvious attempt to attract the wealthy and encourage their migration to the state. Nevada followed suit and enacted its own constitutional amendment in July 1925.[29]

The availability of the federal credit has shaped both the state tax structures as well as the burden imposed by these taxes. In addition, it has contributed to the harmonization of state taxes. Many states have discarded their own tax code in favor of using the federal credit rate schedule as their de facto tax rate schedule, whereby they set the state liability equal to the maximum available credit; the temporary provisions of EGTRRA where the credit is replaced by a deduction has introduced considerable uncertainty into the design and structure of state taxes.

Notwithstanding the availability of the credit, a number of studies find that state estate taxes induce the elderly to migrate. Using U.S. Census migration flow data, Karen Conway and Andrew Houtenville found that the elderly tend to avoid states with high estate taxes. Consequently, states may engage in competition against one another to attract the wealthy elderly with favorable estate, inheritance and gift taxes.[30]

Bakija and Slemrod further ascertained the degree to which wealthy elderly taxpayers migrate or otherwise undertake actions to avoid state taxes by studying the relationship between changes in state tax policies and changes in the number of federal estate tax returns filed in each state over time.[31] They examined how changes in state tax policy affect the number of federal estate tax returns filed in each state, analyzing data on federal estate tax return filings by state and wealth class for eighteen years between 1965 and 1998. The authors found that high state inheritance and estate taxes and sales taxes have statistically significant, but modest, negative impacts on the number of federal estate tax returns filed in a state. This finding is commensurate with the notion that wealthy elderly people change their reported state of residence to avoid high state taxes.

While cross-state differences in tax rates may very well influence location or choice of state for residency, the findings in the literature beg the question of who is actually induced to move by state taxes. With few exceptions, and for the period studied in the literature, the federal credit for state death taxes eliminates much of the cross-state disparity in estate tax rates facing the very wealthy. For the less well off, however, the graduated credit rate schedule (table 3.2) and the steepness of state tax rate schedules may create disparities in the combined state and federal tax rates that may entice some to migrate. But are these differences, and the implied tax savings, truly large enough to offset the migration cost and influence the decision to move? And could they offset the economic gain from residing or remaining in the "high" tax state?

The tax can be an important consideration in shaping location decisions. But other countervailing objectives, such as opportunities to maximize wealth, may be in play that are often omitted in the literature. Consider billionaire Rupert Murdoch, a former citizen of Australia, a country without an estate tax. In 1985, Murdoch applied for U.S. citizenship to legally enable him to acquire a U.S. news network. This act potentially subjects his entire wealth to estate taxation at a rate of 55 percent; and a combined state and federal tax rate of 0.60 when New York taxes are considered.[32]

Tax Avoidance

While tax avoidance undoubtedly takes place, the magnitude of tax base leakages and noncompliance with the estate tax are difficult to gauge. By its very nature, estate planning is geared toward shielding assets from taxation and hiding them from the tax administrators. Lifetime gifts under $10,000 (indexed), for instance, can be used to minimize the estate tax, albeit modestly. Yet such amounts are not reported to the tax authorities, and thus cannot be measured with any reasonable precision.[33]

Some information on the extent of estate planning and tax minimization can be observed from some of the information reported by the taxpayer. Current law, for instance, accords spousal bequests an unlimited marital deduction. Yet it is clear from the information reported on estate tax returns that in the case of the wealthy, the bulk of the assets that qualify for the marital deduction actually do not necessarily benefit the surviving spouse. In many instances, the intended direct beneficiaries are likely to be the children. But as long as these transfers take the form of QTIP trusts, they qualify for the deduction even though the surviving spouse may not necessarily have access to the underlying principle of these assets. With some planning, individuals are thus able to legally defer taxes until the death of the surviving spouse.

Wojciech Kopczuk studied the bequest and wealth accumulation behavior of the wealthy (subject to the estate tax) shortly before death.[34] By examining individual-level estate tax return data for decedents whose tax returns were filed in 1977, Kopczuk was able to compare the estates of individuals who suffered terminal illnesses of different lengths. Individuals who experienced protracted illnesses reported estate values that were 10 percent to 18 percent lower than other taxpayers. While it is possible that medical or long-term care expenses deteriorated the values of these estates, Kopczuk concluded that planning for the disposition of an estate was a more likely explanation. He found that for younger decedents, the drop in net worth was larger and the administrative expenses associated with the estate fell. One interesting innovation is the use of pre-death income to overcome the endogeneity of wealth. But this is also one of the limitations of Kopczuk's paper in that the income of the wealthy is often measured with error. The rate of realized income (i.e., the ratio of reported income to wealth) typically declines with wealth; much of this income, such as accrued gains, is not reported.[35]

To more concretely explore the tax avoidance question, Kopczuk documented changes in the allocation of assets. While he did not find a disproportionate decrease in cash holdings and therefore no evidence of outright tax evasion, Kopczuk highlighted a number of interesting facts that pointed toward tax avoidance behavior. Cash holdings do not fall proportionately, dispelling any notions of liquidity-related problems near the time of death. The category of "other assets" responds strongly for smaller estates. Among taxpayers with moderate wealth, farms and business assets disappear or lose (reported) value following the onset of terminal illness and corporate stock usually fell.

A cursory look at the gift tax figures reported for valuation discounts (tables 4.4 and 4.10), excluded life insurance (table 4.3), and transfers to Crummey Trust transfers (table 5.5), should provide a more direct and accessible picture of the extent of tax avoidance. In another example, the composition of assets held at death and those transferred during life also provides a window on tax minimization. Cash, for instance, makes up about 7 percent of gross estates compared to 44 percent for gifts (tables 4.3 and 4.9). Because assets are stepped up at death and are accorded carryover basis in the case of lifetime transfers, donors are better off making cash transfers during life, and hold on to appreciating assets until death.

Tax Evasion

It should come as no surprise that individuals attempt to minimize taxes, through legal means or otherwise. The estate tax is no exception as it has the potential to appropriate close to one-half of an individual's wealth. This phenomenon is as old as the history of taxation. Indeed, evidence recorded on a papyrus from ancient Egypt describes a pre-death sale of a personal residence from father to a son at a nominal price with the apparent purpose of avoiding the inheritance tax at the former's death.[36] Further evidence also points to considerable evasion and failure to pay such taxes in ancient Greece.[37]

In contrast to legal tax avoidance, however, estate tax evasion is likely to be less widespread. For instance, it is difficult for an estate to escape taxation by not filing an estate tax return. At death, a lien is imposed on all assets, which makes it rather difficult to transfer owner-ship.[38] Because of third-party reporting as ownership changes hands, it may even be difficult to avoid gift taxes on some lifetime transfers. It is generally acknowledged, however, that tax evasion is more of a gift tax problem. And as we have seen from tables 6.5 and 6.6, estate and gift taxes are not always voluntarily paid, and additional taxes are assessed upon audits.

In an attempt to gauge the magnitude of avoided plus evaded estate taxes, Edward Wolff (1996) employed data from the Survey of Consumer Finances on the wealth holding of the U.S. population.[39] To arrive at measures of the taxable estates, Wolff applied mortality rates for the U.S. population, and by statistically killing individuals in the survey, created pseudo estate tax returns. James Poterba replicated this procedure but employed mortality rates that were more representative of the affluent segment of the population.[40] His estimates are in stark contrast to those reported by his predecessor and he finds that much of the tax base is intact.

Reflecting on the lack of coverage of the very wealthy, it is not always clear what light past studies relying on survey data can shed on the potential size of the estate tax gap. In addition, survey data are very unlikely to contain information on the size of deductible estate expenses, charitable bequests, tax preferences, and tax credits. An alternative approach to measuring this gap, albeit with its own imperfections, is to directly employ information from audited estate tax returns.

Martha Eller, Brian Erard, and Chih-Chin Ho employ such data in their 2001 paper using a sample of estates of decedents in 1992.[41] The final data file included complete records for 4,182 returns selected from the 1992 SOI Estate Tax Study sample of 7,559 returns. Of these returns the IRS had audited a subset of 1,357 returns, a portion of a total of 11,338 returns audited that calendar year.[42] The key variable that the authors studied is the tax assessed and how it may have changed upon audit, and not the traditional measure of the gap in the reported activity, or wealth in this case. The authors then proceeded to aggregate to the overall sample using results from the audited sample. More specifically, and using the audited sample of returns, they estimate the probability of getting audited, followed by the probability of a positive tax assessment if audited, followed by an equation for positive tax assessment amount.

They find that around 13 percent of the tax liability is not reported. And they also report that tax assessments, a proxy for the tax gap, decline with the tax rate. This conclusion, however, lacks clarity because the authors also find that assessments rise with an indicator for the presence of credits for state death taxes, presumably employed as an indicator or proxy for state taxes. But in 1992, the latter could be claimed only when the taxable estate is greater than $600,000, that is, when the federal estate tax is typically greater than zero.[43] In other words, this indicator takes the value of one when the tax rate is greater than zero, or more precisely when it is at least 0.37 in value. And so the authors in effect have two tax variables in their estimates, one continuous with a negative sign, and the other a dichotomous variable with a positive sign, rendering the estimated effects rather ambiguous.

As for the gift tax, tax evasion is difficult to quantify given the limitations of data employed in the literature. Jonathan Feinstein, for instance, attempts to gauge the magnitude of such evasion using survey data.[44] Using reported information on gifts in the 1992 waves of HRS and AHEAD surveys, he concludes that the gift tax paid in 1992 should have been $3 billion instead of the reported $1 billion in tax collections. In other words, two-thirds of the tax is never paid. Feinstein along with Chih-Chin Ho revise this estimate by dropping transfers for tuition and medical expenses, which are exempt from taxation, and conclude that about one-half ($1 billion), instead of two-thirds ($2 billion), is evaded.[45] However, a careful examination of the same data would yield an estimated liability closer to zero and not $2 billion to $3 billion they estimate. The latter estimates can only be arrived at by ignoring the unified credit that exempts $600,000 in transfers, and allowing only the annual exclusion of $10,000, in calculating tax liabilities. In other words, Feinstein and Ho calculate the gift tax on gifts in excess of $10,000 and ignore the $600,000 exemption. This does not suggest that individuals paid more in taxes than they owed, but rather highlights the major limitation of the data and errors in calculating tax liability. Indeed, the maximum amount of gifts reported in these surveys is well under $1 million, compared to hundreds of millions reported on gift tax returns.

In my 2007 paper on the gift tax, "The Federal Gift Tax, History, Law, and Economics," I replicate the distribution of total gifts reported in the HRS/AHEAD survey data employed by Feinstein and Ho.[46] Using the HRS data for 1992–1993 yields a population estimate of 15 million individuals making total gifts of $45.8 billion. Of these, however, only 375,000 individuals made gifts in excess of $10,000 per recipient, for a total value of $6.5 billion. It is noteworthy that taxable gifts, those in excess of the annual $10,000 exclusion, are well below the $600,000 exempted by virtue of the unified credit. In other words, it is most likely that the entire population in the HRS/AHEAD data paid zero gift taxes and not the $2 billion to $3 billion reported earlier in Feinstein and Ho.

In contrast to survey data, tax return data contain limited information on transfers as only those with transfers in excess of the annual exclusion are required to file. The data on gift tax returns filed for transfers made in 1993, reported in the right panel of table 8.1, show a total of 208,307 tax returns with total gifts of $23.9 billion, or taxable gifts of $17 billion made by just 138,000 individuals. Of the latter, about

5,800 reported gross gifts in excess of $600,000 each, for a total of roughly $4.5 billion in gifts subject to tax well above the zero amounts observed in the survey data.

Table 8.1 clarifies that survey data, and in particular the HRS/ AHEAD data, fail to point to a significant noncompliance with the gift tax. Indeed, Feinstein and Ho's findings may have resulted from over-looking the unified credit that exempted $600,000 of lifetime gifts in 1992; the authors seem to have considered only the $10,000 annual exclusion in their tax calculation. A tax liability must have been attrib-uted to anyone making a gift in excess of the annual exclusion. But the tax, of course, does not get triggered until cumulative lifetime gifts in excess of the exclusion (and gift for educational and medical purposes) exceeds $600,000.

Portfolio Allocation

While studies have typically focused on the overall effect on savings, James Poterba and Weisbenner studied the portfolio allocation effects

Table 8.1
Gifts Reported in Survey Data and on Tax Returns

Gross Gifts per Individual Donor ($1,000s)	HRS and AHEAD 1992–1993 Data			1993 Gift Tax Returns		
	Taxable Gifts*			Taxable Gifts*		
	Donors	$Millions	Mean	Donors	$Millions	Mean
< 200	372,581	6,517	17,492	110,210	4,773	43,308
200 < 600	-	-	-	22,392	6,791	303,278
600 < 1,000	-	-	-	4,730	2,898	612,685
1,000 < 2,500	-	-	-	880	1,150	1,306,818
2,500 < 5,000	-	-	-	128	423	3,304,688
5,000 < 10,000	-	-	-	54	374	6,925,926
10,000 < 20,000	-	-	-	22	305	13,863,636
20,000 < 30,000	-	-	-	9	212	23,555,556
30,000 and over	-	-	-	8	394	49,250,000
Total	372,581	6,517	17,492	138,433	17,319	125,107

Source: Table 15 in David Joulfaian, "The Federal Gift Tax, History, Law, and Economics," OTA Working Paper 100, U.S. Department of the Treasury, Washington, DC, November 2007.
* Taxable donors and gifts refer to gifts in excess of $10,000 per donee. These become truly taxable when they exceed $600,000. Gifts by married households in HRS and AHEAD are split equally between the spouses. Gifts reported in HRS/AHEAD are not reduced by transfers for educational and medical expenses.

of the estate tax.[47] These authors explored the notion that the estate tax applies at different effective rates across assets, irrespective of special estate-tax provisions for family businesses and for farms. These differences are potentially important when assessing the investment and portfolio allocation effects that are associated with the estate tax.

After comparing the composition of assets reported on estate tax returns with data from the Survey of Consumer Finances, Poterba and Weisbenner found that difficult-to-value assets, especially physical assets that are traded in thin markets and partial interests in businesses whose market value may be reduced by the presence of corporate control concerns, are taxed at effective estate tax rates that are lower than the statutory rates. The estate tax, therefore, may influence households to accumulate wealth in these assets. In turn, estate tax reduction would affect the effective rates on different assets to differing degrees; investments in these difficult-to-value assets should be impacted less by the tax than investments in other assets.

Timing of Death

Much in taxes can be saved by altruistic parents if they were to time their death pending legislative changes. But will parents be able to will themselves to live long enough for their estates to be taxed under legislated lower tax regimes? Alternatively, will they accelerate their death in the case of pending tax increases?

In their 2003 paper "Dying to Save Taxes: Evidence from Estate-Tax Returns on the Death Elasticity," Kopczuk and Slemrod examine how the timing of death may have been influenced by impending estate tax changes.[48] The authors employ estate tax return data for the years between 1916 and 1945, as well as returns filed for the years 1982 through 1984. They focus on thirteen changes in the estate tax, with eight tax increases occurring on March 3, 1917, October 4, 1917, June 2, 1924, June 6, 1932, May 10, 1934, August 30, 1935, June 26, 1940, and September 20, 1941, and five decreases occurring on February 24, 1919, February 26, 1926, October 21, 1942, January 1, 1983, and January 1, 1984. The authors set out to address two questions: do individuals postpone death in anticipation of pending lower taxes? And do they accelerate death in the face of pending tax increases?

The first task Kopczuk and Slemrod undertake is to study tax returns of individuals who passed away a week before or after the tax law changes were made or went into effect, forming two groups of estates.

To minimize errors related to exactly what time of day the changes took effect, they exclude the day that changes were enacted. This yields 8,109 observations for the populations of estate tax decedents before 1945. It also yields 699 observations for samples of returns for decedents near the tax law changes in 1983 and 1984. The latter represent a weighted population of 6,401, but with unreliable sampling properties, and consequently the authors downplay their findings relevant to this group of estates.

With the cleaned data at hand, and for each of the two groups of tax returns, the authors calculate the tax liability under old and new laws. And after doing so, they subtract the tax liability under the low tax regime from the high tax regime to calculate the tax savings from timing deaths under the lower tax regime. Next, they provide tabulations for each law change the mean and median tax liability computed under low and high tax laws, as well as report the tax savings from dying under the low tax law.

Kopczuk and Slemrod then proceed to estimate the probability of dying under the low tax regime given the size of the tax savings. They repeat this exercise for each law change to gauge the effects on the "choice" of dying before taxes increase, or, if taxes are scheduled to decline, after the law change. This generates some mixed results. Then they proceed to pool the data for all the law changes and repeat the exercise by estimating the probability of dying under the low tax regime as a function of the tax savings, and controlling for when each of the laws took effect as well as for age, gender, and marital status. They conclude by stating that a tax saving of $10,000 (in 2000 dollars) increases the probability of dying under the lower tax regime by 1.6 percent. In other words, some individuals will accelerate death and others will delay it to save $10,000.

This paper is quite interesting and innovative at many levels. Yet, and as the authors concede, it is plagued with serious data limitations. As Kopczuk and Slemrod report in the appendix of their paper, they ignore tax credits and deductions for estate-related expenses, among other omissions due to data limitations. The latter deductions can easily account for over 10 percent of the estates. And tax credits play a critical role in determining the net federal tax liability. Equally important, in some years new tax laws introduce changes in the tax base and provide new information on asset holdings, or tax breaks that were not typically captured in the previous tax regime (and vice versa).

With these limitations in mind, it is very difficult to calculate the tax liability with reasonable accuracy. And consequently, the computed tax savings for dying before or after a tax law changes are potentially plagued with measurement errors. As an example, the tax calculations omit any use of tax credits. Consider the case of the state death-tax credit introduced in 1924 and set equal to 25 percent of the federal tax. The Revenue Act of 1924 also raised the maximum federal estate tax rate from 25 to 40 percent. In effect, the act raised the tax rate to a maximum of 30 percent for the residents of many states that levy their own state or inheritance taxes. And so the tax increase of the 1924 act was much larger for those with no inheritance taxes such as Florida, than those who levy such taxes such as Pennsylvania; maximum tax rate increases by 15 versus 5 percentage points. In 1926, federal tax rates were reduced to a maximum of 20 percent (and the exemption expanded from $50,000 to $100,000). But the Revenue Act of 1926 also raised the state credit for death taxes to 80 percent of the federal tax, which effectively reduced the maximum federal tax rate to 4 percent for residences of some states. These tax credits affected federal tax computations from 1924 onward. They also introduced large differentials in savings state by state in the early years.

In another example, charitable bequests were made tax deductible in 1919. For those making such bequests, this deduction is far more valuable than the minor tax rate reductions of 1 to 2 percentage points for taxable estates under $1.5 million. Because of lack of data, however, the benefits of this deduction are ignored. The same enabling legislation in 1919 also extended the estate tax to life insurance proceeds in excess of $40,000. Once again due to lack of information this tax increase is overlooked in the paper, and only tax rate reductions are considered. While the authors treat this regime as one of reducing taxes, the law change is estimated to have raised $60 million in revenues for a net tax increase in its first year of enactment.[49]

Similar evidence is reported for Australia by Joshua Gans and Andrew Leigh in their 2006 paper, "Did the Death of Australian Inheritance Taxes Affect Deaths?"[50] The authors employ daily data on the number of deaths in Australia, and focus on the number of deaths one week before and after the repeal of the inheritance tax on July 1, 1979. Prior to its repeal, the Australian inheritance tax exempted transfers under $200,000, or $100,000 in transfers passing to non-family members, and applied at rates ranging to 27.9 percent in the case of estates of $1 million or more.

More specifically, the authors examine the number of deaths over the period January 1, 1974, through December 31, 2003. By studying records over a thirty-year period, they observe the number of deaths every year and use this information to gauge the effects of repealing the inheritance tax. They report that there were fifty more deaths the week after repeal than the historic trend would suggest, and they conclude that these deaths were likely shifted from the last week in which the inheritance tax applied. One obvious limitation of this study is that the authors cannot tell if these fifty individuals would have been subject to the inheritance tax. And so the paper cannot truly speak to the effects of the estate tax.

In their 2008 paper "Living to Save Taxes," Marcus Eliason and Henry Ohlsson extend the study of the pattern of deaths to Sweden and explore how the repeal of the Swedish inheritance tax may have delayed some deaths.[51] Sweden repealed its inheritance tax for transfers between married spouses and cohabiting couples effective January 1, 2004. It then repealed it altogether for other inheritances effective January 1, 2005.

As with the paper by Gans and Leigh, Eliason and Ohlsson also employ daily data on the number of deaths for the population at large around the dates of inheritance repeal, and do not focus on those touched by the inheritance tax. By comparing the number of deaths before and after the law changes, they report that death decreased by 17 percentage points before repeal took effect. But as with the earlier paper, they do not know whether these decedents would have left behind heirs that would have been subject to the inheritance tax.

Cognizant of the data limitation of their work, the authors revisit the topic in their 2013 paper, "Timing of Death and the Repeal of the Swedish Inheritance Tax. This paper provides an excellent discussion of how death may be timed, but more to the point, the authors provide evidence from Swedish administrative records on how death is delayed in the face of inheritance tax repeal.[52]

Using Tax Registrar records on 1.132 estates, the authors find that those with potential tax savings, relative to those without, were 10 percentage points more likely to postpone death to the day after tax repeal, which was January 1, 2005. For transfers between spouses, they report that individuals with tax savings were 12 percentage points more likely to die on New Year's Day in 2004, again postponing death to the day after repeal. Their extended analysis also suggests that repeal may have affected the timing of deaths during a longer period than the days before and after the changes took effect.

Despite its data limitations, Kopczuk and Slemrod's paper is much richer than more recent studies that employ data for Australia and Sweden. This is primarily due to its use of frequent law changes over numerous years rather than relying on changes in a single year. Equally important, the authors also studied the pattern of deaths for the estate tax-filers and not all decedents, with a majority not touched by the tax. And in addition, they related the probability of death to the size of tax savings from filers' timing of death.

Life Insurance Ownership

Individuals acquire life insurance policies primarily to insure against untimely mortality risks, and in order to provide for their loved ones. Regardless of the motives, however, the estate tax may play an important role in shaping the ownership of acquired policies. Depending on the bequest motive and the desire to control bequests, life insurance contracts maybe owned by the insured or by the beneficiaries. If the insured owns the contract, then she will be able to retain control and the ability to alter beneficiaries at any point in time. The proceeds from such policies will be included in her estate and become subject to the estate tax. Alternatively, the beneficiaries, or a trust formed on their behalf, may own the contracts with the insured relinquishing any control. Because the insured does not own or control the insurance contract, all proceeds bypass the estate and avoid taxation.

In my 2014 study "To Own or Not to Own Your Life Insurance Policy," I employ pooled samples of estate tax returns over a period of twenty-five years to examine how the allocation of life insurance policies between the two forms of ownership (by insured vs. beneficiaries) varies with tax rates.[53] The data from estate tax returns are prepared by SOI and provide rich information on wealth and its disposition for the wealthiest individuals. Information is available on asset categories, debts, and expenses of settling the estate such as attorney fees and executor commissions. More critically, information is also available on life insurance proceeds not included in the estate; proceeds from contracts on the life of the insured but owned by others is reported on Form 712 by insurance companies, which is attached to the estate tax return. Demographic information is available on age, marital status, and gender.

More specifically, I employ data drawn from the estate tax returns of decedents in 1982 through 2003. I exclude observations where individuals are under the age of 30 as well as those with negative wealth, defined as bequeathable wealth and set equal to the gross estate less debts, plus excluded insurance proceeds. And further, I exclude those residing outside the United States. This leaves us with 178,305 estates to work with.

The share of insurance proceeds from policies owned by the insured, the key variable of interest, is defined as the ratio of proceeds from life insurance policies owned by the decedent and hence included in the estate (taxable) to the sum of all life insurance proceeds included and excluded (tax exempt) from the estate. The key explanatory variable, the tax rate, is computed as the average tax rate assuming all insurance proceeds are taxable regardless of whether they are included or not, and is thus exogenous to the form of ownership. More specifically, the tax on insurance proceeds is computed as the difference between tax liability on wealth defined to include all proceeds and that defined to exclude all proceeds.

Estate tax rates varied considerably during the sample period as shown in table 2.1. Prior to 1982, and since 1977, the maximum tax rate was 70 percent, which was reduced in steps to 50 percent by the Economic Recovery Tax Act of 1981. Similarly, the size of the exempted estate was increased between 1977 and 1987, in steps from $120,667 to $600,000. In addition, the deduction for spousal bequests was increased from the greater of $500,000 and 50 percent of the estate to an unlimited deduction in 1982. Furthermore, the special-use valuation exemption for businesses was increased from $500,000 to $750,000. A bubble marginal tax rate of 60 percent was created in 1987 as the benefit of the graduated tax rates and the unified tax credit were phased out. Combined, these changes introduced considerable variation in tax rates independent of the size of the estate.

Looking backward, the fully phased-in tax rates and exemptions are employed in measuring tax incentives. Thus for decedents in 1992, the fully phased-in tax changes anticipated in 1982 are used. Because the maximum tax rate declined from 70 to 65 percent in 1982, and was planned to decline to 50 percent by 1985, the relevant tax rate is assumed to be 50 percent. Similarly, the size of the exempted estate was expanded in steps to $600,000 in 1987. The maximum tax rate was temporarily frozen at 55 percent in 1984, once again in 1987, and permanently in 1993. For these periods, the maximum tax rate is set at 55 percent.

Reflecting on the estate planning process, and following the analysis in Kopczuk and Slemrod's 2001 paper, tax rates are computed using the tax law in effect ten years before the date of death given the date of insurance contract or transfer of policy is not known.

About 113,000 estates reported life insurance proceeds. Of these, 93,289 were individuals who owned their policies, 5,481 who did not own their policies, and 14,052 who owned some of the policies and the beneficiaries owned the remainder. And as illustrated in table 8.2, and for those who own their contracts, as reported in the first column, the mean wealth is $4.4 million with mean life insurance proceeds of $236,033. Their mean age is 67.6 years, with 76 percent male, 64 percent married, 21 percent widowed, and 8 percent never married singles.

Table 8.2
Attributes of Estates by Form of Insurance Ownership

Variable	Owned by Insured		Owned by Beneficiaries		Both Forms of Ownership	
	Mean	Standard Deviation	Mean	Standard Deviation	Mean	Standard Deviation
Wealth	4,385,884	20,000,000	11,000,000	26,300,000	11,300,000	51,100,000
Total insurance	236,033	492,238	1,131,679	2,917,242	1,682,588	34,100,000
Included insurance	236,033	492,238	0	0	351,243	835,139
Excluded insurance	0	0	1,131,679	2,917,242	1,331,345	34,000,000
Owned insurance share	1	0	0	0	0.36	0.30
Age	67.64	15.46	73.25	12.72	67.99	13.33
Male	0.76	0.43	0.59	0.49	0.89	0.32
Married	0.64	0.48	0.61	0.49	0.79	0.41
Widowed	0.21	0.41	0.3	0.46	0.14	0.34
Never married single	0.08	0.28	0.03	0.16	0.02	0.14
Divorced/ separated	0.06	0.24	0.06	0.23	0.05	0.22
Business share	0.07	0.17	0.13	0.22	0.18	0.24
Tax rate	0.28	0.2	0.45	0.12	0.38	0.16
Observations	93,289		5,481		14,052	

Source: David Joulfaian, "To Own or Not to Own Your Life Insurance Policy," *Journal of Public Economics* 118 (2014): 120–127.

Businesses make up 7 percent of their estate, and they face an average tax rate of 28 percent.

In contrast, when the beneficiaries own the policies, shown in the middle column of the table, the decedents are wealthier, have greater insurance coverage, are older, less likely to be male, less likely to be married, less likely to be single, and businesses make up a larger share of their estates (0.13 vs. 0.07). More to the point, their estates face higher tax rates (0.45 vs. 0.28).

For estates where both forms of ownership are present, as in the last column, they are slightly wealthier than those who own their policies. They have greater insurance coverage, the bulk of which is excluded from the estate and owned by the beneficiaries. They are more likely to be male and married, and have greater business presence. The average tax rate is much higher than that faced by those who own all of their policies (0.38 vs. 0.28). Along with column (3), this continues to highlight the role taxes play in shaping the form of life insurance ownership.

Next I employ multivariate analysis to shed further light on the factors that explain the form of ownership (by insured or beneficiary) and estimate of the effect of estate tax rates on the allocation of life insurance contracts between the two forms of ownership. The estimated coefficient on the tax rate is negative and significant, and implies that a 10 percentage point increase in the tax rate leads to a 3.1 percentage point reduction in the owned share of insurance proceeds.

The findings suggest that those facing high tax rates control or own less of their life insurance policies, with beneficiaries owning more, and highlight the incentive effects of taxes. In one of a number of robustness tests, the key variable of interest is defined as the ratio of excluded insurance relative to total wealth, redefined to include all insurance proceeds, and replaces its share of all insurance. The findings show that this share also rises with tax rates, and highlight the importance of excluded insurance as a vehicle for sheltering wealth from taxes.

Political Contributions

Unlike the treatment of charitable gifts and bequests, transfers to all political organizations are not deductible in computing the taxable estate. In contrast, gifts to 527 political organizations have been specifically exempt from the gift tax since 1974. While this exemption is not extended to gifts to other organizations that also intervene in political campaigns, but are legally organized as 501(c)(4) social welfare organizations, they too seem to escape taxation by virtue of a lack of enforcement of the tax code.[54]

Given the asymmetry in the tax treatment of transfers, *de jure and de facto*, an interesting question is whether this has influenced the allocation of transfers by wealthy donors between lifetime gifts and bequests. While gifts, in the aggregate, are observed, little is known about the pattern of bequests.

Conclusion and Limitations

The preceding review of the literature on the behavioral effects critically reviewed some of the shortcomings of the various findings. These include data aggregation, inadequate coverage of the rich, and measurement errors among others. A potentially serious limitation not fully explored, however, is in identifying the economic agents that respond to estate taxation or the margin at which behavior is induced. Typically, researchers examine the behavior of individuals and how much of it is distorted by taxation. But what if decisions are made by households, jointly by husbands and wives and not each separately? And what if what is observed for each individual reflects the budgets and circumstances of the couple and not what typically is revealed on the estate tax return (or probate record) of each?

While the attributes of wealthy decedents can be observed at the individual level only, it is possible to construct household-level observations by linking husbands and wives over time as their respective tax returns are filed. In my 2007 paper, I employ samples of estate tax returns filed during the years 1982 through 2003 in order to examine the divergent pattern of terminal wealth and its disposition by husbands and wives. These samples of estate tax returns, prepared annually by SOI, and many of which have already been described thus far, are designed to over-represent the very wealthy, with returns filed upon the death of an individual.

On each estate tax return, the social security number (SSN) of the deceased is reported, in addition to the size, composition, and ultimate disposition of the estate. The estates of widowed decedents also report the SSN of the pre-deceased spouse. Using the SSN's make it possible to link the estate tax returns of husbands and wives (i.e. married and widowed decedents) filed over time. However, the requirement of reporting the SSN of the pre-deceased (first to die) spouse on the estate tax returns of widowed decedents first went into effect for tax year 1989, and SOI began gathering such information for returns filed in 1991. Accordingly, the starting year for linking couples is the estate tax returns of widowed decedents filed in 1991.

SOI has prepared samples of estate tax returns almost for every year beginning with returns filed in 1982. The universe of estate tax returns that can be linked is subject to a number of limitations. Matching estate tax returns is possible only when both members of the household have passed away, and that the estates of both have filed tax returns. Second, returns are linked only when the SSN for the first to die is reported on the returns of widowed decedents. And third, returns can be linked only when both are selected into the annual SOI samples. Thus the linking of a couple's estate tax returns is contingent on both being filed by 2003, the reporting of the SSN of the first spouse, and the annual sample designs.

To facilitate the comparison of the distribution of terminal wealth, and its disposition, across individuals, wealth for each estate is defined as total assets, or the gross estate, less debts and estate expenses, plus lifetime gifts and gift tax paid. For the household, wealth is defined as the sum of the wealth reported on the estates of husband and wife, less the amount of spousal bequests. All variables are stated in 1989 dollars and estates with wealth under $600,000 are excluded.

As can be gleaned from the frequency distributions reported in table 8.3, the wealth profile of estate tax decedents evaluated at the household level looks much different from that gleaned from estate tax return data on individual decedents filed annually. The last column, when contrasted with the first column, reveals that decedents appear to be much wealthier when their assets are consolidated. This should not be surprising as the individuals typically reported the wealth they own or control. Half the jointly owned property, for instance, will not be reported on the estate tax return of an individual.

Not only may the picture that emerges on the size and distribution of household wealth be different from that commonly gleaned from data on individual estates, but also the disposition of the reported terminal wealth may be at variance as well. Measures of the estate tax burden may look different, and so would the perceived generosity of making bequests and inter vivos gifts. The differences in the observed attributes of individuals and couples gleaned from estate tax returns are large and may have implications for tax policy as well as its behav-

Table 8.3
Wealth Distribution of Husband and Wife Using Linked Estate Tax Returns

	Number of Weighted Estate Tax Returns**			
Wealth ($1,000s)	All	Married (First)	Widowed (Second)	Couple Combined*
600 < 1,000	6,374	4,155	2,219	311
1,000 < 2,500	12,842	6,934	5,908	6,106
2,500 < 5,000	7,263	3,405	3,858	4,232
5,000 < 10,000	5,097	2,029	3,068	3,734
10,000 < 20,000	2,652	893	1,759	2,087
20,000 < 50,000	1,229	406	823	1,084
50,000 and over	453	133	320	400
Total	35,910	17,955	17,955	17,955

Source: David Joulfaian, "What if Estate Taxpayers Were Viewed as Households Rather Than as Individuals?," mimeo, 2007.
Notes: Limited to estate tax returns of decedents 1982–2003. Exclude estates with wealth under $600,000 in 1989 dollars.
* Wealth is defined as the sum of terminal wealth of the first to die plus the wealth of the second to die less spousal bequests.
** Weights are obtained from the annual SOI samples. They are not representative of the matched universe of the estate tax returns of husbands and wives.

ioral consequences. The appropriate definition of the tax unit, be it the individual or the household, can be critical to tax policy design and to evaluating the behavioral effects of taxing wealth transfers. The evidence suggests that the "burden" of taxation is greater than commonly reported when the unit of observation is the household. Similarly, the wealthy appear to be more generous in providing for charitable bequests and making inter vivos gifts. In many ways, the attributes of households seem to have much in common with those of widowed decedents.

While there is considerable merit to evaluating the behavior and circumstances of husbands and wives on a household basis, and hence reason to be critical of the existing literature, a case can be made that individuals may very well be the appropriate unit of study. Indeed, the evidence on income pooling for living individuals is at best mixed. Shelley Phipps and Peter Burton, for instance, find that the influences on the household expenditures by male and female income earners are not identical.[55] They find some support for pooling in the case of expenditures on housing, but reject it for other categories of expenditures. The notion that households maximize a single utility function, or that their behavior is independent of who controls resources or earns the income have also been challenged by Shelly Lundberg and Robert Pollak, among others.[56] A similar outcome is possible in the case of bequests, where control of household wealth changes hands. This has important implication for identifying the margin at which the wealthy react to estate taxation. Future research should focus on these behavioral concerns as well as on the appropriate definition for the taxable unit.

9   A Critical Assessment

All taxes, including inheritance-type taxes, share a common objective, which is to raise revenue to fund government expenditures. Income, excise, and estate taxes were enacted, or their reach broadened, at times of critical fiscal needs. Unlike most taxes, however, the estate tax has also been more forcefully advanced as a corrective tax. It is advocated as a mechanism to protect the income tax and reduce its erosion, and has been promoted as an instrument to shore up the progressivity of the tax system, reduce wealth concentration, and enhance equal opportunity.

Preempting income tax avoidance is one of the earliest arguments advanced in support of the estate tax. For example, under a Haig-Simon definition of "income," capital gains would be taxed as they accrue. For practical reasons, only realized gains are taxed under current law. However, gains held until death escape taxation as the basis is stepped up, even though these gains would be taxed under a more practical comprehensive income tax. In addition to the deferral of gains, taxpayers engage in a number of tax planning and avoidance schemes to minimize lifetime taxes that ultimately lead to the formation of larger estates. And as such, the estate tax may be considered as a recapture tax of sorts, a delayed or deferred income tax.[1]

Much of the often-repeated objectives of the estate tax, however, can be addressed through a revamped income tax. This would involve reforming and broadening the base of the income tax, improving its administration, and modifying its rate of progression. But absent such reforms, a strong case can be made on practical grounds that the estate tax is perhaps the second-best to "overcoming" the limitations of reforming the income tax. This gains further credibility when considering that the wealthy realize very little in capital income, and that sheltering their income and deferring income taxes is not terribly difficult. As an example, Eugene Steuerle demonstrated that the wealthy realize disproportionately less of their capital income, resulting in smaller amounts reported for income tax purposes.[2]

Given the way it is structured, the estate tax seems in some ways to be intended more as a tax on transfers. Different tax regimes apply depending on the relationship and nature of the beneficiary. Spousal bequests are exempt from taxation, grandchildren and similar or older generations are double taxed (GSTT) to insure each generation is taxed, and businesses are preferentially treated. In addition spousal bequests benefit from step-up in basis, thereby avoiding income taxation as well. Hence, the emerging tax structure does not reflect the income of the donor, and not even that of the recipients.

Indeed, the tax seems more of a hybrid inheritance tax featuring elements of both a transfer tax and a backstop to the income tax, which are not always in harmony. For example, the unlimited marital deduction under the estate tax, along with the portability of the exemption to the surviving spouse ($10 million, indexed, in 2018), treat husband and wife as one taxpaying unit while the step-up in basis provision under the income tax treats them as two separate individuals. This lack of focus and divergent treatments may have contributed to the inevitable narrow base and high rates feature of the tax.

The imperfections of the estate tax, and in particular the manufactured valuation discounts, have led some reformers to call for its replacement with another form of wealth transfer tax. As an example, Henry Aaron and Alicia Munnell attempt to assess the role of transfer taxes in their 1992 paper "Reassessing the Role for Transfer Taxes."[3] In another example, Lily Batchelder proposed a more comprehensive inheritance tax in her 2007 paper "Taxing Privilege More Effectively: Replacing the Estate Tax with an Inheritance Tax."[4] Alternative tax systems, however, such as a pure inheritance tax (or hybrid variants), are likely to introduce a number of complexities in defining the tax base as well as the ability to identify, locate, and expand the number of taxpayers. More important, proposed inheritance taxes do not replace the estate tax. The starting point is the division of bequests reported on the estate tax return (or some future variant of it). Indeed, they merely shift the statutory incidence of the tax to the heirs while leaving in place all the existing complexities of deriving the size of the estate to be divided among the heirs. Unless the shortcomings of the current estate tax are addressed, proposed inheritance taxes fall far short from a meaningful contribution to reforming the tax system.

Notwithstanding the heightened attention to estate taxation over the past decade, as well as the empirical findings reported in the literature, the estate tax has attracted relatively little attention from researchers and scholars in particular when compared to the voluminous economics literature on personal and corporate income taxes. There is little validation of the existing studies and many pressing aspects of the estate tax have yet to be explored.

Returning to the remarks made by Gregory Mankiw, at the time he served as the chairman of President Bush's Council of Economic Advisers, "The estate tax unfairly punishes frugality, undermines economic growth, reduces real wages, and raises little, if any, federal revenue. There are no principles of good tax policy that support this tax."[5] Of course, there is little in the way of support to Mankiw's propositions in the empirical literature.[6] Nevertheless, they do highlight a number of areas of research topics to pursue.

The small yield of the estate tax cited by Mankiw and often by other critics of the estate should not come as a surprise since the scope of the tax is limited to a very small number of the estates of wealthy decedents. Indeed, about 5,000 reported estate tax liability on returns filed in 2016, or 33,000 at the time of Mankiw's writing, compared to about 100 million with tax liability for the individual income tax, or to the 800,000 for corporations.

And despite its small contribution to government revenues, it is important not to underestimate the importance of the estate tax paid in shaping income distribution in the long run. As an example, Frank A. Cowell, Dirk Van de gaer, and Chang He, in their 2017 paper "Inheritance Taxation: Redistribution and Predistribution," illustrate how important the estate tax is, despite its low governmental revenue yield, in shaping long-run distribution of wealth.[7]

Of course we should not be deceived by the low yield of the tax. One consideration in evaluating the size or the burden of the estate tax is to compare the tax liability to that the decedents had faced during life under the income tax. By this yardstick, the estate tax is quite sizeable. For estate tax returns filed in 2008, mostly representing decedents in 2007 at a time when the estate exemption was $2 million, the tax paid by the estates of widowed decedents is about twenty-six times as large as the income tax paid in the year prior to death. Alternatively stated, the estate tax liability is about twice as large as the sum of income taxes paid in the previous ten years.[8]

Well over a century ago, Andrew Carnegie spoke passionately about his preference to have bequests taxed heavily to fund the public sector. Yet at the same time, he was a strong opponent of income taxation. For the entrepreneur like Carnegie, the implications are that estate taxation is a more efficient way to raise tax revenues. But are corporate taxes or personal taxes on the rich less efficient ways of raising revenues than the estate tax? And could the latter raise the same amount of revenues needed to fund public expenditures?

The structure of the estate tax has evolved over the years and currently reflects a number of historical developments and political compromises. Its salient features are a fluid, narrow tax base with high tax rates and a complex code. While many of the tax's shortcomings—noted in the often-cited 1979 work of George Cooper—have been addressed by Congress over the years, many other new ways of avoiding the tax have taken shape as well.[9] The estate tax continues to be porous and unnecessarily disruptive to succession planning. Indeed, it is not always clear who is being taxed and what is being taxed. And reforms over the years have primarily focused on tax rates and size of exempted estate with little attention to the underlying structure of the tax. But if history is likely to repeat itself, either in terms of budgetary needs or changes in the political landscape, policymakers may need to turn their attention to estate tax reform. Perhaps this book will contribute in meaningful ways to the ensuing debate on the proper structure and place of the estate tax in shaping the size and distribution of the nation's taxes.

Notes

Chapter 1

1. Max West, *The Inheritance Tax*, 2nd ed. (New York: Columbia University Press, 1908), 11–13.
2. Ibid., 60–61.
3. Ibid., 88.
4. The federal government does not levy annual wealth taxes. Annual property taxes imposed by cities and counties are the only form of wealth taxation observed in the United States.
5. See Internal Revenue Service tabulations at https://www.irs.gov/statistics/soi-tax -stats-estate-tax-statistics-filing-year-table-1, last updated November 5, 2018. The returns of taxable estates filed in 1977 represent slightly over 7 percent of deaths.
6. See Adam Smith, *An Inquiry into the Nature and Causes of the Wealth of Nations* (New York: Modern Library, [1776] 1930), book 5, chap. 2, part 2:appendix to articles I and II; David Ricardo, *On the Principles of Political Economy and Taxation* (London: John Murray, 1821), chap. 8. Unlike Ricardo, Smith was not opposed to taxing inheritances of adult or otherwise "emancipated" children and other relations.
7. West, *Inheritance Tax*, 204; Michael J. Graetz, "To Praise the Estate Tax, Not to Bury It," *Yale Law Journal* 93 (1983): 259, 270; James R. Repetti, "Democracy, Taxes, and Wealth," *NYU Law Review* 76 (2001): 825, 851–852.
8. See Irving Fisher, "Some Impending National Problems," *Journal of Political Economy* 26 (1916): 697–712; Andrew Carnegie, *The Gospel of Wealth, and Other Timely Essays* (1900; repr., Garden City, NY: Doubleday, Doran and Company, 1975), 10; and Theodore Roosevelt, *Presidential Addresses and State Papers: April 14, 1906 to January 14, 1907* (New York: The Review of Reviews Company, 1910), 712–724.
9. Remarks by Dr. N. Gregory Mankiw, Chairman of the Council of Economic Advisers, at the National Bureau of Economic Research Tax Policy and the Economy Meeting, National Press Club, November 4, 2003, http://georgewbush-whitehouse.archives.gov/cea/NPressClub20031104.html.
10. Michael J. Graetz and Ian Shapiro, *Death by a Thousand Cuts: The Fight over Taxing Inherited Wealth* (New Jersey: Princeton University Press. 2006).
11. See "Death (Tax) Takes a Holiday," *CBS News*, March 14, 2001, last updated March 20, 2001, http://www.cbsnews.com/stories/2001/03/14/politics/main278884.shtml.

Chapter 2

1. Jonathan D. Jones and David Joulfaian, "Federal Government Revenues and Expenditures in the Early Years of the American Republic: Evidence from 1792 to 1860," *Journal of Macroeconomics* 13, no. 1 (Winter 1991): 133–155.

2. As stated earlier, a stamp tax was enacted in 1797 for a short period and applied to legacies at roughly the equivalent rate of 0.2 percent.
3. West, *Inheritance Tax*, 90–91.
4. Sidney Ratner, *American Taxation* (New York: W. W. Norton, 1942), chap. 9.
5. Pollock v. Farmers' Loan and Trust Co., 158 U.S. 601 (1895).
6. Knowlton v. Moore, 178 U.S. 41 (1900). The Supreme Court took issue with the exemptions and the rate schedule being based on the size of the estate instead of on the shares of the beneficiaries.
7. William J. Shultz, *The Taxation of Inheritance* (Boston: Houghton Mifflin Company, 1926), 150–155.
8. Ratner, *American Taxation*, 239.
9. Roosevelt, *Presidential Addresses and State Papers*, 720–721.
10. See Charles J. Bullock, "The Position of the Inheritance Tax in American Taxation," in Proceedings of the National Tax Association (1907), 230–240; Andrew Mellon, *Taxation: The People's Business* (New York: The Macmillan Company, 1924), 111.
11. Roy G. Blakey, "The New Revenue Act," *American Economic Review* 6 (December 1916): 837–850.
12. See Shultz, *Taxation of Inheritance*, 156. Under a pure inheritance tax, the tax is determined by the relationship of the heir and the amount of transfers from the estate to each beneficiary. Under an estate tax, the tax liability is determined by the size of the estate.
13. See *Annual Report of the Secretary of the Treasury 1915* (Washington, DC: Government Printing Office, 1915), 50.
14. *Internal Revenue Service Annual Report 1918*, 98–99.
15. Roy G. Blakey, "The War Revenue Act of 1917," *The American Economic Review* 7, no. 4 (1917): 791–815.
16. Roy G. Blakey and Gladys C. Blakey, "The Revenue Act of 1918," *The American Economic Review* 9, no. 2 (1919): 214–243.
17. *Annual Report of the Secretary of the Treasury 1924* (Washington, DC: Government Printing Office, 1924), 11.
18. Schultz, *Taxation of Inheritance*, 161–162.
19. Increases in tax liability, both on estates and gifts, attributable to the 1924 Act were refunded (per Section 325 of the Revenue Act of 1926) over a number of years. The amounts of refunds are reported in the *Annual Report of the Commissioner of Internal Revenue for the Fiscal Year Ended June 30, 1927*(Washington, DC: Government Printing Office), 30 and that of 1928, 45.
20. See United States Seventy-Second Congress, House of Representatives Report 608, reprinted in *Internal Revenue Cumulative Bulletin* 1939 (1), part 2 (Washington, DC: Government Publishing Office, 1932), 462; also see United States Seventy-Second Congress, Senate Report 665, reprinted in *Internal Revenue Cumulative Bulletin* 1939 (1), part 2 (Washington, DC: Treasury Department, 1932), 525.
21. Harriss, C. Lowell, *Gift Taxation in the United States* (Washington, DC: American Council on Public Affairs, 1940), 147.
22. When an investor sells assets that have appreciated in value over the years held, the increases in value are subject to capital gains taxes. If the very same assets are instead held until death and bequeathed to heirs, the gains accrued by the donor will not be subject to capital gains taxes when the assets are sold in the future. Consider the example of an individual buying stocks for $5 million and selling them when they appreciate at $8 million. The $8 million selling price less the $5 million acquisition cost (or basis of the investor) represents a gain of $3 million, which is subject to capital gains taxes. If held until death, the heirs' basis in the property rises (is stepped-up) from $5 to $8 million,

and the $3 million in gains accrued by the deceased donor are never taxed when the stocks are sold by the beneficiaries.

23. The DEFRA froze the rate at 55 percent in 1984 for three years; OBRA87 froze it for another five years; OBRA93 made the 55 percent rate permanent.

24. EGTRRA also repealed the step-up in basis on bequeathed assets, thereby potentially subjecting heirs to future capital gains taxes.

Chapter 3

1 The tax advantages of making non-cash gifts, however, are in part offset by the income tax treatment of capital gains. Assets are accorded a step-up in basis in the case of bequests and a partial basis carryover in the case of gifts; the basis of the donee in the case of a gift is the donor's basis increased by the gift tax multiplied by the share of appreciation in the property transferred—Internal Revenue Service (IRC) Section 1015(d) (6). An expanded discussion is provided in David Joulfaian, "Choosing between Gifts and Bequests: How Taxes Affect the Timing of Wealth Transfers," *Journal of Public Economics* (2005): 2069–2091.

2. IRC Section 2032.

3. IRC Section 2032A.

4. Assets may be valued based on capitalized income or the value of properties employed in similar enterprises.

5. Prior to ERTA in 1981, the waiting period was fifteen years.

6. This valuation method may seem reasonable in the case of active businesses, but the potential for abuse is significant in the case of passive businesses. A growing practice in recent years is for investors to bundle their stocks, bonds, or personal residences into partnerships and make fractional transfers to their heirs.

7. IRC Section 2042.

8. IRC Section 2039.

9. IRC Section 4981A, relabeled as 4980A by the Technical and Miscellaneous Revenue Act of 1988 (TAMRA).

10. John B. Shoven and David A. Wise, "The Taxation of Pensions: A Shelter Can Become a Trap," in *Frontiers in the Economics of Aging*, ed. David A. Wise (Chicago: University of Chicago Press, 1998), 173–212.

11. IRC Section 2057.

12. IRC Section 2031(c).

13. IRC Section 2503(b).

14. IRC Section 2631(a).

15. IRC Section 2056.

16. See Joseph A. Pechman, *Federal Tax Policy*, 4th ed. (Washington, DC: Brookings Institution, 1987), 241; and Carl S. Shoup, *Federal Estate and Gift Taxes* (Washington, DC: Brookings Institution, 1966).

17. IRC Section 2055.

18. IRC Section 2053(a).

19. IRC Section 2053.

20. For the tax-minimizing estate, the choice of whether to claim the expenses against the income tax or the estate tax depends on the respective tax rates.

21. IRC Section 2010.

22. IRC Section 2011.

23. IRC Section 2012. Because tax rates and the sizes of exempted gifts and estates vary over time with law changes, the previously paid gift taxes are recomputed to reflect the law for the most recent year when gifts are made or death occurs.

24. IRC Section 2013.
25. IRC Section 6161.
26. IRC Section 6651.
27. IRC Section 6166.
28. IRC Section 6161.

Chapter 4

1. See "Mortality Data," *National Vital Statistics System (NVSS)*, National Center for Health Statistics, https://www.cdc.gov/nchs/nvss/deaths.htm.
2. There are a number of small deductions related to estate expenses that add up to less than $1 billion not reported here.
3. These political organizations are typically referred to as Section 527 organizations, as the exemption for gifts is sanctioned by IRC Section 527.
4. Annuity distributions to grantor are not taxable income because in effect assets are passed between the grantor and his/her trust.

Chapter 5

1. David Joulfaian, "The Distribution and Division of Bequests," OTA Working Paper 71 (U.S. Department of the Treasury, Washington, DC, 1994).
2. Crummey et al. v. Commissioner of Internal Revenue, 397 F.2d 82 (9th Cir.1968).
3. Wealth is defined as net worth, or gross estate less debts, reduced by estate expenses.
4. See Robert N. Gordon, David Joulfaian, and James M. Poterba, "Choosing Between an Estate Tax and a Basis Carryover Regime: Evidence from 2010," *National Tax Journal* 69, no. 4 (2016): 981–1002.
5. Recall that the filing threshold was $5.34 million in 2014.

Chapter 6

1. David Joulfaian, "The Federal Estate and Gift Tax: Description, Profile of Taxpayers, and Economic Consequences," OTA Working Paper 80 (U.S. Department of the Treasury, Washington, DC, 1998), table 19.
2. David Cay Johnston, "IRS to Cut Auditors," New York Times, July 23, 2006.
3. Charles Davenport and Jay A. Soled, "Enlivening the Death-Tax Death-Talk," *Tax Notes* 84, no. 4 (July 26, 1999 special report): 591–630.

Chapter 7

1. Carnegie, *Gospel of Wealth*.
2. See Michael D, Hurd, "Mortality Risk and Bequests," *Econometrica* 57, no. 4 (July 1989):779–813; Menahem E. Yaari, "Uncertain Lifetime, Life Insurance, and the Theory of the Consumer," *Review of Economic Studies* 32, no. 2 (April 1965): 137–150.
3. See Robert J. Barro, "Are Government Bonds Net Wealth?," *Journal of Political Economy* 82, no. 6 (1974): 1095–1117.
4. See James Andreoni, "Impure Altruism and Donations to Public Goods: A Theory of Warm-Glow Giving," *Economic Journal* 100, no. 401 (1990): 464–477.
5. See B. Douglas Bernheim, Andrei Shleifer, and Lawrence H Summers, "The Strategic Bequest Motive," *Journal of Political Economy* 93, no. 6 (1985): 1045–1076; Donald Cox,

"Motives for Private Income Transfers," *Journal of Political Economy* 95, no. 3 (June 1987): 508–546.

6. See Max Weber, *The Protestant Ethic and the Spirit of Capitalism*, trans. ed. (New York: Charles Scribner's Sons, [1905] 1958); Smith, *Wealth of Nations*.

7. "Andrew Carnegie: Pioneer. Visionary. Innovator, *Andrew Carnegie's Story*, Carnegie Corporation of New York, n.d., https://www.carnegie.org/interactives/foundersstory/#!/#giving-legacy (accessed May 25, 2018).

8. John Laitner, "Simulating the Effects on Inequality and Wealth Accumulation of Eliminating the Federal Gift and Estate Tax," in *Rethinking Estate and Gift Taxation*, ed. William G. Gale, James Hines, and Joel B. Slemrod (Washington, DC: Brookings Institution Press, 2001).

9. William G. Gale and Maria G. Perozeh, "Do Estate Taxes Reduce Saving?," in *Rethinking Estate and Gift Taxation*, ed. William G. Gale, James Hines, and Joel Slemrod (Washington, DC: Brookings Institution Press, 2001), 206–247.

10. Marco Cagetti and Mariacristina De Nardi, "Estate Taxation, Entrepreneurship, and Wealth," *American Economic Review* 99, no. 1 (2009): 85–111.

11. Wojciech Kopczuk, "Taxation of Intergenerational Transfers and Wealth," in *Handbook of Public Economics*, vol. 5, ed. Alan J. Auerbach, Raj Chetty, Martin Feldstein, and Emmanuel Saez (Amsterdam: Elsevier, 2013), 329–390.

12. Douglas Holtz-Eakin and Donald Marples, "Distortion Costs of Taxing Wealth Accumulation: Income Versus Estate Taxes," NBER Working Paper No. 8261, National Bureau of Economic Research, 2001.

13. Wojciech Kopczuk and Joel Slemrod, "The Impact of the Estate Tax on the Wealth Accumulation and Avoidance Behavior of Donors, in *Rethinking Estate and Gift Taxation*, ed. William G. Gale, James R. Hines Jr., and Joel Slemrod (Washington, DC: Brookings Institution Press, 2001), 299–343.

14. David Joulfaian, "The Behavioral Response of Wealth Accumulation to Estate Taxation: Time Series Evidence," *National Tax Journal* 59 (2006): 253–268.

15. James Poterba, "The Estate Tax and After-Tax Investment Returns," in *Does Atlas Shrug? The Economic Consequences of Taxing the Rich*, ed. Joel Slemrod (Cambridge, MA: Harvard University Press, 2000), 329–349.

16. William G. Gale and Joel B. Slemrod, "Rhetoric and Economics in the Estate Tax Debate," *National Tax Journal* 54, no. 3 (September 2001): 613–627.

17. Kenneth Chapman, Govind Hariharan, and Lawrence Southwick Jr., "Estate Taxes and Asset Accumulation," *Family Business Review* 9, no. 3 (Fall 1996): 253–268.

18. Franklin D. Roosevelt, *The Public Papers and Addresses*, vol. 4 (New York: Random House 1938), 313–314.

19. To simplify the discussion, assets are assumed to appreciate at the beneficiary discount rate.

20. Joulfaian, "Choosing between Gifts and Bequests."

21. This is based on data from long-term gains realized reported in Gerald Auten and Janette Wilson, "Sales of Capital Assets Reported on Individual Income Tax Returns, 1985," *Internal Revenue Service SOI Bulletin* (Spring 1999): 113–136.

22. David Joulfaian, "Gift Taxes and Lifetime Transfers: Time Series Evidence," *Journal of Public Economics* 88 (2004): 1917–1929.

23. Auten and Wilson, "Sales of Capital Assets Reported."

24. David Joulfaian and Kathleen McGarry, "Estate and Gift Tax Incentives and Inter Vivos Giving," *National Tax Journal* 57, no. 2, part 2 (June 2004): 429–444.

25. For opposing view, see Barro, "Are Government Bonds Net Wealth?"

26. David N. Weil, "Intergenerational Transfers, Aging, and Uncertainty," in *Advances in the Economics of Aging*, ed. David A. Wise (Chicago: University of Chicago Press, 1996), 321–342.

27. See David Joulfaian, "Inheritance and Saving," NBER Working Paper No. 12569, National Bureau of Economic Research, 2006.

28. David Joulfaian and Mark O. Wilhelm, "Inheritance and Labor Supply," *Journal of Human Resources* 29, no. 4 (1994): 1205–1234.

29. David N. Weil, "The Saving of the Elderly in Micro and Macro Data," *Quarterly Journal of Economics* 109, no. 1 (1994): 55–81.

30. For details on how the proxy was developed, see Jonathan Skinner, "A Superior Measure of Consumption from the Panel Study of Income Dynamics," *Economics Letters* 23, no. 2: 213–216.

31. Jay Zagorsky, "Do People Save or Spend Their Inheritances? Understanding What Happens to Inherited Wealth," *Journal of Family and Economic Issues* 34, no. 1 (2013): 64–76.

32. Douglas Holtz-Eakin, David Joulfaian, and Harvey S. Rosen, "The Carnegie Conjecture: Some Empirical Evidence," *Quarterly Journal of Economics* 108, no. 2 (1993): 413–435.

33. Joulfaian, "Inheritance and Saving."

34. Jeffrey R. Brown, Courtney C. Coile, and Scott J. Weisbenner, "The Effect of Inheritance Receipt on Retirement," *Review of Economics and Statistics* 92, no. 2 (2010): 425–434.

35. Jeffrey R. Brown, Courtney C. Coile, and Scott J. Weisbenner, "The Effect of Inheritance Receipt on Retirement," NBER Working Paper 12386, National Bureau of Economic Research, 2006.

36. Holtz-Eakin, Joulfaian, and Rosen, "Carnegie Conjecture."

37. Mikael Elinder, Oscar Erixson, and Henry Ohlsson, "The Impact of Inheritances on Heirs' Labor and Capital Income," *B. E. Journal of Economic Analysis & Policy* 12, no. 1 (2012): 1–35.

38. Douglas Holtz-Eakin, David Joulfaian, and Harvey S. Rosen, "Estimating the Income Effect on Retirement," Princeton, NJ: Center for Economic Policy Studies, Princeton University, 1999.

39. Douglas Holtz-Eakin, David Joulfaian, and Harvey S. Rosen, "Entrepreneurial Decisions and Liquidity Constraints," *The RAND Journal of Economics* 25, no. 2 (1994): 334–347.

40. Douglas Holtz-Eakin, David Joulfaian, and Harvey S. Rosen, "Sticking It Out: Entrepreneurial Survival and Liquidity Constraints," *Journal of Political Economy* 102, no. 1 (1994): 53–75.

41. Douglas Holtz-Eakin, "The Death Tax: Investments, Employment, and Entrepreneurs," *Tax Notes* 84, no. 5 (August 1999): 782–792.

42. Erik Hurst and Annamaria Lusardi, "Liquidity Constraints, Household Wealth, and Entrepreneurship," *Journal of Political Economy* 112, no. 2 (April 2004): 319–347.

Chapter 8

1. Giving USA 2017: *The Annual Report on Philanthropy for the Year 2016*, Giving USA Foundation, Indiana University Lily Family School of Philanthropy.

2. Michael Boskin, "Estate Taxation and Charitable Bequests," *Journal of Public Economics* 5, no. 1–2 (1976): 27–56.

3. See Charles T. Clotfelter, *Federal Tax Policy and Charitable Giving* (Chicago: University of Chicago Press, 1985), 241; Thomas Barthold and Robert Plotnick, "Estate Taxation and Other Determinants of Charitable Bequests," *National Tax Journal* 37, no. 2 (June 1984):

225–237; Martin Feldstein, "Charitable Bequests, Estate Taxation, and Intergenerational Wealth Transfers," vol. III, Special Behavioral Studies of Foundations and Corporations (Washington, DC: U.S. Department of the Treasury), 1485–1500, research paper, sponsored by the Commission on Private Philanthropy and Public Needs; Boskin, "Estate Taxation and Charitable Bequests."
4. Barthold and Plotnick, "Estate Taxation and Other Determinants of Charitable Bequests."
5. David Joulfaian, "Charitable Bequests and Estate Taxes," *National Tax Journal* 44 (1991): 169–180.
6. See Boskin, "Estate Taxation and Charitable Bequests;" Clotfelter, *Federal Tax Policy and Charitable Giving*, 241; Barthold and Plotnick, "Estate Taxation and Other Determinants of Charitable Bequests."
7. David Joulfaian, "Estate Taxes and Charitable Bequests by the Wealthy," *National Tax Journal* 53, no. 3, part 2 (September 2000): 743–763.
8. David Joulfaian, "Estate Taxes and Charitable Bequests: Evidence from Two Tax Regimes," U.S. Department of the Treasury, mimeo, 2006. This updates an earlier version released as U.S. Department of the Treasury, OTA Working Paper 92, March 2005.
9. See David Joulfaian, "The Federal Estate and Gift Tax."
10. Regressing the log of wealth of decedents in 1982 on the year an estate tax return is filed yields a coefficient of 0.13 (se=0.01), implying that reported wealth is on average 13 percent higher for each year returns are filed late.
11. Jon M. Bakija, William G. Gale, and Joel B. Slemrod, "Charitable Bequests and Taxes on Inheritances and Estates: Aggregate Evidence from across States and Time," *American Economic Review* 93, no. 2 (2003): 366–370.
12. Jon M. Bakija and William G. Gale, "Effects of Estate Tax Reform on Charitable Giving," *Tax Policy Issues and Options* No. 6 (Washington, DC: Urban–Brookings Tax Policy Center, July 2003).
13. Robert McClelland, "Charitable Bequests and the Repeal of the Estate Tax," Technical Paper 2004–08 (Washington, DC: Congressional Budget Office, July 2004).
14. I am grateful to Robert McClelland for sharing his SAS program code.
15. Indeed, and in the context of studying charitable bequests, table 1 of their paper is very misleading as it implies a wide wedge between the average and marginal tax rates, in particular for the wealthiest of estates. The measurement errors also go beyond the treatment of the credit for state taxes. Furthermore, the average tax rate they employ is effectively reduced by transfers to spouses and charities, as well as by estate-related expenses. In addition, the 20 percent tax rate they report for taxable estates over $20 million is very misleading, as this rate is likely to be closer to the maximum statutory tax rate. See Bakija and Gale, "Effects of Estate Tax Reform on Charitable Giving," table 1; p. 6.
16. Paul G. Schervish and John J. Havens, "Gifts and Bequests: Family or Philanthropic Organizations?," in *Death and Dollars: The Role of Gifts and Bequests in America*, ed. Alicia H. Munnell and Annika Sundén (Washington, DC: Brookings Institution Press, 2003), 130–158.
17. Gerald Auten and David Joulfaian, "Charitable Contributions and Intergenerational Transfers," *Journal of Public Economics* 59 (1996): 55–68.
18. On the pattern of giving by the wealthy using 1976 estate collation data, see also Eugene Steuerle, "Charitable Giving Patterns of the Wealthy," in *America's Wealthy and the Future of Foundations*, ed. Teresa Odendahl (New York: The Foundation Center, 1987), 203–221.
19. Pamela Greene and Robert McClelland, "Taxes and Charitable Giving," *National Tax Journal* 54, no. 3 (2001): 433–453.

20. David Joulfaian, "Charitable Giving in Life and at Death," in Gale, Hines Jr., and Slemrod, *Rethinking Estate and Gift Taxation*, 350–374.

21. Ibid., table 9. The paper notes a number of limitations in carrying out this exercise.

22. Charles C. Holt and John P. Shelton, "The Lock-In Effect of the Capital Gains Tax," *National Tax Journal* 15, no. 4 (1962): 337–352; and Joseph E. Stiglitz, "Some Aspects of the Taxation of Capital Gains," *Journal of Public Economics* 21 (1983): 257–294.

23. The maximum federal estate-tax rate of 0.55 percent reflects a state tax rate of 0.16, for a net federal estate-tax rate of 0.39. The maximum federal capital-gains tax rate is 0.20, which becomes roughly equal to 0.25 when state taxes are accounted for.

24. Gerald Auten and David Joulfaian, "Bequest Taxes and Capital Gains Realization," *Journal of Public Economics* 81, no. 2 (2001): 213–229.

25. Poterba, "Estate Tax and After-Tax Investment Returns."

26. Douglas B. Bernheim, "Does the Estate Tax Raise Revenue?," in *Tax Policy and the Economy*, vol. 1, ed. Lawrence H. Summers (Cambridge, MA: MIT Press, 1987): 113–138.

27. David Joulfaian, "A Quarter Century of Estate Tax Reforms," *National Tax Journal* 53, no. 3 (2000): 343–360.

28. Shultz, *Taxation of Inheritance*, 337.

29. Ibid., 131.

30. Karen Smith Conway and Andrew J. Houtenville, "Elderly Migration and State Fiscal Policy: Evidence from the 1990 Census Migration Flows," *National Tax Journal* 54, no. 1 (2001): 103–123.

31. Jon M. Bakija and Joel B. Slemrod, "Do the Rich Flee from High State Taxes? Evidence from Federal Estate Tax Returns," NBER Working Paper No. 10645, National Bureau of Economic Research, 2004.

32. See "Murdoch Becomes U.S. Citizen, Can Buy TV Network," *LA Times*, September 4, 1985, at 1.

33. Using survey data, some have attempted to measure such gifts. See James Poterba, "Estate and Gift Taxes and Incentives for Inter Vivos Giving in the US," *Journal of Public Economic* 79, no. 1 (2001): 237–264; and Kathleen McGarry, "Inter Vivos Transfers or Bequests? Estate Taxes and the Timing of Parental Giving," *Tax Policy and the Economy* 14 (2000): 94–121. A major shortcoming of survey data is that the wealthy are under-represented. Another is their inability to distinguish between gifts potentially taxable and those not taxable (tuition and medical expenses).

34. Wojciech Kopczuk, "Bequest and Tax Planning: Evidence from Estate Tax Returns," *Quarterly Journal of Economics* 122, no. 4 (2007): 1801–1854.

35. See Steuerle, "Wealth, Realized Income," who also uses 1976 estate tax data.

36. West, *Inheritance Tax*, 11–12.

37. Shultz, *Taxation of Inheritance*, 4.

38. IRC Section 6324.

39. Edward N. Wolff, "Commentary Colloquium on Wealth Transfer Taxation," *Tax Law Review* 51, no. 3 (1996): 517–522.

40. James Poterba, "The Estate Tax and After-Tax Investment Returns," in *Does Atlas Shrug? The Economic Consequences of Taxing the Rich*, ed. Joel Slemrod (Cambridge, MA: Harvard University Press, 2000), 329–349.

41. Martha Britton Eller, Brian Erard, and Chih-Chin Ho, "The Magnitude and Determinants of Federal Estate Tax Noncompliance," in *Rethinking Estate and Gift Taxation*, ed. William G. Gale, James Hines, and Joel Slemrod (Washington, DC: Brookings Institution Press), 375–410.

42. See table 6.5 for fiscal year figures.

43. The only and rare exception is when all assets are located and the person resides outside the United States, and when the person is not a legal resident of any state in the United States. Then the credit is zero regardless of the size of the taxable estate; there are no state taxes.

44. Jonathan Feinstein, "Approaches for Estimating Noncompliance: Examples from Federal Taxation in the United States," *Economic Journal* 109, no. 456 (June 1999): 360–369.

45. Jonathan Feinstein and Chih-Chin Ho, "Predicting Estate Tax Filings and Taxable Gifts," Internal Revenue Service, *IRS Research Bulletin*, Publication 1500 (Rev. 11-99) (1999): 39–45.

46. David Joulfaian, "The Federal Gift Tax, History, Law, and Economics," U.S. Department of the Treasury. OTA Paper 100, November 2007.

47. James M. Poterba and Scott J. Weisbenner, "Inter-asset Differences in Effective Estate-Tax Burdens," *American Economic Review* 93, no. 2 (2003): 360–365.

48. Wojciech Kopczuk and Joel Slemrod, "Dying to Save Taxes: Evidence from Estate-Tax Returns on the Death Elasticity," *Review of Economics and Statistics* 85, no. 2 (2003): 256–265.

49. Blakey and Blakey, "The Revenue Act of 1918."

50. Joshua S. Gans and Andrew Leigh, "Did the Death of Australian Inheritance Taxes Affect Deaths?" *B. E. Journals in Economic Analysis and Policy* 6, no. 1 (2006): 1–7.

51. Marcus Eliason and Henry Ohlsson, "Living to Save Taxes," *Economics Letters* 100, no. 3 (2008): 340–343.

52. Marcus Eliason and Henry Ohlsson, "Timing of Death and the Repeal of the Swedish Inheritance Tax," *Journal of Socio-Economics* 45 (2013): 113–123.

53. David Joulfaian, "To Own or Not to Own Your Life Insurance Policy," *Journal of Public Economics* 118 (2014): 120–127.

54. Ellen April provides an excellent discussion of the treatments of transfers to 501(c)(4) organizations in her article "Once and Future Gift Taxation of Transfers to Section 501(c)(4) Organizations: Current Law, Constitutional Issues, and Policy Considerations," *NYU Journal of Legislative and Public Policy* 15 (April 2012): 289–327.

55. Shelley A. Phipps and Peter S. Burton, "What's Mine Is Yours? The Influence of Male and Female Incomes on Patterns of Household Expenditure," *Economica* 65, no. 260 (November 1998): 599–613.

56. Shelly Lundberg and Robert A. Pollak, "Bargaining and Distribution in Marriage," *Journal of Economic Perspectives* 10, no. 4 (1996): 139–158.

Chapter 9

1. West, *Inheritance Tax*, 204.

2. Eugene Steuerle, "Wealth, Realized Income, and the Measure of Well-Being," in *Horizontal Equity, Uncertainty, and Economic Well-Being*, ed. Martin David and Timothy Smeeding (Chicago: University of Chicago Press, 1985), 91–124.

3. Henry J. Aaron and Alicia H. Munnell, "Reassessing the Role for Transfer Taxes," *National Tax Journal* 45, no. 2 (June 1992): 119–143.

4. Lily L. Batchelder, "Taxing Privilege More Effectively: Replacing the Estate Tax with an Inheritance Tax," NYU Law and Economics Research Paper No. 07–25, 2007.

5. Remarks by Dr. N. Gregory Mankiw Chairman of the Council of Economic Advisers at the National Bureau of Economic Research Tax Policy and the Economy Meeting, November 4, 2003.

6. In theory, and depending on a number of assumptions on the reach of the tax and bequest motives, the estate tax may influence economic growth. See, for example, Joseph

E. Stiglitz, "Notes on Estate Taxes, Redistribution, and the Concept of Balanced Growth Path Incidence," *Journal of Political Economy* 8 (1978): 5137–5150.

7. Frank A. Cowell, Dirk Van de gaer, and Chang He, "Inheritance Taxation: Redistribution and Predistribution," STICERD—Public Economics Programme Discussion Papers 35, Suntory and Toyota International Centres for Economics and Related Disciplines, LSE, November 2017.

8. David Joulfaian, "What Do We Know About the Behavioral Effects of the Estate Tax?" *Boston College Law Review* 57, no. 5 (2016): 843–858.

9. George Cooper, *A Voluntary Tax? New Perspectives on Sophisticated Estate Tax Avoidance* (Washington, DC: Brookings Institution, 1979).

References

Aaron, Henry J., and Alicia H. Munnell. 1992. "Reassessing the Role for Transfer Taxes." *National Tax Journal* 45, no. 2 (June): 119–143.

April, Ellen. 2012. "Once and Future Gift Taxation of Transfers to Section 501(c)(4) Organizations: Current Law, Constitutional Issues, and Policy Considerations." *NYU Journal of Legislative and Public Policy* 15 (April): 289–327.

Andreoni, James. 1990. "Impure Altruism and Donations to Public Goods: A Theory of Warm-Glow Giving." *Economic Journal* 100, no. 401: 464–477.

Auten, Gerald, and David Joulfaian. 2001. "Bequest Taxes and Capital Gains Realization." *Journal of Public Economics* 81, no. 2: 213–229.

Auten, Gerald, and David Joulfaian. 1996. "Charitable Contributions and Intergenerational Transfers." *Journal of Public Economics* 59, no. 1: 55–68.

Auten, Gerald, and Janette Wilson. 1999. "Sales of Capital Assets Reported on Individual Income Tax Returns, 1985." *Internal Revenue Service SOI Bulletin* (Spring): 113–136.

Bakija, Jon M., and William G. Gale. 2003. "Effects of Estate Tax Reform on Charitable Giving." *Tax Policy Issues and Options*, no. 6, July. Washington, DC: Urban–Brookings Tax Policy Center.

Bakija, Jon M., and Joel B. Slemrod. 2004. "Do the Rich Flee from High State Taxes? Evidence from Federal Estate Tax Returns." NBER Working Paper No. 10645, National Bureau of Economic Research.

Bakija, Jon M., William G. Gale, and Joel B. Slemrod. 2003. "Charitable Bequests and Taxes on Inheritances and Estates: Aggregate Evidence from across States and Time." *American Economic Review* 93, no. 2 (May): 366–370.

Barro, Robert J. 1974. "Are Government Bonds Net Wealth?" *Journal of Political Economy* 82, no. 6: 1095–1117.

Barthold, Thomas, and Robert Plotnick. 1984. "Estate Taxation and Other Determinants of Charitable Bequests." *National Tax Journal* 37, no. 2 (1984): 225–237.

Batchelder, Lily L. 2007. "Taxing Privilege More Effectively: Replacing the Estate Tax with an Inheritance Tax." NYU Law and Economics Research Paper No. 07-25.

Bernheim, Douglas B. 1987. "Does the Estate Tax Raise Revenue?" In *Tax Policy and the Economy*, vol. 1, ed. Lawrence H. Summers, 113–138. Cambridge, MA: MIT Press.

Bernheim, B. Douglas, Andrei Shleifer, and Lawrence H. Summers. 1985. "The Strategic Bequest Motive." *Journal of Political Economy* 93, no. 6: 1045–1076.

Blakey, Roy G. 1917. "The War Revenue Act of 1917." *American Economic Review* 7, no. 4: 791–815.

Blakey, Roy G. 1916. "The New Revenue Act." *American Economic Review* 6 (December): 837–850.

Blakey, Roy G., and Gladys C. Blakey. 1919. "The Revenue Act of 1918." *The American Economic Review* 9, no. 2: 214–243. http://www.jstor.org/stable/1823605.

Blumkin, Tomer, and Efraim Sadka. 2003. "Estate Taxation with Intended and Accidental Bequests." *Journal of Public Economics* 88, no. 1: 1–21.

Boskin, Michael J. 1976. "Estate Taxation and Charitable Bequests." *Journal of Public Economics* 5, no. 1–2: 27–56.

Brown, Jeffrey R., Courtney Coile, and Scott J. Weisbenner. 2006. "The Effect of Inheritance Receipt on Retirement." NBER Working Paper No. 12386, National Bureau of Economic Research.

Bullock, Charles J. 1907. "The Position of the Inheritance Tax in American Taxation." Proceedings of the National Tax Association, Columbus, OH, 230–240.

Cagetti, Marco, and Mariacristina De Nardi. 2009. "Estate Taxation, Entrepreneurship, and Wealth." *American Economic Review* 99, no. 1: 85–111.

Carnegie, Andrew. 1900. *The Gospel of Wealth, and Other Timely Essays*. Reprint, Garden City, NY: Doubleday, Doran and Company, 1975.

Chapman, Kenneth, Govind Hariharan, and Lawrence Southwick Jr. 1996. "Estate Taxes and Asset Accumulation." *Family Business Review* 9, no. 3: 253–268.

Clotfelter, Charles T. 1985. *Federal Tax Policy and Charitable Giving*. Chicago: University of Chicago Press.

Congressional Budget Office. 2007. "The Budget and Economic Outlook: Fiscal Years 2008 to 2017." U.S. Congress, Washington, DC.

Conway, Karen Smith, and Andrew J. Houtenville. 2001. "Elderly Migration and State Fiscal Policy: Evidence from the 1990 Census Migration Flows." *National Tax Journal* 54, no. 1: 103–123.

Cooper, George. 1979. *A Voluntary Tax? New Perspectives on Sophisticated Estate Tax Avoidance*. Washington, DC: Brookings Institution.

Cowell, Frank A., Chang He, and Dirk Van de gaer. 2017. "Inheritance Taxation: Redistribution and Predistribution." STICERD—Public Economics Programme Discussion Papers 35, Suntory and Toyota International Centres for Economics and Related Disciplines, LSE.

Cox, Donald. 1987. "Motives for Private Income Transfers." *Journal of Political Economy* 95, no. 3 (June): 508–546.

Davenport, Charles, and Jay A. Soled. 1999. "Enlivening the Death-Tax Death-Talk." *Tax Notes* 84, no. 4 (July 26, special report): 591–630.

Eliason, M., and Ohlsson, H. 2008. "Living to Save Taxes." *Economics Letters* 100, no. 3: 340–343.

Elinder, M., O. Erixson, and H. Ohlsson. 2012. "The Impact of Inheritances on Heirs' Labor and Capital Income." *B. E. Journal of Economic Analysis & Policy* 12, no. 1: 1–35.

Eller, Martha Britton. 1997. "Federal Taxation of Wealth Transfers, 1992–1995." *Statistics of Income Bulletin.* Internal Revenue Service, Washington, DC.

Eller, Martha Britton, Brian Erard, and Chih-Chin Ho. 2001. "The Magnitude and Determinants of Federal Estate Tax Noncompliance." In *Rethinking Estate and Gift Taxation,* ed. William G. Gale, James Hines, and Joel Slemrod, 375–410. Washington, DC: Brookings Institution Press.

Feinstein, Jonathan. 1999. "Approaches for Estimating Noncompliance: Examples from Federal Taxation in the United States." *Economic Journal* 109, no. 456 (June): 360–369.

Feinstein, Jonathan, and Chih-Chin Ho. 1999. "Predicting Estate Tax Filings and Taxable Gifts." Internal Revenue Service, *IRS Research Bulletin,* Publication 1500 (Rev. 11-99), 39–45.

Feldstein, Martin. 1997. "Charitable Bequests, Estate Taxation, and Intergenerational Wealth Transfers." Vol. III, Special Behavioral Studies of Foundations and Corporations, 1485–1500. Washington, DC: U.S. Department of the Treasury. Research paper, sponsored by the Commission on Private Philanthropy and Public Needs.

Fisher, Irving. 1916. "Some Impending National Problems." *Journal of Political Economy* 26: 694–712.

Gale, William G., and Maria G. Perozeh. 2001. "Do Estate Taxes Reduce Saving?" In *Rethinking Estate and Gift Taxation,* ed. William G. Gale, James Hines, and Joel Slemrod, 206–247. Washington, DC: Brookings Institution Press.

Gale, William G., and Joel B. Slemrod. 2001. "Rhetoric and Economics in the Estate Tax Debate." *National Tax Journal* 54, no. 3 (September): 613–627.

Gans, Joshua S., and Andrew Leigh. 2006. Did the Death of Australian Inheritance Taxes Affect Deaths? *B. E. Journals in Economic Analysis and Policy* 6, no. 1: 1–7.

Graetz, Michael. 1983. "To Praise the Estate Tax, Not to Bury It." *Yale Law Review* 93: 259–286.

Graetz, Michael J., and Ian Shapiro, 2006. *Death by a Thousand Cuts: The Fight over Taxing Inherited Wealth.* Princeton, NJ: Princeton University Press.

Gordon, Robert N., David Joulfaian, and James M. Poterba. 2016. "Choosing Between an Estate Tax and a Basis Carryover Regime: Evidence From 2010." *National Tax Journal* 69, no. 4: 981–1002.

Greene, Pamela, and Robert McClelland. 2001. "Taxes and Charitable Giving." *National Tax Journal* 54, no. 3: 433–453.

Harriss, C. Lowell. 1940. "Gift Taxation in the United States." American Council on Public Affairs, Washington, DC.

Holtz-Eakin, Douglas. 1999. "The Death Tax: Investments, Employment and Entrepreneurs." *Tax Notes* 84, no. 5 (August): 782–792.

Holtz-Eakin, Douglas. 1996. "The Uneasy Empirical Case for Abolishing the Estate Tax." *Tax Law Review* 51: 495–516.

Holtz-Eakin, Douglas, and Donald Marples. 2001. "Distortion Costs of Taxing Wealth Accumulation: Income vs. Estate Taxes." NBER Working Paper No. 8261, National Bureau of Economic Research.

Holtz-Eakin, Douglas, David Joulfaian, and Harvey S. Rosen. 1994. "Entrepreneurial Decisions and Liquidity Constraints." *The RAND Journal of Economics* (Summer): 334–347.

Holtz-Eakin, Douglas, David Joulfaian, and Harvey S. Rosen. 1994. "Sticking It Out: Entrepreneurial Survival and Liquidity Constraints." *Journal of Political Economy* 102, no. 1: 53–75.

Holtz-Eakin, Douglas, David Joulfaian, and Harvey S. Rosen. 1993. "The Carnegie Conjecture: Some Empirical Evidence." *Quarterly Journal of Economics* 108, no. 2: 413–436.

Holtz-Eakin, Douglas, David Joulfaian, and Harvey S. Rosen. 1999. "Estimating the Income Effect on Retirement." Center for Economic Policy Studies Working Paper Series, Princeton University, Princeton, NJ.

Holt, Charles C., and John P. Shelton. 1962. "The Lock-In Effect of the Capital Gains Tax." *National Tax Journal* 15, no. 4 (December): 337–352.

Hurd, Michael D. 1989. "Mortality Risk and Bequests." *Econometrica* 57, no. 4 (July): 779–813.

Hurst, Erik, and Annamaria Lusardi. 2004. "Liquidity Constraints, Household Wealth, and Entrepreneurship." *Journal of Political Economy* 112, no. 2 (April): 319–347.

Jones, Jonathan D., and David Joulfaian. 1991. "Federal Government Revenues and Expenditures in the Early Years of the American Republic: Evidence from 1792 to 1860." *Journal of Macroeconomics* 13, no. 1: 133–155.

Joulfaian, David. 2016. "What Do We Know About the Behavioral Effects of the Estate Tax?" *Boston College Law Review* 57, no. 5: 843–858.

Joulfaian, David. 2014. "Intergenerational Transfers under an Uncertain Estate Tax." Mimeo, August, U.S. Department of the Treasury.

Joulfaian, David. 2014. "To Own or Not to Own Your Life Insurance Policy." *Journal of Public Economics* 118 (October): 120–127.

Joulfaian, David. 2009. "On Estate Tax Repeal and Charitable Bequests." *Tax Notes* 123, no. 10 (June): 1221–1229.

Joulfaian, David. 2007. "The Federal Gift Tax: History, Law, and Economics." OTA Paper 100. U.S. Department of the Treasury, Washington, DC.

Joulfaian, David. 2007. "What if Estate Taxpayers Were Viewed as Households Rather Than as Individuals?" Mimeo, U.S. Department of the Treasury.

Joulfaian, David. 2006. "Estate Taxes and Charitable Bequests: Evidence from Two Tax Regimes." Mimeo, U.S. Department of the Treasury, Washington, DC.

Joulfaian, David. 2006. "Inheritance and Saving." NBER Working Paper No. 12569, National Bureau of Economic Research.

Joulfaian, David. 2006. "The Behavioral Response of Wealth Accumulation to Estate Taxation: Time Series Evidence." *National Tax Journal* 59: 253–268.

Joulfaian, David. 2005. "Choosing between Gifts and Bequests: How Taxes Affect the Timing of Wealth Transfers." *Journal of Public Economics*: 2069–2091.

Joulfaian, David. 2005. "Estate Taxes and Charitable Bequests: Evidence from Two Tax Regimes." OTA Working Paper 92, March. U.S. Department of the Treasury, Washington, DC.

Joulfaian, David. 2004. "Gift Taxes and Lifetime Transfers: Time Series Evidence." *Journal of Public Economics* 88: 1917–1929.

Joulfaian, David. 2001. "Charitable Giving in Life and at Death." In *Rethinking Estate and Gift Taxation*, ed. William G. Gale, James R. Hines Jr., and Joel Slemrod, 350–374. Washington, DC: Brookings Institution Press.

Joulfaian, David. 2001. "Choosing Between an Income Tax and a Wealth Transfer Tax." *National Tax Journal* 54, no. 3 (September): 629–643.

Joulfaian, David. 2000. "A Quarter Century of Estate Tax Reforms." *National Tax Journal* 53, no. 3, part 1 (September): 343–360.

Joulfaian, David. 2000. "Estate Taxes and Charitable Bequests by the Wealthy." *National Tax Journal* 53, no. 3, part 2 (September): 743–763.

Joulfaian, David. 2000. "Taxing Wealth Transfers and Its Behavioral Consequences." *National Tax Journal* 53, no. 4 (December): 933–957.

Joulfaian, David. 1998. "The Federal Estate and Gift Tax: Description, Profile of Taxpayers, and Economic Consequences." OTA Working Paper 80. U.S. Department of the Treasury, Washington, DC.

Joulfaian, David. 1994. "The Distribution and Division of Bequests: Evidence from the Collation Study." OTA Paper 71. U.S. Department of the Treasury, Washington, DC.

Joulfaian, David. 1991. "Charitable Bequests and Estate Taxes." *National Tax Journal* 44: 169–180.

Joulfaian, David, and Kathleen McGarry. 2004. "Estate and Gift Tax Incentives and Inter Vivos Giving." *National Tax Journal* 57, no. 2, part 2 (June): 429–444.

Joulfaian, David, and Mark O. Wilhelm. 1994. "Inheritance and Labor Supply." *Journal of Human Resources* 29, no. 4: 1205–1234.

Kopczuk, Wojciech. 2013. "Taxation of Intergenerational Transfers and Wealth." In *Handbook of Public Economics*. Vol. 5, ed. Alan J. Auerbach, Raj Chetty, Martin Feldstein, and Emmanuel Saez. Amsterdam: Elsevier, 329–390.

Kopczuk, Wojciech. 2007. "Bequest and Tax Planning: Evidence from Estate Tax Returns." *Quarterly Journal of Economics* 122, no. 4: 1801–1854.

Kopczuk, Wojciech. 2003. "The Trick Is to Live: Is the Estate Tax Social Security for the Rich?" *Journal of Political Economy* 111, no. 6: 1318–1341.

Kopczuk, Wojciech, and Joel Slemrod. 2003. "Dying to Save Taxes: Evidence from Estate-Tax Returns on the Death Elasticity." *Review of Economics and Statistics* 85, no. 2: 256–265.

Kopczuk, Wojciech, and Joel Slemrod. 2001. "The Impact of the Estate Tax on the Wealth Accumulation and Avoidance Behavior of Donors." In *Rethinking Estate and Gift Taxation*, ed. William G. Gale, James R. Hines Jr., and Joel Slemrod, 299–343. Washington, DC: Brookings Institution Press.

Laitner, John. 2001. "Simulating the Effects on Inequality and Wealth Accumulation of Eliminating the Federal Gift and Estate Tax." In *Rethinking Estate and Gift Taxation*, ed. William G. Gale, James Hines, and Joel B. Slemrod. Washington, DC: Brookings Institution Press.

Lundberg, Shelly, and Robert A. Pollak. 1996. "Bargaining and Distribution in Marriage." *Journal of Economic Perspectives* 10, no. 4: 139–158.

Mankiw, N. Gregory. 2003. Remarks at the National Bureau of Economic Research Tax Policy and the Economy Meeting, National Press Club, November 4. http://georgewbush -whitehouse.archives.gov/cea/NPressClub20031104.html.

McGarry, Kathleen. 2000. "Inter Vivos Transfers or Bequests? Estate Taxes and the Timing of Parental Giving." *Tax Policy and the Economy* 14: 94–121.

McClelland, Robert. 2004. "Charitable Bequests and the Repeal of the Estate Tax." Technical Paper 2004-08, Congressional Budget Office, July.

Mellon, Andrew. 1924. *Taxation: The People's Business*. New York: The Macmillan Company.

Paul, Randolph E. 1954. *Taxation in the United States*. Boston: Little, Brown, and Co.

Pechman, Joseph A. 1987. *Federal Tax Policy*, 4th ed. Washington, DC: Brookings Institution.

Phipps, Shelley A., and Peter S. Burton. 1998. "What's Mine Is Yours? The Influence of Male and Female Incomes on Patterns of Household Expenditure." *Economica*, New Series 65, no. 260: 599–613. http://www.jstor.org/stable/2555190.

Poterba, James. 2001. "Estate and Gift Taxes and Incentives for Inter Vivos Giving in the US." *Journal of Public Economic* 79, no. 1: 237–264.

Poterba, James. 2000. "The Estate Tax and After-Tax Investment Returns." In *Does Atlas Shrug? The Economic Consequences of Taxing the Rich*, ed. Joel Slemrod, 329–349. Cambridge, MA: Harvard University Press.

Poterba, James M., and Scott J. Weisbenner. 2003. "Inter-asset Differences in Effective Estate-Tax Burdens." *American Economic Review* 93, no. 2: 360–365.

Ratner, Sidney. 1942. *American Taxation: Its History as a Social Force in Democracy*. New York: W. W. Norton & Company, Inc.

Roosevelt, Theodore. 1910. *Presidential Addresses and State Papers: April 14, 1906 to January 14, 1907*. New York: The Review of Reviews Company, 712–724.

Schervish, Paul G., and John J. Havens. 2003. "Gifts and Bequests: Family or Philanthropic Organizations?" In *Death and Dollars: The Role of Gifts and Bequests in America*, ed. Alicia H. Munnell and Annika Sundén. Washington, DC: Brookings Institution Press, 130–158.

Shoup, Carl S. 1966. *Federal Estate and Gift Taxes*. Washington, DC: Brookings Institution.

Shoven, John, and David Wise. 1996. "The Taxation of Pensions: A Shelter Can Become a Trap." NBER Working Paper No. 5815, National Bureau of Economic Research.

Shultz, William J. 1926. *The Taxation of Inheritance*. New York: Houghton Mifflin, The Riverside Press.

Skinner, Jonathan. 1987. "A Superior Measure of Consumption from the Panel Study of Income Dynamics." *Economics Letters* 23, no. 2: 213–216.

Smith, Adam. [1776] 1930. *An Inquiry into the Nature and Causes of the Wealth of Nations*. New York: Modern Library.

Steuerle, Eugene. 1987. "Charitable Giving Patterns of the Wealthy." In *America's Wealthy and the Future of Foundations*, ed. Teresa Odendahl, 203–221. New York: The Foundation Center.

Steuerle, Eugene. 1985. "Wealth, Realized Income, and the Measure of Well-Being." In *Horizontal Equity, Uncertainty, and Economic Well-Being*, ed. Martin David and Timothy Smeeding, 91–124. Chicago: University of Chicago Press.

Stiglitz, Joseph E. 1983. "Some Aspects of the Taxation of Capital Gains." *Journal of Public Economics* 21: 257–294.

Stiglitz, Joseph E. 1978. "Notes on Estate Taxes, Redistribution, and the Concept of Balanced Growth Path Incidence." *Journal of Political Economy* 8: 5137–5150.

United States Seventy-Second Congress. 1932. House of Representatives Report 608. Reprinted in *Internal Revenue Cumulative Bulletin* 1939 (1), part 2, 457–495. Washington, DC: Government Publishing Office.

United States Seventy-Second Congress. 1932. Senate Report 665. Reprinted in *Internal Revenue Cumulative Bulletin* 1939 (1), part 2, 496–526. Washington, DC: Government Publishing Office.

Wagner, Richard E. 1993. "Federal Transfer Taxation: A Study in Social Cost." *Fiscal Issues* 8, Institute for Research on the Economics of Taxation.

Weber, Max. [1905] 1958. *The Protestant Ethic and the Spirit of Capitalism*. Trans. ed. New York: Charles Scribner's Sons.

Weil, David N. 1996. "Intergenerational Transfers, Aging, and Uncertainty." In *Advances in the Economics of Aging*, ed. David A. Wise, 321–342. Chicago: University of Chicago Press.

Weil, David N. 1994. "The Saving of the Elderly in Micro and Macro Data." *Quarterly Journal of Economics* 109, no. 1: 55–81.

West, Max. 1908. *The Inheritance Tax*. 2nd ed. New York: Columbia University Press, the Macmillan Company, agents.

Wolff, Edward N. 1996. "Commentary Colloquium on Wealth Transfer Taxation." *Tax Law Review* 51, no. 3: 517–522.

Yaari, Menahem E. 1965. "Uncertain Lifetime, Life Insurance, and the Theory of the Consumer." *Review of Economic Studies* 32, no. 2: 137–150.

Zagorsky, Jay. 2013. "Do People Save or Spend Their Inheritances? Understanding What Happens to Inherited Wealth." *Journal of Family and Economic Issues* 34, no. 1: 64–76.

Zaritsky, Howard. 1980. "Federal Estate, Gift, and Generation-Skipping Taxes: A Legislative History and a Description of Current Law." *CRS Report* No. 80-76A.

Index

Aaron, Henry, 176
Accession tax, 8
Act of August 30, 1935, 12
Act of March 3, 1917, 9
Act of May 10, 1934, 12
Act of October 21, 1942, 12, 27
Act of September 20, 1941, 12
Adjusted Gross Estate, 30
Adjusted taxable estate, 34
American Taxpayer Relief Act of 2012, 16, 34
Applicable credit amount, 33
Asset and Health Dynamics study (AHEAD), 115
Assets
 bonds, 48, 59
 business, 50
 capital gains, 150–154, 175
 corporate, 47
 gifts, 59–61, 75
 portfolio allocation, 162–163
 real estate, 49–50, 59
 retirement, 13–14, 28, 50
 step-up in basis, 109, 112, 150
 tax avoidance, 158–159
Asset valuation, 13, 26–27, 50–51
 discounts, 51, 61
 gifts, 61
 special use valuation, 13, 26
Attorney fees, 31
Audits, 95–98
Australia, 165
Auten, Gerald, 147, 151

Bakija, Jon, 144–146, 156
Barthold, Thomas, 136–137
Basis carryover, 13, 76–78, 109, 112

Batchelder, Lily, 176
Behavioral effects, 101, 171
 capital gains realizations, 151
 charitable bequests, 136–148
 charitable contributions during life, 148
 choice between gifts and bequests, 108
 entrepreneurship and self-employment, 104, 129–132
 gift timing, 107–114
 interstate migration, 156
 labor supply, 121–129
 life insurance ownership, 167
 redistribution, 177
 saving and wealth accumulation, 102–121
 tax avoidance, 157
 tax evasion, 159
 timing of death, 163–166
Beneficiaries, 65–83. See also Charitable bequests; Heirs; Lifetime gifts; Spousal transfers
 children, 68–73
 income, 66, 69–72
 inheritance size, 72
 types of, 65–69
Bernheim, Douglas, 155
Blockage rule, 26
Bonds, 48, 59
Boskin, Michael, 136–137
Brown, Jeffrey, 124
Buffett, Warren, 103
Businesses
 assets, 50
 closely held, 13
 family-owned, 28–29
 special use valuation, 13

Cagetti, Marco, 103
California, 64
Capital gains, 150–154, 175
Carnegie, Andrew, 101, 103, 178
Cash, 61
Chapman, Kenneth, 106
Charitable bequests, 31, 46, 56–58, 75–83, 165
    charitable organizations, 65
    at death, 135–147
    lifetime contributions, 147–150
    married/widowed decedents, 140–143
    and spousal transfers, 138–139, 141–142, 144
    tax preferential treatment of, 136–138
Children (as beneficiaries), 68–73
Civil War, 7
Clinton administration, 15
Clotfelter, Charles, 136–137
Collation Studies, 66
Conservation easements, 29
Consumer Expenditure (CEX), 148
Consumption, 119–121
Conway, Karen, 156
Cooper, George, 178
Corporate equity, 47
Corporate income tax, 8
Cowell, Frank A., 177
Crude Oil Windfall Profit Tax Act of 1980, 13
Crummey trusts, 74–75

Davenport, Charles, 99
Death
    charitable bequests at, 135–147
    taxes, 1–2, 10–11, 30, 34, 53, 132, 157
    timing of, 163–167
Debts, 31, 46
Decedent spouse's unused exemption (DSUE), 51–52
Deductions, 30–31. See also Marital deduction
    family-owned businesses, 28–29
    interest payments, 37–38
Deficit Reduction Act of 1984, 15, 28
Discounts, valuation, 51, 61
"Distortion Costs of Taxing Wealth Accumulation: Income Versus Estate Taxes," 103–104
"Distribution and Division of Bequests, The" 66

"Does the Estate Tax Raise Revenue?," 155
Donors, entrepreneurial, 131–132
Donor saving, 102–107
"Dying to Save Taxes," 163

Economic Growth and Tax Relief Reconciliation Act of 2001, 15, 42, 91, 93
Economic Recovery Tax Act of 1981, 13, 41, 139–140, 151–155, 168
Efficiency of taxation, 3
Elderly
    migration, 156–157
    saving, 120
    working heirs, 128–129
Eliason, Marcus, 166
Elinder, Mikael, 127
Eller, Martha, 160
Emergency Revenue Act of 1916, 8–9
Employer securities, 31
Employment. See Labor supply
England, 2
Entrepreneurial heir/donor, 130–132
Equity, 3
Estate planning, 157–159
Estate profile, 43–47
Estate tax (2017), 25–39. See also Generation-skipping transfer tax (GSTT); Gift tax; Taxpayer profile (estate tax)
    conservation easements, 29
    deductions, 30–31
    due dates, 36–37
    exemptions and exclusions, 17, 28–30
    life insurance, 27
    pension assets, 28
    tax base, 25–26
    tax credits, 33–36
    tax deferral, 37–38
    tax rate schedule, 31–33
    valuations, 26–27
Estate taxes, 2, 9–12, 178. See also Estate tax (2017); Generation-skipping transfer tax (GSTT); Gift tax; Revenue contribution; Taxpayer profile (estate tax)
    as deferred income tax, 175
    and democratic ideals, 3
    efficiency and equity, 3
    enactment of, 9
    historical features, 17, 22–23

income and substitution effects, 101–102
and inflation, 90
installment payments, 13
marital property, 12–13
net worth, 47
opposition to, 4, 10–11
receipts and liability, 2–3
returns, 41–44, 114–116, 172
and state taxes, 10–11
tax base, 9–10
tax credit, 10, 12–13
tax liability, 47
temporary features, 19
Exemptions and exclusions, 17–20, 90
DSUE, 51–52
family-owned businesses, 28–29
gift tax, 18, 29, 55, 58
GSTT, 19, 29–30, 93
life insurance, 27
pension assets, 28
state taxes, 34
unified credit, 33–34, 90–91

Farm assets, 50–51, 59
Federal estate tax. *See* Estate tax (2017);
    Estate taxes; Revenue contribution
"Federal Gift Tax, History, Law, and
    Economics, The" 161
Federal unified transfer tax, 2. *See also*
    Estate taxes
Feinstein, Jonathan, 161–162
Feldstein, Martin, 136
Filing threshold, 53, 76
Florida, 10–11, 156

Gale, William, 103, 132
Gans, Joshua, 165
Generation-skipping transfer tax (GSTT),
    2, 13–16, 26, 113. *See also* Estate taxes
due date, 37
exemptions and exclusions, 19, 29–30,
    93
historical features, 19
rate, 33
revenues, 93
"Gifts and Bequests: Family or Philan-
    thropic Organizations?," 147
Gift tax, 2, 10–11, 13, 15–16, 53–62. *See
    also* Estate taxes; Lifetime gifts;
    Taxpayer profile (gift tax)
asset types and valuations, 59–61, 75

audits, 96–97
due date, 36–37
and estate tax returns, 61–62, 92
exemptions and exclusions, 29, 55, 58
filing threshold, 53
historical features, 18
lifetime gift tax credit, 34–35, 46, 61–62
number of returns, 55
revenues, 85, 87, 91–94, 111–114
spousal transfers, 56
state returns, 62
tax avoidance, 159
tax evasion, 161–162
tax-exclusive nature of, 109
tax rates, 20–22, 33, 92–94, 107–109
temporary features, 19
timing of gifts, 110–114
Grandchildren (as beneficiaries), 68, 72,
    74
Grantor-retained annuity trust (GRAT),
    58
Great Depression, 11
Greece, ancient, 159
Greene, Pamela, 148
Gross estate, 25, 51

Health and Retirement Study (HRS), 104,
    114–115, 124
Heirs, 116–132
children, 68–73
elderly working, 128–129
entrepreneurial, 130–131
grandchildren, 68, 72, 74
hours of work, 126–128
labor force exit, 121–124
retirement, 124–126
saving, 116–121
self-employment, 129–132
work effort, 121
Holt, Charles, 150
Holtz-Eakin, Douglas, 103–104, 121,
    124–132
Households
behavior, 171–174
saving, 103–104
wealth profile, 172
Hurst, Erik, 133

Income
beneficiaries, 66, 69–72
distribution, 177

Income (cont.)
  effect of estate tax, 101–102
  and inheritance size, 72
Income taxes, 7–9, 11
  deferred, 175–176
  and estate/gift tax receipts, 85–86
  returns, 118–119
  step-up in basis, 176
Income tax revenue, 85–86, 177–178
Inflation, 90
Inheritance
  and consumption, 119–121
  labor force exit, 121–124
  and retirement, 124–126, 128–129
  and saving, 117–119
  and self-employment, 129–132
  and wages, 126
Inheritance taxes, 1–2, 176–177. See also
  Estate taxes
  forms of, 1–2
  history, 1–2, 7
  as income taxes, 7
  progressive, 8
Insurance, 1
Interest rates, 37–38
Internal Revenue Act of 1954, 12, 27,
  34
Internal Revenue Service budget, 98–99
Internal Revenue Service Restructuring
  and Reform Act of 1998, 28
Interstate competition, 156–157

Kopczuk, Wojciech, 103–104, 106, 158,
  163–164, 167

Labor supply, 101, 121
  elderly working heirs, 128–129
  labor force exit, 121–124
  retirement, 124–126, 128–129
  self-employment, 129–132
  work effort, 121, 126–128
Laitner, John, 103
Legacy tax, 2, 7
Life insurance, 27, 50, 75, 167–170
Lifetime gifts, 72–75. See also Gift tax
  and bequests, 108–110
  charitable contributions, 147–150
  and tax avoidance, 101, 107–108
  tax credit, 34–35, 46, 61–62
  and tax rates, 108–109, 111, 115–116
  timing, 110–114

Liquidity constraints, 129, 133
"Living to Save Taxes," 166
Lundberg, Shelly, 174

Mankiw, Gregory, 4, 177
Marginal tax rate, 112
Marital deduction, 30, 91, 93, 139
  household unit, 176
  surviving spouses, 158
  tax deferrals, 154–155
Marital property, 12–13
Marples, Donald, 103–104
McClelland, Robert, 145, 148
McGarry, Kathleen, 114
Minority discounts, 26
Murdoch, Rupert, 157

National Longitudinal Survey of Youth
  1979, 120
Nevada, 11, 156
New York, 64, 111
Noncompliance, 96
Nonprofit organizations, 135

Omnibus Budget Reconciliation Act of
  1987, 15
Omnibus Budget Reconciliation Act of
  1989, 31
Orphan children, 31

Panel survey of income dynamics (PSID),
  119, 126–127
Payne-Aldrich Tariff Act of 1909, 8
Pension assets, 28
Perozek, Maria, 103
Personal income tax, 8–9
Phipps, Shelley, 173
Political contributions, 170–171
Portfolio allocation, 162–163
Poterba, James, 160, 162–163
"Premium paid" test, 27
Prior federal tax paid credit, 35–36
Progressive inheritance tax, 8

Qualified terminable interest property
  (QTIP) trusts, 13, 155, 158
"Quarter Century of Estate Tax Reforms,
  A," 155

Reagan administration, 15
Real estate, 49–50, 59

"Reassessing the Role for Transfer Taxes," 176
Retirement
  assets, 13–14, 28, 50
  and inheritance, 124–126, 128–129
Revenue Act of 1918, 10, 27, 31, 35
Revenue Act of 1924, 10, 34, 165
Revenue Act of 1926, 89, 165
Revenue Act of 1932, 11
Revenue Act of 1940, 12
Revenue Act of 1948, 12
Revenue Act of 1978, 13
Revenue contribution, 9, 85–100
  administration costs, 98–99
  audits, 96–97
  enforcement and tax evasion, 85–87, 94–98
  estate tax, 85, 87–91, 155
  gift tax, 85, 87, 91–94, 111–114
  historical trend, 85
  and income tax, 85–86, 177–178
  and tax rates, 107
Ricardo, David, 3
Roosevelt, Theodore, 8
Rosen, Harvey, 121, 124–131

Saving, 116–121. *See also* Heirs
  bequest motives, 102–105
  donor, 102–116
  elderly, 120
  firms, 103
  and gift timing, 110–114
  households, 103–104
  lifetime gifts versus bequests, 108–110
  simulation models, 103
  and tax rates, 105–107, 112
  tax returns, 114–116
  and timing of transfers, 107–108
  wealth mobility, 118–119
"Saving of the Elderly in Micro and Macro Data, The" 120
Schervish, Paul, 147
Shelton, John, 150
Shoven, John, 28
Siblings (as beneficiaries), 68–69, 73
Skinner, Jonathan, 120
Slemrod, Joel, 104, 106, 132
Small Business Tax Revision Act of 1958, 13, 37
Smith, Adam, 3
Soled, Jay, 99

Special use valuation, 13, 26
Spousal transfers, 16, 46
  and charitable bequests, 138–139, 141–142, 144
  DSUE, 51–52
  gifts, 56
  marital deduction, 30, 91, 93, 139, 154–155, 158, 176
  QTIP trusts, 13, 155
  surviving spouses, 68, 82, 91, 158
  and tax deferrals, 154–156
Stamp Act of 1797, 2
Stamp tax, 2
State Death Tax Credit, 30, 34, 165
State taxes
  death tax, 1–2, 10–11, 30, 34, 53, 132, 157
  estate tax, 10–11, 46–47
  as exclusions, 34
  and federal credit, 156–157
  gift tax, 62
  interstate competition, 156–157
  taxpayer profiles, 53, 62
Statistics of Income (SOI) Program, 66, 151, 172
Step-up in basis, 109, 112, 150, 176
Steuerle, Eugene, 176
Stiglitz, Joseph, 150
Survey of Consumer Finances (SCF), 148
Sweden, 127–128, 166

Taxation
  efficiency, 3
  purposes of, 1, 175
Tax audits, 95–96, 160
Tax avoidance, 11, 85–87, 94–98, 175
  and estate planning, 157–159
  gift tax, 159
  and lifetime gifts, 101, 107–108
Tax credits, 10, 12–13, 33–36
  lifetime gifts, 34–35, 46, 61–62
  state death tax, 30, 34, 165
Tax Cuts and Jobs Act of 2017, 16, 33, 147
Tax deferrals, 37–38, 154–156
Tax Equity and Fiscal Responsibility Act of 1982, 13–14, 28
Tax evasion, 85–87, 94–98, 159–162
Tax gap, 160
"Taxing Privilege More Effectively," 176

Taxpayer profile (estate tax), 41–53,
    62–63
  asset composition, 47–50
  asset valuation, 50–51
  DSUE, 51–52
  estate profile, 43–47
  filing comparison (2001), 52–53
  filing threshold, 46
  number of returns, 41–44
  state, 53
Taxpayer profile (gift tax), 53–64
  asset types and valuations, 59–61
  number of returns, 55
  state, 62
Taxpayer Relief Act of 2012, 34
Tax planning, 99
Tax rates, 9–12, 20–22, 90–94
  and charitable bequests, 139
  and incentives, 112
  and lifetime gifts, 108–109, 111, 115–116
  and saving, 105–107, 112
Tax rate schedules, 31–33
Tax Reform Act of 1969, 31
Tax Reform Act of 1976, 13, 26, 33, 41, 90,
    92, 139
Tax Reform Act of 1986, 15, 26, 28
Tax Relief, Unemployment Insurance
    Authorization, and Job Creation Act of
    2010, 16, 51
Tax Relief Act of 1997, 15, 28, 96
Tax returns (2016), 44–46. See also
    Taxpayer profile (estate tax)
Terminal wealth, 85
Transfer taxation, 2–3, 13–14. See also
    Estate taxes
Trusts
  beneficiaries, 74
  Crummey, 74–75
  and GSTT, 13–14
  QTIP, 13, 155, 158

Unified credit, 33–34, 90–91, 140
Unified transfer tax, 13. See also Estate
    taxes
United States
  Civil War taxation, 7
  Great Depression, 11
  progressive inheritance tax, 8
  Spanish-American war taxes, 8
  Stamp Act of 1797, 2
  World War I, 9

Valuation date, 26. See also Asset
    valuation
Vicesima hereditatium, 1

Wages, 126
War Revenue Act of 1898, 8
War Revenue Act of 1917, 9–10
Wealth accumulation. See Saving
Wealth levies, 1–2
Wealth mobility, 118–119
Wealth transfer taxation, 2–3
Weil, David, 120
Wilhelm, Mark, 119, 126
Wise, David, 28
Wolff, Edward, 159
Work effort of heirs, 121
World War I, 9

Zagorsky, Jay, 120